creative actions

EMBEDDING CREATIVE COMPETENCIES IN EVERY CLASSROOM

Tim Patston, James C Kaufman and David Cropley

Published in 2025 by Amba Press, Melbourne, Australia
www.ambapress.com.au

First published 2022 by Hawker Brownlow Education

© 2025 Tim Patston, James C Kaufman and David Cropley

All rights reserved. No part of this book may be reproduced or transmitted in any form or by any means, electronic or mechanical, including photocopying, recording or by any information storage and retrieval system, without prior permission in writing from the publisher.

Cover photo: William Patston
Icon design: Peter Bajer
Maths creativity advisor: David Dimsey
Designer: Zoe Burdack

ISBN: 9781923403406 (pbk)
ISBN: 9781923403413 (ebk)

A catalogue record for this book is available from the National Library of Australia.

TABLE OF CONTENTS

DEDICATION		iv
ACKNOWLEDGEMENTS		v
ABOUT THE AUTHORS		v
PREFACE		vii
ABOUT THIS BOOK		viii
CHAPTER 1	*The history of creativity and of creativity in education*	1
CHAPTER 2	*Myths and barriers to creativity in education*	11
CHAPTER 3	*The creative place: How physical and social environments enhance creativity*	25
CHAPTER 4	*The creative person: What are the key attitudes and attributes of creativity?*	53
CHAPTER 5	*The creative process: From generating ideas to presenting solutions*	93
CHAPTER 6	*Evaluating creativity: Measuring and assessing the components of creativity*	133
CHAPTER 7	*The creative school: How can whole-school climate build organisational creativity?*	169
CHAPTER 8	*The creative independent learner: Being creative inside and outside the classroom*	187
CHAPTER 9	*The creative parent: How can families build creative competencies in their children?*	211
CHAPTER 10	*Where to from here?*	223
REFERENCES		232
INDEX		261

DEDICATION

TIM PATSTON

To my family

JAMES C KAUFMAN

For Allison, Jacob and Asher – the foundation of my world

ACKNOWLEDGEMENTS

The authors wish to acknowledge the teachers around the globe who embrace their own creativity and seek to nurture creativity in their students. You are our future.

ABOUT THE AUTHORS
DR TIM PATSTON

Dr Tim Patston has been involved in creativity in his professions as an educator, researcher and performer. Tim was the inaugral Coordinator of creativity and innovation at Geelong Grammar School. His framework of creative education was recognised as one of the top ten innovations in Victorian education by the HundrEd organisation of Finland. Previously he designed innovative curriculum as Head of music at the National Institute of Dramatic Art (NIDA). He was also a Principal singer with Opera Australia and Victoria State Opera.

Tim is currently Senior adjunct at Uni SA STEM, University of South Australia, senior fellow at the Melbourne Graduate School of Education, The University of Melbourne, and teaching associate at Monash University. Tim's interests lie in the use of data-based evidence from the science of creativity to improve educational practice and student outcomes. His research has identified positive links between elements of creativity and academic performance.

Tim is the featured expert on creativity in the 2021 documentary *Finding creativity*. In his consultancy work, Tim is Senior partner at Creative Actions creativeactions.com.au.

DR JAMES C KAUFMAN

Dr James C Kaufman is a Professor of Educational Psychology at the Neag School of Education at the University of Connecticut. He is the author or editor of more than fifty books (including the forthcoming *The creativity advantage*) and has written more than four hundred papers, including theoretical contributions such as the Four-C model of creativity (with Ron Beghetto).

He is a past president of Division 10 (Society for Psychology of Aesthetics, Creativity, and the Arts) of the American Psychological Association (APA) and has won many awards, including Mensa's research award, the Torrance Award from the National Association for Gifted Children, and APA's Berlyne, Arnheim, and Farnsworth awards. He co-founded two major journals (*Psychology of Aesthetics, Creativity, and the Arts*, and *Psychology of Popular Media Culture*).

James has tested Dr Sanjay Gupta's creativity on CNN, appeared in the hit Australian show *Redesign my brain* (2013) and narrated the comic book documentary *Independents* (2007). He wrote the book and lyrics to *Discovering Magenta*, which had its premiere in 2015. He has co-authored books on bad baseball pitchers (with his father Alan), pseudoscience (with his wife Allison), and is finishing one on creativity and musical theatre (with Olivier-nominated composer Dana Rowe).

DR DAVID CROPLEY

Dr David Cropley is the Professor of Engineering Innovation at the University of South Australia. He specialises in helping people and organisations become better, more effective problem-solvers.

David joined the School of Engineering at the South Australian Institute of Technology (SAIT) in 1990 after serving for four years in the United Kingdom's Royal Navy, including deployments to the Caribbean and Middle East. Following the establishment of the University in 1991, he completed a PhD in measurement systems engineering in 1997, and a Graduate Certificate in Higher Education in 2002.

David is author or co-author of nine books including *Creativity and crime: A psychological analysis* (Cambridge University Press, 2013); *Creativity in engineering: Novel solutions to complex problems* (Academic Press, 2015); *The psychology of innovation in organizations* (Cambridge University Press, 2015), and *Femina problematis solvendis – problem-solving woman: A history of the creativity of women* (Springer, 2020).

Now a recognised expert in creative problem-solving and innovation, Dr David Cropley was a scientific consultant and on-screen expert for the Australian ABC TV documentaries *Redesign my brain* (2013 and 2015) and *Life at 9* (2014). For more than twenty years, he has helped schools and organisations in Australia, the US and Europe develop more effective, creative problem-solvers.

PREFACE

What do Iceland, Nigeria, India, Brazil, Canada and Australia have in common? They all have creativity as an expected competency to be integrated into their national curriculums. Increasingly in the last ten years, creativity as a key competency has appeared in curriculum documentation globally. Teachers around the world now know that they should integrate creativity into their subject areas. They know that students need to finish their schooling with not only subject knowledge and skills but also creative competencies to survive and thrive in a rapidly evolving global landscape.

Despite education systems around the globe calling for creativity in education, there is much inconsistency in approach, definition and assessment. We know that education systems have not supported teachers effectively in transitioning the focus to building creative competencies in their students. Our experience in working with teachers shows that educators are increasingly developing their practice to build their own creative competencies and those of their students.

The purpose of this book is threefold. Firstly, we look at creativity through the lens of research. What is creativity in education? Why is it essential? Where is the evidence? What are the challenges teachers face when implementing creativity in their classrooms? How can school management, parents and students foster a climate of creativity? Secondly, we celebrate those teachers leading the way in creative education. Our unique experience, always striving to build a bridge between theory and practice, has led us to offer a series of practical, sensible and implementable solutions for teachers, school leaders and students in the classroom. We provide templates of lesson plans from a range of countries in a variety of subjects, to guide educators in the practice of implementing creative education. Thirdly, we offer students a toolkit of creative practices to build their independent learning to be more efficient and effective, both at school and in life.

WHAT IS CREATIVITY?

> *Creativity is the interaction among aptitude, process, and environment by which an individual or group produces a perceptible product that is both novel and useful as defined within a social context.* (Plucker et al., 2004, p. 90)

Human creativity has ensured the survival of our species. Through the science of creativity, we now understand that creativity is a system, involving attitudes, environments, knowledge and processes. Creativity can only occur with the following components in place:

1. All creativity is built on some form of knowledge, even at its most basic level in infants. Creativity is the manipulation of knowledge to pose and solve problems.
2. Everyone needs the right attitudes and attributes to be creative.
3. Creative problem-solving and problem-posing are processes that can be taught and learned.
4. For creativity to occur, it needs the right physical and social environments.
5. Creativity is context dependent. A creative chef may also be a creative shot-putter, but their skills are different and they have different problems to solve.

ABOUT THIS BOOK

CHAPTER 1: THE HISTORY OF CREATIVITY AND OF CREATIVITY IN EDUCATION

We know everyone has the capacity to be creative in some aspects of their lives. We also know that 'creativity can be taught, learned and assessed' (Patston, 2019, para. 12). This chapter explores how creativity as a science has evolved since the 1960s, from the first attempts to integrate creativity into education and its sporadic appearance to the new drive for creative education in the early 2000s. We explore how countries in all continents around the globe are increasingly including creative competencies in their national curriculums.

CHAPTER 2: MYTHS AND BARRIERS TO CREATIVITY IN EDUCATION

This chapter busts some of the common myths associated with creativity and explains why teachers, parents, school management and students should not subscribe to these myths in the classroom. We also discuss the inconsistencies regarding definition, professional development, implementation and measurement of creativity that exist in education systems in many countries. We acknowledge the additional challenges teachers face in building their own creative competencies, integrating creativity into a crowded curriculum, and providing formative and summative feedback to students when the main modality for feedback is test results.

CHAPTER 3: THE CREATIVE PLACE

Classroom environments can help or hinder creativity. While the physical environment is important, it only accounts for approximately 40 per cent of the effect of the context on creativity. The social environment accounts for the remaining 60 per cent. As creativity is a human activity, this is not surprising. The social environment refers to the style and type of interaction between teachers and students in the classroom. This chapter looks at the elements that make up physical and social environments and discusses why they are important. It also includes examples from real teachers in real classrooms.

CHAPTER 4: THE CREATIVE PERSON

This chapter looks at the personal side of creativity. Our personal beliefs strongly influence how and what we do. How can teachers both model and foster these attitudes and build on attributes such as openness, intellectual risk-taking and resilience?

We explore the developmental trajectory of creativity. Creativity begins with the mini-c level – the spark that comes at the beginning of the creative process – or what we might consider personal creativity. It is the discovery of something new, at least to the person having that insight. Little-c creativity is 'one level up from the mini-c level, in that it involves feedback from others combined with an attempt to build knowledge and skills in a particular area' (Patston, 2019, para. 5). The little-c level of creativity is experienced by the majority of students during their schooling.

Pro-c creativity is demonstrated by educators as they develop pedagogies and build their own competencies. Lesson plans from a variety of countries demonstrate how attitudes and attributes of creativity can be built in students.

CHAPTER 5: THE CREATIVE PROCESS

The creative process is the engine room of creativity. This chapter will explore the most cited methods of idea generation, idea recording, idea summarising, critical thinking and presenting solutions as well as problem-posing. This chapter offers students and teachers a toolkit of skills that can be developed from primary to high school and beyond.

CHAPTER 6: EVALUATING CREATIVITY

This chapter looks at the results, or outputs, of creativity. We know that assessment, or evaluation, is an integral part of the education process. What should teachers be looking for, and what are some of the formative and summative assessments and measures of creativity that could be used by teachers in classrooms?

CHAPTER 7: THE CREATIVE SCHOOL

School climate and the professional development of teachers are hot topics in education. In this chapter we will explore how school climate impacts creativity, and some of the models of professional learning that will support teachers in being more creative educators and enable them to build the competencies of creativity in their students.

CHAPTER 8: THE CREATIVE INDEPENDENT LEARNER

Student learning is not exclusively the responsibility of teachers and does not end at the classroom door. Students take their knowledge and skills between classes and then home. This chapter looks at the learning and study behind subject content and skills. Does being creative in study improve test results? How can students build their competency as creative independent learners?

CHAPTER 9: THE CREATIVE PARENT

Environment, attitudes and attributes also live in the home. This chapter looks at the role of parents in developing creativity in their children through modelling and fostering creativity in the home.

CHAPTER 10: WHERE TO FROM HERE?

Where to next? Is developing creative competencies in teachers and students possible, globally, at scale? Where could this lead us? What will happen if we do not build a future of creative generations? We share our conclusions and thoughts on how creativity in education may develop.

WHY THIS BOOK

We believe that schools can significantly improve the creative competencies of both teachers and students by leveraging assets they already have, learning a few new things and striving for sensible and sustainable incremental change. In other words – slow food creativity, gradually building complexity over time, rather than fast food, or 'instant' creativity.

We also believe that teachers can learn a lot from each other, both within their own subjects but more importantly from teachers who teach other subjects. We have included examples from teachers and subjects around the world to show you that teachers have the capacity and curiosity to succeed. We also offer examples from our experiences as educators. Our experience in schools shows us that teachers are willing and able to face the challenges and opportunities in building their competencies as creative educators, despite some of the barriers they are facing.

For students, the science of creativity can build creative competencies while maintaining or improving academic outcomes in standardised testing and preparing students for life in a rapidly changing world. This book is a practical guide for teachers, school leaders, students and parents to help them understand what creativity is and how it can be implemented and integrated to give students the future that they deserve and need.

We do not promise a magic pill to fix the ills of education. This book is more a menu than a prescription. We encourage you to read, think, question, experiment and prototype new ideas and approaches. In other words, use this book as a tool to build your own creative competencies.

HOW TO USE THIS BOOK

We would like you to think of this book as a selection of healthy and nourishing recipes using a range of ingredients and techniques to build a menu of creativity. Each chapter from 3 to 7 begins with a section on the latest research in the field of creativity in education. We will explain the terms you can learn to build understanding of your creativity and that of your students. Think of these sections as discussing the ingredients and tools of creativity. We then offer teaching examples from a range of subjects from educators in every continent. Every lesson plan is from a peer-reviewed journal and reveals the incredible range and diversity of creative education practice around the globe. These are the recipes for applied creativity.

You can search this book by topic, by components or facets of creativity, by subject, by level of schooling, or by country. We encourage you to be curious and explore beyond your own subject and cultural horizons, then take a risk and experience new, relevant and useful creative opportunities in your classroom. The lesson examples all follow the same format as the following (example 5.6).

Mathematics, secondary, Pakistan

WHAT THE TEACHER FOUND

"Use of everyday familiar analogies increased interest and motivation level of the students of the experimental group and contributed to their high achievement and better understanding of abstract concepts of mathematics." (Khan & Mahmood, 2018, p. 193)

Component of creativity	Facet(s) of creativity	Teaching with or for creativity
Process	Critical thinking and analogous thinking	For
Attitudes and attributes	Tolerance for ambiguity	For
Environment	Collaboration	For

PURPOSE OF LESSON: SUBJECT KNOWLEDGE OR SKILLS

The purpose of this lesson was for students to develop an understanding of abstract concepts in mathematics knowledge and skills in the topics of sets, polynomials and fundamentals of geometry.

PURPOSE OF THE LESSON: TEACHING WITH OR FOR CREATIVITY

In terms of creativity, the purpose of this lesson was for students to build their tolerance for ambiguity and analogous thinking by giving examples of experiences with mathematical concepts from their personal lives. The control group completed exercises from the textbook without training in analogous thinking while the experimental group received explicit instruction and had group discussions on the analogies they developed.

REFERENCE

Khan, A. A., & Mahmood, N. (2018). Effect of synectics model of teaching in enhancing students' understanding of abstract concepts of mathematics. *Pakistan Journal of Distance and Online Learning, 4*(1), 185–198. https://files.eric.ed.gov/fulltext/EJ1267261.pdf

ACCESS

You can then design lessons to build creative competencies in your classroom according to your particular context. We would strongly suggest that you begin any lesson involving creativity with a brief introduction about creativity – which component or facet of creativity you are using or teaching, why you are using it and how it will help the students develop subject knowledge and skills as well as creative knowledge and skills.

For those wishing to learn more and explore their intellectual curiosity, there is a QR code at the end of each example. This will give you a link to the study from which the example came.

CONTENTS — GUIDE TO ALL LESSON PLANS

Subject Area	Year Level	Pg No	Ex No
Art	Lower Secondary	39	3.4
Art	Secondary	66	4.4
Art and Environmental Science	Secondary	33	3.2
Biology	Secondary	107	5.4
Biology	Secondary	198	8.3
Business Studies	Secondary	157	6.5
Chemistry	Secondary	70	4.5
Engineering and Design	Lower Secondary	58	4.1
English	Secondary	103	5.2
English	Upper Secondary	119	5.7
English	Secondary	141	6.2
English as a Foreign Language	Secondary	83	4.9
English as a Foreign Language	Secondary	112	5.5
English as a Second Language	Upper Primary/ Lower Secondary	86	4.11
Environmental Science	Primary	75	4.7
French Language	Secondary	193	8.1
Geography	Secondary	87	4.12
History	Secondary	64	4.3
History	Secondary	126	5.9
History	Secondary	197	8.2
Interdisciplinary real-world problem- solving	Secondary	183	7.3
Mathematics	Lower Secondary	44	3.5
Mathematics	Upper Primary	59	4.2
Mathematics	Secondary	80	4.8
Mathematics	Secondary	84	4.10
Mathematics	Secondary	89	4.13
Mathematics	Secondary	115	5.6
Mathematics	Secondary	138	6.1
Mathematics	Primary	181	7.2
Music	Upper Primary/ Lower Secondary	32	3.1
Music	Lower Secondary	131	5.10
Native tongue (Finnish)	Secondary	105	5.3
Physics	Secondary	151	6.3
Religious Education	Secondary	36	3.3
Science	Secondary	72	4.6
Science	Primary	101	5.1
Science	Primary	174	7.1
Science	Primary and Secondary	185	7.4
Science and STEM	Lower Secondary	121	5.8
STEAM – Science, Technology, Engineering, Art, Mathematics	Upper Primary/ Lower Secondary	50	3.6
STEM	Secondary	156	6.4

CHAPTER 1
THE HISTORY OF CREATIVITY AND OF CREATIVITY IN EDUCATION

Human civilisation is inextricably entwined with creativity. We have built physical and social environments to enable creativity, demonstrated the attitudes and attributes necessary for creativity, invented problem-solving processes, posed problems that needed solving and created a vast array of products, from great ideas to great achievements.

The creativity that enabled our species to flourish did not start with a single genius with one big idea. Many small problems needed to be solved, the attitudes of successful problem-solving needed to be developed, and the processes of problem-solving needed to be discovered. Through success and failure, increasingly complex cognitive processes, larger scale collaboration, and tireless iteration and prototyping, we crept incrementally towards the twenty-first century. Creativity became a human competency, combining knowledge, attitudes, dispositions and skills, to pose and solve problems in an incredible range of contexts. Humanity has also explored the dark side of creativity, at times being architects of our own destruction through weaponry and war.

Given the importance of creativity throughout human history, it is essential that we understand what it is, how it develops, how it can be taught and learned, and how we can continue to use it, not only in education but also in our global society. This chapter will discuss the origins of what is now called the *science of creativity*, from ancient civilisations to the present day. We will also explore how and why creativity is considered an essential competency to be taught to students. Finally, we will look at how creativity develops in students.

THE HISTORY OF CREATIVITY

CONTEXT

The word *creativity* has its etymological roots in the Latin word *creare*, meaning 'to make', but the term itself was not coined until the nineteenth century. In global terms, the Western construct of creativity, with its associated elements of environment, attitudes, processes and results, is the dominant model in government, economics and education (Glăveanu & Kaufman, 2019). Consequently, this model is the focus of this book.

The history of humanity is the history of problem-solving. Those who demonstrated the ability to solve problems, uncertain and ambiguous problems in particular – from basic existential issues to the more complex – were the ones who survived and thrived. In all cultures across history, problem-solving methods were, and still are, passed from one generation to the next. Creativity matters.

You will see the word *context* a lot in this book. Creativity is not some vague and abstract concept that occurs in a vacuum inside someone's head – it is always relevant to the context in which it occurs. Context can of course refer to both time and place – sometimes the right idea comes at the wrong time (Bach and van Gogh being two artists whose creativity was not fully recognised and appreciated until after their deaths).

ANCIENT HISTORY

Ancient civilisations, such as China, India, Mesopotamia, Egypt and Greece, valued and appreciated different kinds of creativity in different ways (Cropley, 2020). Essentially, creativity was divided into two kinds: what Cropley and Cropley (2005) call functional creativity, the development of new ideas or objects that had practical and useful application in everyday life, from tools to buildings; and aesthetic creativity, related to the arts. As civilisations became more stratified, functional creativity had an impact on most individuals in society, but aesthetic creativity increasingly became the realm of the rich and powerful. This growing divide may be responsible for several pervasive myths about creativity, what it is, who it is for and how it occurs (see Chapter 2 for more details on the myths of creativity).

For the Greeks, 'creativity was a gift from the gods' (Patston, 2019, para. 2). Homer was inspired by the divine and Plato by the Muses (Glăveanu & Kaufman, 2019). This belief was sill prevalent in the Middle Ages when, at least in Western Europe, creativity was not attributed to humans, but rather was a prerogative of God (Glăveanu & Kaufman, 2019).

THE FOURTEENTH TO NINETEENTH CENTURIES

This idea gradually shifted during the Renaissance, when the responsibility for creativity shifted from God to humans and creators were accredited and compensated for their creations (Glăveanu & Kaufman, 2019). This cultivated creative production in the sciences, arts, trade guilds and beyond (Glăveanu & Kaufman, 2019). Highly creative individuals began to be associated with the term genius, laying the foundation for the myth that only the exceptional can be creative.

The Enlightenment saw another attitudinal shift, toward a more individual notion of creativity based on the power of human reason and the belief that mankind could manipulate and change the world (Glăveanu & Kaufman, 2019). Problem-solving became a pragmatic way of expressing one's creativity. The Enlightenment was followed by Romanticism, arguably one of the eras that had the deepest impact on modern conceptions of creativity. In contrast to rationality, Romanticism brought torment, unhinged fantasy, and the idea that genius was a pathology for the psychotically gifted.

The Industrial Revolution saw a return to a more pragmatic view of creativity, as the association between creativity and economic gains raised the popularity of this phenomenon to a new level (Glăveanu & Kaufman, 2019). Early work in creativity considered it as an ability, such as intelligence; subsequent scholars considered it a trait, similar to personality; today, both cognitive and social perspectives are emphasised.

THE TWENTIETH CENTURY TO NOW

The field now known as the science of psychology emerged at the turn of the twentieth century through researchers and practitioners such as Freud, Jung and Pavlov. This interest in the human mind led to a series of attempts to examine the cognitive processes behind creativity in the 1920s.

The applied science of creativity – the concept that facets of the system of creativity can be understood and described through observation and experiment – began with Graham Wallas's *The art of thought* (1926). Wallas, an English economist and later political scientist, was interested in how people generated thoughts and ideas in a range of fields. He examined an eclectic sample of writings from Greek philosopher Aristotle, English playwright Shakespeare, French poet Remy de Gourmon, British poet Robert Graves, Belgian psychologist Julien Varendonck, French mathematician Henri Poincaré, and – most prominently – the German physician and physicist Hermann von Helmholtz. From these thinkers, Wallas constructed a four-stage model of the thought processes involved in generating ideas (Sadler-Smith, 2015). Wallas's (1926) four-stage model of the creative process consisting of 'preparation, incubation, illumination and verification' (p. 10) is foundational in creativity research.

Wallas' work showed that creative problem-solving is in fact a systematic process. By exploring a range of fields in the arts and sciences, he identified that the cognitive processes involved appear to be generic rather than domain-specific but are applied uniquely within each area. Unfortunately, his exclusive emphasis on cognitive processes meant these became the central focus of creativity research for the next few decades. (In fact, this focus on the cognitive side of creativity is one of the failings of many curriculum documents around the world. We discuss this in more detail in Chapter 2.) As you will discover throughout this book, creativity is much more than just thinking.

The next major step in viewing creativity as a science came with J. P. Guilford's 1950 address to the American Psychological Association, in which he galvanised the field and generated a new enthusiasm and focus. The timing of this address was not coincidental. World War I had seen the development of psychological testing to determine people's ability to solve problems, and World War II demonstrated the demand for problem-solving and the competitiveness across the globe – in particular, the United States' deep concern about the scientific progress in the Soviet Union (Glăveanu, 2019).

It is not the first or last time that politics and economics drove creativity in education. Guilford (1950) made some key points which are still important and relevant today:

1. Anyone has the capacity to be creative.
2. Creativity is not a genetically endowed gift.
3. It is a myth that only people with high IQ can be creative.
4. Motivation and temperament (what we will call in this book attitudes and attributes) affect a person's ability to be creative. (Guilford was the first to identify that creativity requires personal qualities.)
5. Creativity can be defined, analysed and measured.
6. Creativity involves problem-solving, which requires a process. (Guilford focused on divergent thinking but paved the way for others to articulate more explicitly the process of creative problem-solving.)
7. Human intellectual ability is defined too narrowly by what we call convergent thinking (only one solution to a problem) and needs to include the ability to find alternatives (divergent thinking).
8. It is essential that teaching and learning creativity be a part of school education.

Rhodes (1961) followed Guilford, adding two crucial elements to the holistic understanding of creativity: the environment and the product. He was also the first researcher to mention convergent thinking as part of the creative process. Rhodes proposed that for creativity to occur, it requires four elements working in tandem. He called these the four Ps – person, process, product and press (in his desire to use a catchy acronym Rhodes used the term press to describe the environmental or social factors; most now prefer to use the term *environment*). In addition to the attitudes and attributes, processes, analyses, and cognitive and material resources required to develop a tangible product, creativity cannot happen in an unsupportive environment.

The past seventy years since Guilford's address have seen an explosion in the science of creativity in terms of research, models, methods, measures and applications, but the key ideas and principles, if not the exact terminology, of Wallas and Rhodes remain (we focus our discussions in the next section to those in the world of education).

THE HISTORY OF CREATIVITY IN EDUCATION

Politics, economics and education all impact one another: the history of creativity in education is no exception. The earliest conversations about creativity in the modern era were conversations about education. Early research in the 1950s explored creativity in school curriculums (Hill, 1954), while there was a great deal of interest in creativity as a facet of intelligence (Guilford, 1950; Meer & Stein, 1954). The launch of Sputnik I in 1957 was a driving force behind the United States' formal attempts to introduce creativity into educational system curriculums as a central and key component, as opposed to a supplement (Steeves et al., 2009). From the 1958 US National Defense Education Act onward, the primary focus was to promote problem-solving in science, technology, engineering and mathematics (STEM) disciplines (Herold, 1974). It embraced creativity within science programs for gifted students at the elementary level, focusing on independent projects and the study of science in everyday life.

Into the 1960s that interest grew, exploring creativity more explicitly in the classroom (Torrance, 1965), even as it continued to be studied in terms of the relationship between creativity, intelligence and school achievement (Cropley, 1967).

Creativity's role in education continued to push forward in the 1970s, but this progress lagged until the early 2000s. This lag was caused by top-down management of school structures, student outcomes designed to meet perceived societal needs, age-based classrooms, and an increasing focus on memorisation and testing to produce student results.

In contrast, education in the United Kingdom in the 1960s was shaped by the Plowden Report (CACE, 1967). The report was based on Piagetian theory of childhood psychology linking creativity to a child-centred, discovery-based pedagogical approach and the arts. In the United States, influence from the UK led to the rise of student-centred 'open education'. This approach to education subsequently formed part of the critique of child-centred education practices. The chief criticism was that students often failed to achieve academic competence, particularly in English and mathematics, and that more discipline and structure was needed. This paved the way for the introduction of a subject- and content-based national curriculum at the end of the 1980s. The 1988 Education Reform Act in the United Kingdom imposed a subject-based national curriculum and introduced a regime of testing and published league tables, forcing schools to focus on teaching for good test results. Creativity became consigned almost exclusively to the arts, a place it still remains in some national education systems.

It is noteworthy that, while creativity remained a topic of interest in education throughout the decades since, it may be said creativity never really caused a decisive, fundamental change in education – that is, until now.

Scholarship from the United Kingdom in the 1990s (Hubbard, 1996; Jeffrey & Woods, 1997) pushed the creative agenda forward. Ultimately, this work resulted in the important National Advisory Committee on Creative and Cultural Education's (1999) report, which recommended a return of creativity in the classroom in all subjects. However, perhaps the greatest change to the global economy and education in the 1990s was the rise of digital devices, the internet and truly global communication.

As information has become more readily accessible, students require creative competencies more than ever. Skills that lie within creativity, such as critical thinking, are necessary for students to determine what information is relevant and useful for the problems they are trying to solve. In a world of increasing complexity, problem-posing and problem-solving are essential skills for life, while the attitudes of openness, curiosity, risk-taking and tolerance for ambiguity are required to navigate growing uncertainty. The need for these competencies was called for as early as

2000 by European business leaders (UNICE, 2000), calling for education systems to build creative competencies in students to prepare them for a fluid future.

Unfortunately, the push for creativity and the emergence of digital technologies at the same time meant that academic testing results could be compared between countries, expanding competition in education internationally. The first Programme for International Student Assessment (PISA) tests, administered in 1997, shone a spotlight on education around the world and international league tables led to education reform across the globe. This rise to international standardisation of education is not without its critics:

> *The foundation upon which PISA has built its success has been seriously challenged. First, there is no evidence to justify, let alone prove, the claim that PISA indeed measures skills that are essential for life in modern economies. Second, the claim is an imposition of a monolithic and West-centric view of societies on the rest of the world. Third, the claim distorts the purpose of education.* (Zhao, 2020, p. 249)

This conflict, between the stated need for creative competencies and the world of standardised testing, means we are currently in a state of tension regarding the place of creativity in education. While global organisations including the Organisation for Economic Co-operation and Development (OECD, 2008) picked up the call for increased curricular creativity, there is notable work left to be done (Patston et al., 2021). The important thing about this expanded view is that this defines creativity as a competency. Creativity is no longer considered exclusively in the domain of traditional arts (Kaufman, 2016), it is rather a 'travelling concept' (Nordin & Sundberg, 2016) being increasingly accepted and used in educational policy, even at the point of being considered a core competency. It is seen as strongly tied to modern society (Rosenstock & Riordan, 2017) and as a driving economic force (Florida, 2012). No longer should creativity be seen as a luxury or supplement to curriculums, but rather an essential piece of what is needed to succeed in an increasingly global yet divided world.

So, what has changed in early twenty-first century education that is causing, for the first time, a shift from creativity as interesting to creativity as essential? What is driving the appearance of creativity as a core component of school curriculums in countries around the world in the current era?

The answer is: digital transformation, or in more formal terms, the rapid growth of artificial intelligence (AI), big data, robotics and automation. The practical consequence of a tipping point in the capability of digital technologies is a change in what is now ubiquitously called the *future of work*. As AI becomes a viable alternative to humans, we recognise that the impact of this on labour is quite specific. AI is ideally suited to quite specific kinds of work. In particular, the jobs that are under threat from AI are those that are characterised by repetitive, algorithmic, cognitive and physical labour: factory work, data processing, paralegal tasks, accounting, driving cars, tending bars and more!

Creativity is truly essential now because, for the first time, we face an existential threat to human labour. As humans are replaced in many jobs by better, faster and cheaper AI-powered robots, where does that leave us? The answer is that it leaves us with those things that AI and robots cannot do, and that includes, at its core, the ability to find new and effective solutions to unprecedented problems. In other words, the key human ability for twenty-first century work is creativity.

Creativity is now essential because it is the key to preparing young people for the future of work (Cropley, 2022; Kettler et al., 2021). With creativity as a core professional competency, young people entering the workforce can look forward to vibrant careers solving problems that involve uncertainty, change and unpredictability. Without creativity, young people risk entering the workforce with a very narrow range of options.

Nonetheless, many countries continue to buy into myths surrounding creativity (Baas et al., 2015). These range from continuing to assume that creativity is restricted to the arts (Patston et al., 2018) to believing that creativity is more dependent on luck or sudden insight as opposed to extensive practice and high levels of expertise (Benedek et al., 2021). We will discuss this in more detail in our next chapter.

CONCLUSION

So, what solutions do we have in this book? In addition to the person, product, process and environment, we remind you that creativity also depends on domain knowledge – for example, knowledge of mathematics or physics – and depends on other domain-specific skills (for example, perhaps the ability to code). Skills are specific, focused and often not transferable, whereas competencies are broader, general and transferable. These must be acquired through some form of education.

Is it possible to integrate creative competencies into current curriculum? Our answer is a resounding yes, and this book is full of examples to help you do just that. It is relatively straightforward to construct physical and social environments that enable and enhance creativity. By modelling and fostering the attributes of creativity, teachers will demonstrate that students can build their attitudinal capacity for creativity. Short, explicit, incremental instruction in the processes of creative problem-solving and problem-posing will build students' competencies over their journey through school, and relatively simple and straightforward changes to school reporting can capture the developmental trajectory of creative competencies in a student's schooling. We will also show that students with creative competencies have better academic outcomes at school.

CREATIVE ACTIONS

The authors of this book are both optimistic and pragmatic. We do not propose storming the ramparts of education around the world demanding a creative utopia. The history of human creativity has been a history of incremental change. We propose a solution created by enthusiastic, evidence-informed, incremental change in individual classrooms around the world. In Chapter 2 we will explore and expose some of the myths of creativity that may hinder our solution for a more creative future in education.

CHAPTER 2

MYTHS AND BARRIERS TO CREATIVITY IN EDUCATION

2

When discussing the idea of creativity and, more importantly, creativity in education, it is essential that education systems, school management, teachers, students and parents understand what creativity is and what it is not. Despite over seventy years of empirical research, there are still pockets of misunderstanding regarding creativity. This has led to some research positing that teachers prescribe to particular myths, and as a result integrating creativity into education is extremely difficult (Mullet et al., 2016). Fortunately, the research we, the authors, have been conducting on this matter is far more optimistic than earlier studies. In fact, our findings show nearly the opposite. Despite there being a great deal of inconsistency and incomplete information regarding creativity in international curriculum documentation (Patston, Kaufman et al., 2021) and variance between subject areas, teachers are open to professional learning and know more about creativity than they have previously been given credit for (Cropley et al., 2019; Patston et al., 2018). This does not mean that the myths are no longer an issue in education; they may still influence parents and other stakeholders in the education system, including students. This is why we need to tackle and dispel the myths.

The profession of teaching is rapidly evolving around the world. Teachers are expected to be aware of the latest developments in an increasing range of fields: to know not only the latest evidence-based types of pedagogy, but also digital literacy, child psychology, neuroscience and creativity, among others. However, education can also be beset by myth and misconception (Ferrero et al., 2020). Given the acceleration in research over the last twenty years, it seems unfair to blame teachers for not being up to date with all the latest theories and trends in creativity. While teachers, like all professionals, bear some responsibility for maintaining their professional learning, tertiary teacher trainers, curriculum designers, policymakers and education systems hold the bulk of responsibility for informing teachers about contemporary best practice and how this is manifest in the classroom.

This chapter will explore the key myths and misconceptions of creativity and related fields such as psychology and neuroscience. We will discuss who holds these misconceptions and why, and how some of these may be barriers to building creative competencies in education. For example, it is extremely difficult for teachers to have a complete understanding of creativity in education if they are provided with incomplete or incorrect information by their education system. Key additional challenges for teachers are having the time and the opportunity to build their own creative competencies; finding time to integrate creativity into a crowded curriculum; and how to provide formative and summative feedback to students when the main modality for feedback is test results.

MYTHS ABOUT CREATIVITY

As you saw in Chapter 1, the history of creativity has been the history of changing ideas and perceptions about creativity. The past few years have seen an explosion in creativity research, but it can take many years for a scientific finding to be implemented as practice in a classroom.

In practical terms, the longer someone believes in a myth the more strongly they believe it. These become implicit beliefs, based on experience rather than evidence, and can be difficult to shift. If a myth becomes an implicit belief, a range of strategies is needed to change the perception, rather than a mere correction (Ferrero et al., 2020).

The following myths are those that still seem to have some prevalence and credence in the general population, even if not held by educators. We will explain the potential negative impacts that each myth can have on education.

MYTH 1: CREATIVITY IS BORN AND NOT MADE

This is possibly one of the most pervasive and stubborn myths relating to creativity (Plucker et al., 2021). This myth has two potential origins: it may be a hangover from ancient Greece and the nineteenth century Romantics, or the mass media focus on what Kaufman and Beghetto (2009) call *Big-C creativity*. Big-C creativity is the creativity of individuals who changed the world (Mozart and Einstein are typical examples). As recently as 2017, a special edition on creativity in *Scientific American* (Stover, 2014) perpetuated this myth, and unforunately, the myth of mental illness and creativity being linked.

THE FACTS

It is possible for almost anyone to show some level of creativity. We all have the potential to be creative to some degree, from the modest recipe changes to make a meal more appetising, to the prolonged focus and problem-solving involved in writing this book. There are many variables that influence when and how creativity is manifested, but we all have creative potential.

WHAT TEACHERS CAN DO

The best way to bust this myth is to challenge it whenever it raises its head. In Tim's class, he would begin with a discussion about mini-c and little-c creativity in people's lives. Students would often give examples of creativity in their hobbies and how their interest and motivation built their creative competency over time. Teachers can also give personal illustrations of their own creativity in their professional or private lives, in addition to the elements of creativity which they will be exploring in a particular subject.

MYTH 2: CREATIVITY IS ALL IN THE MIND

The idea that there is something different in the brains of creative people is a myth that manifests itself in a variety of different ways, none of which help educators to build creative competency in their students.

YOU NEED TO BE A LITTLE CRAZY TO BE CREATIVE

The graphic example of Van Gogh cutting off his ear in a fit of madness is one that tends to stay with you. Was he mad because he was creative? Was he creative because he was mad? Or was he both creative and mad with no link between the two? Human beings like to label those who are different, and the mystery of creative talent is something that has been the cause of much speculation. Popular books, such as *An unquiet mind* (1995) or *Touched with fire* (1993) by Kay Redfield Jamison, as well as other media, romanticise the idea of a connection between creativity and mental illness.

This area is too large to cover in adequate detail here for a number of reasons. Although there are countless studies on the topic, many are not by creativity researchers. As a result, the populations studied, the techniques applied and the measures used are often not ideal. Even the core question 'Is mental illness and creativity related?' is hard to parse; when we say *mental illness*, we are lumping together so many different conditions that finding a consistent pattern would be difficult even if one was there. While there is some evidence that certain fields of creative genius (Big-C) may be more likely to show signs of mental illnesses (Kaufman, 2001, 2014), such research is flawed (Schlesinger, 2009).

More importantly, these types of connections mean nothing for the classroom. Acknowledging some caveats (Taylor, 2017), personal or everyday creativity shows little to no relationship with diagnosable, life-impacting mental illness, and such creativity is generally associated with positive mental health (Kaufman, 2018).

Life in the classroom is overwhelmingly concerned with the early developmental stages of creativity. The impact of the mental illness myth is two-fold: it implies that only a certain, pre-disposed group of people can ever be creative and, therefore, suggests futility in trying to develop creative competencies in schools and students.

SOME PEOPLE HAVE 'CREATIVE' PERSONALITIES

This myth has had a potentially negative impact on education over the last thirty years. The phrase 'they are just being creative' can be used in a negative sense to explain poor behaviour. It implies that creativity is associated with non-conformity of behaviour rather than non-conformity of ideas. Some frequently cited studies indicated that, even though teachers profess to value creativity, they do not like the non-conformist attitudes of creative students and see them as potential troublemakers (Chan & Chan, 1999; Westby & Dawson, 1995). However, these studies in particular were both conducted with small monocultural samples (N204 in Chan and Chan and N32 in Westby and Dawson). A more recent international cross-cultural study of over nine hundred teachers reported that educators are more aligned with current evidence-based views regarding the creative attitudes of students (Karwowski et al., 2020). These positive attributes include intellectual curiosity, motivation, resilience and a tolerance for ambiguity.

LEFT BRAIN AND RIGHT BRAIN

Another myth that is also highly prevalent regarding creativity is the functionality of the so-called *left brain* and *right brain*. This began with the idea that left-handers and right-handers must have brains that function differently. This was combined with the idea that both left-handers and creative types were in the minority and, therefore, related.

This myth has been well and truly busted by the field of neuroscience and our understanding of neuroplasticity in the last ten years (Nielsen et al., 2013). A multitude of studies have since added further evidence to put away such ideas (Allen & van der Zwan, 2019; Krammer et al., 2020). Creativity is not confined exclusively to one hemisphere as confirmed by functional magnetic resonance imaging (fMRI) studies. As Demarin and Derke (2020) assert, creativity 'is a dynamic interplay of many different brain regions, emotions and our unconscious and conscious processing systems' (p. 4).

THE FACTS

There are many variables that influence both our ability and opportunity to be creative. There is no evidence that mental illness, a 'creative' personality, or one side of the brain being dominant is a prerequisite for any element of creativity. Recent findings show teachers consider characteristics such as curiosity, initiative and the ability to look at problems from multiple perspectives as being representative of student creativity.

WHAT TEACHERS CAN DO

In the case of these myths, a discussion of the positive attitudes and attributes of creativity is necessary. It may also be worthwhile discussing the difference between non-conformist ideas and non-conformist behaviour, and how creativity flourishes in an environment of respect and psychological safety.

MYTH 3: CREATIVITY IS ONLY FOUND IN THE ARTS

The origins of this myth lie in the historical distinction between technical or artisanal creativity and aesthetic creativity, combined with the creative genius fallacy. For some reason, over seventy years of applied research in creativity has not put this myth to bed. The busting of this particular myth is not helped by certain occupations still being described as *creatives* and universities offering degrees such as a Bachelor of Creative Industries.

Do teachers believe in this myth? Although a comprehensive literature review of historical studies conducted by Mullet and colleagues in 2016 suggested that the arts bias is alive and well in education, our recent work suggests such false beliefs are not as pronounced as previously thought (Patston et al., 2018). Broadly, teachers did not endorse the arts bias. There was some minor variation in attitudes between subject areas and plenty of support for the idea of teachers requiring professional learning in creativity within their subject.

THE FACTS

There is overwhelming evidence that creativity can be found in any area of human endeavour, from golf to gardening to nuclear physics.

WHAT TEACHERS CAN DO

In the case of this myth teachers can actively model creativity in their own subject area. They could also give examples of creativity in a range of non-artistic areas, such as sport or science. A discussion of 'Who is more creative – Messi or Ronaldo? Marie Curie or Ada Lovelace? Why?' (Cropley, 2020) with a variety of figures from a range of fields could stir some fruitful debate and assist students in seeing the full scope of creativity.

MYTH 4: ONLY HIGHLY INTELLIGENT PEOPLE CAN BE CREATIVE

This myth draws together two of the big questions in education. What is intelligence? And what is the relationship, if any, between creativity and standard measures of intelligence? Each of these questions could take up a whole book, so we will answer them briefly according to the latest research findings.

The short answer is creativity is significantly and positively associated with both standardised test scores and grades (Dollinger, 2011; Gajda et al., 2017; Grigorenko et al., 2009; Powers & Kaufman, 2004). Our recent work (Kaufman et al., 2021) and that of others (Toivainen et al., 2021) shows that creativity not only predicts educational achievement but also does so even when other attributes such as intelligence, previous grade point average (GPA), motivation and conscientiousness are taken into account.

THE FACTS

While creativity depends on the knowledge of a particular subject or domain area, and the processes, attitudes and environments necessary for creativity to be effective, it is not necessarily linked to intelligence as described, for instance, in the gifted and talented literature.

WHAT TEACHERS CAN DO

Students can find many ways to approach, solve and discuss a problem if allowed and encouraged to do so. We encourage teachers to be open to ideas expressed in novel ways and to respond to such ideas with open-ended questions such as 'What makes you say that?' or 'Could you explain that another way?' to further creative stimulation and examination.

MYTH 5: CREATIVITY CANNOT BE TAUGHT, LEARNED OR ASSESSED

If you subscribe to the previous myths, this myth must be also true …

You can see the problem: the myths all roll together like a giant snowball, leading to an overall big picture misconception of what creativity is. Sometimes unpacking myths can seem a little bit like trying to unscramble an egg. Our job in writing this book is to make sure that when you are learning about creativity, discussing creativity or teaching creativity, you understand what the ingredients of the system are.

THE FACTS

As with the other myths discussed so far, there is overwhelming evidence that the components of 'creativity can be taught, learned and assessed' (Patston, 2019, para. 12). Otherwise there is no point in us writing this book. Scott et al. (2004) states:

> *Based on 70 prior studies, it was found that well-designed creativity training programs typically induce gains in performance with these effects generalizing across criteria, settings, and target populations. Moreover, these effects held when internal validity considerations were taken into account.* (p. 361)

In all seriousness, this myth has significant negative implications for education if it continues to be believed.

WHAT CAN TEACHERS DO?

This next section on overcoming barriers will demonstrate that this not only is possible but also will have tangible and positive benefits for you as a teacher and the students in your classroom. This is a book not about what but about the detailed *how*.

BARRIERS TO IMPLEMENTING CREATIVITY IN EDUCATION

Previous research has shown that, yes, creativity can be taught, but this is generally in an artificial setting. So it makes the basic point, but doesn't address the real issue for teachers: 'How do I actually teach it in a real classroom?' To move from the abstract to the real world, you have to know what the real-world constraints and barriers are.

We know that the profession of teaching is becoming more complex and demanding. We also know that governments, industry and education departments need and want creative competencies to be built into the school education system in many countries around the world. What are some of the barriers to making this possible and how can these barriers be overcome? We acknowledge that curriculum, politics and policy may at times seem disconnected to life in the classroom (Banaji et al., 2013), and may in fact appear to contradict each other (Patston, Kaufman et al., 2021). In the interests of practicality, we will address the barriers over which individual schools and teachers have some control (some of these will be mentioned only briefly in this section and will be covered in more detail in later chapters in the book).

BARRIER 1: DEFINITION OF CREATIVITY IN CURRICULUM POLICY AND DOCUMENTATION

Many countries continue to buy into myths surrounding creativity (Baas et al., 2015). These range from continuing to assume that creativity is restricted to the arts to believing that creativity is more dependent on luck or sudden insight as opposed to extensive practice and high levels of expertise (Benedek et al., 2021; Patston et al., 2018).

Two studies are of key interest in this area. Banaji and colleagues (2013), building on the work of Heilmann and Korte (2011), conducted analyses of the role and relevance, contexts and implementation of creativity and innovation in compulsory education and teacher training within twenty-seven European education systems through interviews with eighty-one experts in education. Disappointingly, despite creativity being seen as valued, important, and even essential in policy documents, 'National curricula rarely seem to provide any guidance as what to do in order to achieve creativity in subjects other than arts' (Banaji et al., 2013, p. 8).

A qualitative study of national curriculum documentation in twelve countries by Patston, Kaufman and colleagues (2021) reported that only four of the countries had an explicit definition of creativity in their curriculum, while not one country mentioned the importance of the creative environment. There was also a scarcity of suggestions as to how creativity may be assessed. The majority of countries focused on the processes and personal elements of creativity. This study's findings are summarised as follows:

> **❝** *Across these 12 curricula that reflect diverse cultures and locations, there is … consistency in creativity as self-expression and an overall emphasis on the arts. There appears to be little evidence of a systemic and logical approach toward creative education, but rather an ad hoc grab bag for teachers to dip into with little understanding as to place and purpose from a broader perspective. There appears to be no effort to align the central policy directive across the disciplines.* **❞** *(Patston, Kaufman et al., 2021, p. 14–15).*

These findings make it very difficult for teachers to achieve the policy objectives of governments. How is it possible for students to be leaving school as competent, creative, collaborative individuals, having the necessary attitudes and attributes to be creative and a toolkit of problem-solving processes, when there are such flawed inconsistencies in the documentation teachers use?

The problem also lies with the silo-based nature of most school education. It is clear from reading international curriculum documentation that a holistic overview of the place and purpose of creativity in education has been hijacked by subject-based priorities in the curriculum.

This lack of international consensus regarding the definitive position of creativity in curriculum is the biggest challenge faced by teachers. Our book will provide you with a comprehensive, practical, evidence-based approach to building your creative competency and that of your students.

BARRIER 2: SCHOOL CLIMATE

Schools are complex places. The term *school climate* has four main dimensions: physical, cultural, social and individual (we cover this in more detail in Chapter 7). School management is primarily responsible for the first two dimensions, but can certainly influence the last two, while teachers can influence all four within their classroom and the last three outside of the classroom. The development of creativity in school necessitates focus and differentiation in all four dimensions; it is not enough to attempt to foster creativity in a general manner. At the whole school level, the development of creativity depends on a dynamic approach that accounts for the interaction of key components – the environments, the people and the processes. From an internal perspective this means offering supported opportunities for the development of creative competencies in staff and students. From an external perspective, this means effectively communicating to parents and other stakeholders that creative competencies are integrated into the education system of the school and have tangible benefits for both academic outcomes and the life that students will lead after school. There is ample evidence that the school climate has a significant impact on both teacher and student creativity (Mousena & Raptis, 2020). Teachers of course have primary control for their classroom climate (see Chapter 3 for how teachers can influence the physical and social environment of their classroom).

BARRIER 3: PROFESSIONAL LEARNING

For teachers to have the knowledge and skills to build their own creative competencies, and that of their students, they require a certain level of professional learning. The following two quotes demonstrate the state of tension that exists between teachers and their needs for professional development:

> *"Usually, the management invites someone from a consultancy to organize the days. These consultants always work with a world-famous method that often includes positioning yourself and your colleagues with the help of colours, team activities with objects (among which Lego) and giving honest feedback to each other – which no wise person ever does."* (Swennen, 2017, p. 157)

> *"To be successful, professional development must be seen as a process, not an event, providing teachers with specific, concrete, and practical ideas that directly relate to the day-to-day operation of their classrooms. According to*

> *teachers' self-reported data, PD activities that present these features tend to have positive effects on their knowledge and instructional practices.* **"** *(Bautista & Ortega-Ruíz, 2015, p. 245)*

Ineffective professional development, or professional development that is seen as irrelevant, is worse than none. Professional learning is a significant investment, both for the school and for the individual teachers.

In terms of creativity the current prevailing view in the science is that creativity is primarily domain- or subject-specific:

> **"** *As a teacher, I don't assume that because my students have learned how to dribble a basketball, they will also be able to diagram sentences, nor do I assume that teaching them one of these skills have any impact on their skill performing the other.* **"** *(Baer, 2019, p. 121)*

In the same way that teachers conduct professional learning in their subject area, we would strongly suggest that teachers seek professional development in creative competencies within their subject area (throughout the book you will see that we always give examples within a particular subject area). What is true of skills is always true to a certain extent of attitudes – a student who shows intellectual curiosity in chemistry does not necessarily have an intellectual curiosity for poetry. The same can be said for learning environments – there is a reason that classroom layouts and resources work for certain subjects.

It is true that some of the processes of creativity, such as problem-solving, can share methodologies between subject areas. Further, there are some personal attributes, which we will address in Chapter 4, that will enhance a student's creativity in many areas. (For more details on how we propose professional learning can be shaped to build creative competencies across the school please refer to Chapter 7.)

BARRIER 4: NOT BELIEVING IN YOUR OWN CREATIVITY

All of us have views about ourselves that develop over time in a variety of ways following a variety of circumstances. These translate into beliefs. The beliefs we have about ourselves and creativity are called *creative self-efficacy* – essentially how creative we think we are or can be in a particular field or endeavour. If you subscribe to the myths of creativity discussed earlier, or fundamentally believe that you are not creative, then trying to become creative starts with a significant disadvantage.

In Tim's experience, two types of teachers tend to struggle with creative self-efficacy: recent graduates and teachers teaching outside their subject. For those new to teaching this makes sense. They are building their portfolio of pedagogic practice. For these teachers, learning from mentors, either by example or observation, is a useful strategy.

For teachers who find themselves teaching outside their subject area, we would suggest an asset-based approach to building creative self-efficacy. Where has your pedagogy been creative in your core subject? Were there any creative approaches which can be translated to your new subject area? Does anyone else in the department have any creative ideas in pedagogy which they can share with you?

A common theme throughout this book is that everyone has the capacity to be creative. As with learning anything else, it requires knowledge, skills, some teaching, either by yourself or by others, and building experience through trial and error. Teachers who demonstrate and model creative self-efficacy to their students will find that students also develop a sense of creative self-efficacy.

BARRIER 5: IMPLEMENTING CREATIVITY PRACTICALLY

There is an argument that since education systems introduced standardised testing, teachers have become more focused on teaching to the test than educating their students (Marshall, 2017). While it is true that in most countries there is some form of external assessment, national or international benchmark testing at the end of high school, a lot of testing precedes these examinations. Education is not, or at least should not be, a relentless round of rote learning and regurgitation through narrow recall in tests. As discussed in the previous chapter, international standardised testing and the rise of creativity in international curriculums have occurred at approximately the same time. It is a challenge for teachers to meet both sets of needs.

There is also another, more important consideration here. We are not proposing that every lesson needs to include some form of creativity, nor are we proposing students need to build beyond the competency of mini-c and little-c creativity while they are at school. We believe that most steps that enhance creativity are completely supportive of the overall goal of education. Students can learn and practise creativity as they build knowledge, skills and competencies, from both a subject and social perspective, which they can use in life after school. Exposure to the environments, attitudes, processes and products of creativity can happen incrementally in small doses across of range of subjects through all year levels.

The approach we articulate throughout the book is relatively simple and straightforward. If a facet of creativity is to be included in a lesson or series of lessons, there must be, even if only briefly, some explicit instruction about the facet which is to be included, or reflection if the students are already aware of this particular element. The purpose for this facet of creativity, whether it be to build a student creative competency or to deepen student knowledge and skills in a subject area, also needs to be clearly stated. Of equal importance is having time to discuss or reflect at the end of a lesson or a unit of work how these creative competencies have developed and what their impact has been on the learning. Incremental gain through the process of interleaving (reviewing concepts in addition to knowledge and weaving them together) is the most effective way to build the creative competencies of students.

The same is true for the assessment of creativity, which we discuss in Chapter 6. While we do not suggest giving a student a mark out of ten in terms of their tolerance for ambiguity or resilience when solving a problem, facets of creativity can be observed and discussed. Our preferred approach is for formative assessment. However, there is no reason why summative assessment cannot be used when constructing a creative product. The most important element of assessment is timely and useful feedback.

Two other points are worthy of inclusion in the discussion of how to implement creativity in schools. One important place for creativity in schools lies within the pedagogic approaches of teachers. Teachers who are able to teach confidently with a wide range of strategies, while concurrently building students' subject knowledge and skills, improve both student outcomes and student engagement. It is possible to teach with creativity, and we have many examples of this from around the world in a range of subjects throughout the book.

It is also vital that students build their creative competencies as independent learners. By that we mean finding a range of strategies to transfer information and knowledge within a classroom, summarise and store that information and knowledge in a format or formats which deepen learning and understanding, and enable that information and knowledge to be retrieved for use in assessments or exams. Students who are creative independent learners will carry this competency into life after school, when explicit teaching is less likely to occur in the same manner it does at school. (We discuss how students can do this and provide a range of strategies in Chapter 8).

CONCLUSION

In summary we believe that the field of creativity has the power to make a positive impact on education around the world. As the science of creativity has evolved over the last seventy years, many myths have been disproved. While some of these may still be present in the media (or even in the name of some university subjects), teachers are increasingly less likely to subscribe to these myths. While inconsistencies exist between government policy and the definition and application of creativity in international curriculum documentation, the practical day-to-day barriers that could possibly impede creativity can in fact be managed successfully by school leaders, teachers, parents and students. Given that creativity is now considered essential, teachers must be supported in embedding creativity in every classroom.

CHAPTER 3

THE CREATIVE PLACE: HOW PHYSICAL AND SOCIAL ENVIRONMENTS ENHANCE CREATIVITY

3

All education happens in a particular space and place. In a school where David taught, a maths teacher came to him with a problem. They were teaching a topic in senior maths. It appeared that half the class understood a particular concept and half did not. The textbook they were using was not very helpful, and the teacher had tried a variety of ways of explaining the topic with little success. After some discussion the teacher agreed to trial a change to the physical and social environment of the classroom. Poster-sized sheets of blank paper were put on each of the four walls of the classroom. Four students who understood the topic were asked to devise and write a question (which they could answer) on four different posters. Students who felt they did not understand the topic were asked to attempt to solve a question of their choosing from the four available. If they became stuck or had any questions, they were to ask the student who had written the question. This approach proved very successful. It took the locus of control from the teacher and diluted it around the room. The teacher observed that when students were asking questions of each other they were more willing to admit some basic misunderstandings to a classmate that they may be reluctant to admit to the teacher. The teacher also gained an insight into how students explained the process of solving the problems and the language they used with their peers. A relatively simple adaptation to the physical and social learning environment had an immediate and positive impact on student learning. In terms of creativity, this approach was new, relevant and useful to both the teacher and their students, and therefore creative.

This chapter discusses the importance of two of the fundamental elements that impact creativity: the physical and the social environment. It is clear that these two elements have an individual and a combined effect on creativity and are pivotal in the flourishing or floundering of creativity in schools (Amabile, 1998; Fan & Cai, 2020; Mokhtar Noriega et al., 2013; Richardson & Mishra, 2018). We know that students experience a variety of learning environments at school (Benavides et al., 2008) and that teachers understand that both physical and social environments impact learning. Research shows that, while the physical environment is important, it only accounts for approximately 40 per cent of the contextual effect on creativity.

CREATIVE ACTIONS

The social environment accounts for the remaining 60 per cent (Dul, 2019). Students need explicit instruction about how environments impact their learning to build their creative capacities from an informed perspective.

This chapter will explore how these may affect the development of creative competency in students, as well as build teacher efficacy in creative approaches to teaching and learning. We also introduce a recurring aspect of the book – wherever possible, we offer peer-reviewed evidence provided by teachers who have trialled the creative ideas in their classrooms. If peer-reviewed evidence is lacking, we acknowledge it and endeavour to inform the discussion with our own teaching experience and a sensible and logical perspective.

When it comes to discussing the importance of the physical and social environments in education, there appears to be a disconnect between the research and education policy globally. A recent paper (Patston, Kaufman et al., 2021) analysed curriculum documentation from twelve different countries and found that not one of the countries mentioned the importance of the social and physical environments in creativity.

When writing this book, we have always had to consider that every teacher in every school operates in a different context with differing available resources. There are many products that claim to make the classroom a better space for learning. However, when it comes to the physical environment, it can be difficult to see the difference between the actual evidence that a particular paint colour makes students more creative and the marketing spin offered by a furniture manufacturer (Barrett et al., 2015). Teachers need professional learning and development if they are to build their pedagogic competencies in teaching about, with and for creativity in physical and social environments. Learning environments need to be pedagogically flexible, not just physically flexible (Blackmore et al., 2011; Lackney, 2008).

We realise that few teachers have bottomless budgets and the ability to reconfigure their physical space whenever they enter a classroom. We will focus on some of the elements that are accessible to teachers who wish to expand their creative teaching and their students' creative competencies. We begin by looking at the physical environment.

PHYSICAL ENVIRONMENT

The physical environment of the classroom can be considered from three perspectives. The first is the internal physical space of the classroom, including where the teacher is positioned in relation to the students, and where the students are positioned in relation to each other. The second element is the resources, or affordances, students have in the classroom. These vary from items such as paper, card, scissors, coloured markers or sticky notes to areas where students can demonstrate work. The third element lies outside the classroom. This can range from holding lessons outside to travelling to other physical environments to stimulate students' creative processes.

ORGANISATION OF SPACE

The didactic model of students sitting in rows of solo desks being dictated to by a teacher should now be obsolete in school education. Or should it? A key component of all environments that enhance creativity is flexibility and adaptability (Davies et al., 2013). As with any other element of creativity, any considerations regarding the physical environment must be made in relation to the overall learning objectives regarding content and skills in the subject area, or in the creative competencies being developed in that particular lesson. Context is key in creativity – not every classroom environment needs to be creative. In other words, sometime the mood and purpose might be highly convergent as well.

Sometimes direct instruction is the most effective way to introduce students to new ideas or remind them of ideas that have already been covered. Short sharp targeted instruction to students who are sitting individually gives the teacher the opportunity to observe individual student responses – feedback is more immediate. In this type of seating arrangement teachers can very quickly read the visual, physical and verbal cues of their students as they respond to the information being given. However, we would suggest a scaffolded approach. Once it is clear that students understand what is required as individuals, they can then move into groups if it is appropriate. It is at this point that the physical elements of the learning space begin to have a new impact.

One of the biggest trends in education in the developed world over the last twenty years has been the move to flexible learning spaces (Kariippannon et al., 2019). The essence of the flexible learning space is to provide variation in both orientation of desks and seating and construction of learning groups within a classroom. The premise behind this is that variation in the physical learning environment builds a more positive and effective social environment, in terms of both student engagement and wellbeing, and that learning can be more student-centred. This premise may well be valid. However, a new learning space also needs some new pedagogy, as a change in the physical environment will also impact the social interaction between students. For example, these types of spaces may require the students to be more self-disciplined – if students need more deliberate management, these new learning environments may be unsuccessful. For a new physical configuration to be an efficient and effective space for learning, teachers should plan their pedagogy to adapt to the new environment. We also recommend they explain to the students the purpose behind this adjustment and how they anticipate it will benefit student learning. Teachers and students need to build their competence in working in an open shared space together, over time.

In terms of creativity, if students are sitting at individual desks or in pairs facing the front of the room, there is a limited range of opportunities to share ideas; the natural focus is the teacher. This arrangement determines the pace of the lesson and positions the teacher as the key holder of knowledge and skills. It also establishes relatively immovable social relationships between students and a fixed social distance between individual students and the teacher. Teachers frequently observe anecdotally that the 'smart' and 'good' students sit at the front of the classroom, an idea confirmed by research (Pichierri & Guido, 2016). This research also reported that introverts tended to sit towards the back of the classroom, indicating the need for teachers to consider individual personalities when organising seating plans.

One simple change has been shown to increase both individual and group creativity in the classroom: putting desks into clusters (Tobia et al., 2020). As demonstrated in the beginning of this chapter, when students operate in groups rather than individually or in pairs, there is an increase in social interaction between students that is not possible when students are sitting in rows. Students are also more likely to ask questions they may be reluctant to ask the teacher.

Alternatively, the Harkness arrangement places students and the teacher in an oval configuration (Catterall et al., 2019). This arrangement is excellent for building group creativity as all students can both see and be seen by others and generate collaborative solutions to problems. The teacher is also in a more neutral position regarding their influence on the group. To facilitate an equal distribution of problem-solving tasks and the generation of creative ideas, it might be necessary for the teacher to find either a scripted or randomised allocation for students to contribute to the group.

The most flexible learning spaces inside a traditional classroom are the zoned classrooms (Barrett et al., 2017). In their simplest form these classrooms position different configurations of desks and seating in different parts of the room. Each zone is designated to a particular type of task. This might be group collaboration on a whiteboard in one area or quiet individual work in another. In their most complex form, these spaces have varied sizes and heights of both tables and chairs, ranging from standing desks to bean bags. In each of these arrangements, teachers must consider the purpose of the lesson and the individual learning needs of all students. Flexible physical learning environments promote flexible thinking, which is an important part of creativity, and allow students to understand that various elements of the creative process may be more or less effective in different physical environments. By experimenting with a range of physical configurations, teachers and students will come to understand which physical environments are most conducive to creative learning for them and the class.

THE CONTEXT OF THE LESSON

At times it is necessary for students to build and apply their creative competencies as individuals and as a group. The choice you make as a teacher will always depend on content and context. There are similarities, but also some differences, between the skills and attitudes needed for individuals or groups in the creative process. In terms of development, it is preferable that students feel comfortable with their individual attitudes and skills of creativity before embarking on collaborative creativity.

In a school where Tim worked, a particular class was always held in one of the dreaded portable classrooms. The space lacked the richness of the home rooms, where teachers created learning environments that they believed most effectively met the needs of their students. However, it is easy to blame a stark physical environment for creating an unhealthy or inefficient learning atmosphere. Tim's solution was twofold. Before the students sat down he discussed the purpose of the lesson and why a particular seating arrangement would enhance the learning for that class. The students then took a few minutes to construct this arrangement. Over the course of a term students began to understand that reorganising their physical space could have a positive impact on their learning. He also brought butchers' paper, removeable adhesives and whiteboard markers into each lesson. These could be used to create a 360-degree classroom where students could explore their ideas. Over time students began to actively contribute to the seating arrangements, the composition of groups and the learning materials used and displayed.

For an individual teacher to establish the efficacy of a particular seating arrangement we would advise a relatively simple experimental design. As previously mentioned, if a teacher is seeking divergent responses to questions this may be inhibited by students sitting individually in rows. A simple solution is to ask a series of questions and note how many students respond and the way they respond. A similar approach can then be tried with desks in clusters of four or by sitting students in an oval arrangement following the Harkness model. By noting the changes in student responses, you will develop an understanding of how the creative variation in the physical environment has affected students' learning.

RESOURCES

In addition to the physical space, other elements, known as affordances, can influence the teaching and learning environment in terms of creativity. Affordances can be both material and personal (Glăveanu, 2013). In this instance, the term is applied to material resources within the environment. These may include books, musical instruments, computers, a hammer or saw or any other physical objects. Personal resources, which may include relevant knowledge or expertise (such as speaking a foreign language), or access to people with such skills (such as being able to consult an expert), are social affordances. In terms of creativity the richer the variety of affordances, the richer the opportunities for creative thinking. Creative thinking can be stimulated by words, images, sounds, people or objects.

MATERIAL AFFORDANCES

Narrowing or limiting the resources students can use in the creative process can be a powerful stimulus for creativity. Having constraints can force students to consider highly creative uses for materials if they are the only materials available, increasing their cognitive load by drawing more deeply from their pre-existing knowledge and looking at ideas from new perspectives (Mansour et al., 2018). For example, in an English class students could create a poem which must include

CREATIVE ACTIONS

some specific words, or alternatively, must not contain any nouns. In mathematics students may have to demonstrate the use of more than one mathematical process to solve a problem. In the following examples constraints are used to build student creativity in a music classroom (Davis, 2018) and develop art and environmental science knowledge and skills (Mansour et al., 2018).

Music, upper primary and lower secondary, Australia

WHAT THE TEACHER FOUND

> *For those who invest in the process, it can be testing and uncomfortable, but the rewards are multi-dimensional. The findings of this research confirm that creativity can be stimulated through the use of productive constraints.* (Davis, 2018, p. 352)

Component of creativity	Facet(s) of creativity	Teaching with or for creativity
Environment	Constraints	With
Attitudes and attributes	Risk-taking	For
Process	Inquire, ideate and implement	For

PURPOSE OF LESSON: SUBJECT KNOWLEDGE OR SKILLS

The purpose of this lesson was for students to build subject content and skills in music by using the pentatonic scale. Students were required to explore both individual notes and chords within the scale with improvised instruments and explore simple rhythms.

PURPOSE OF LESSON: TEACHING ABOUT CREATIVITY OR TEACHING FOR CREATIVITY

In terms of creativity, the purpose of this lesson was for students to learn that creativity can happen effectively with constraints by engaging in practical music-making with limited resources. The aim was to teach the concept of risk-taking by using familiar objects in an unfamiliar context. In this case a range of barbecue tools were used to explore pitch. Students used a process of inquiry (exploring the pitches of the tools), ideation (think about how the pitches of different tools related) and implementation (play the scale and create chords). The students that were given constraints thought more deeply, were more creative and achieved higher grades than those without constraints.

REFERENCE

Davis, S. (2018). *Flexibility, constraints and creativity: Cultivating creativity in teacher education.* In K. Snepvangers, P. Thomson & A. Harris (Eds.), *Creativity policy, partnerships and practice in education* (pp. 331–352). Palgrave Macmillan. https://doi.org/10.1007/978-3-319-96725-7_15

ACCESS

THE CREATIVE PLACE

Art and environmental science, secondary, Oman

WHAT THE TEACHER FOUND

> *The Department of art education ... aims through its programs to achieve creativity and functionality in art work. This provides students with several teaching strategies that develop critical thinking and problem-solving skills. Also, it enables students to give aesthetic and critical judgments in the field of fine arts.* (Mansour et al., 2018, p. 83)

Component of creativity	Facet(s) of creativity	Teaching with or for creativity
Environment	Constraints	With
Attitudes and attributes	Intellectual curiosity	For
Process	Design and iteration (sketching)	For

PURPOSE OF LESSON: SUBJECT KNOWLEDGE OR SKILLS

The purpose of this lesson was for students to build subject content and skills knowledge in both art and environmental science by examining resources and combinations. This was achieved in art by exploring the relationship between elements in an artwork in creating visual effects, and how artistic composition can be achieved through combining different elements. Students were required to evaluate how the aesthetic values of balance, diversity and rhythm contributed to the final artwork. In environmental science this was achieved by building an appreciation of finite resources and the need for sustainability in art.

PURPOSE OF THE LESSON: TEACHING WITH OR FOR CREATIVITY

In terms of creativity, the purpose of this lesson was for students to build an understanding that creativity can happen effectively with constraints, by creating artworks with limited resources. Students developed their intellectual curiosity by combining a range of materials in novel and interesting ways. Students were also introduced to the problem-solving process through researching, sketching, iteration and drafting.

REFERENCE
Mansour, H., & Al-yahyai, F., & Heiba, E. (2018). The recycling concept in art education at Sultan Qaboos University. *Journal of Education and Social Development, 2*(2), 82–87. https://zenodo.org/record/2526431#.Yu_BHHZBy3A

ACCESS

We also stress that not every classroom environment needs to be creative. Sometimes the mood and the purpose might be highly convergent. Given the majority of examinations conducted in classrooms around the world happen in a seating plan of individual desks, it is essential that students are comfortable learning and thinking convergently as individuals. It is also likely that different subjects will require different physical spaces for optimal learning, and we encourage you to experiment in your classrooms (Barrett et al., 2017).

SOCIAL ENVIRONMENT

The social environment refers to the style and type of interaction between teachers and students in the classroom. There are many other things teachers can consider when striving to build an environment for creativity in their classroom. These include modelling the attitudes and attributes of creativity, which will be explained in more depth in Chapter 4. There are times when students' learning is best served by peer-to-peer or group collaboration, and others where knowledge can be delivered to a whole class simultaneously. As with all the other aspects of creativity, context is key (Beghetto & Kaufman, 2014).

TEACHER-CONSTRUCTED ENVIRONMENT

The construction of the social environment begins at the very start of a lesson. Part of the creative environment is the mood of the classroom, and the teacher can set the tone. Rather than beginning a lesson by students opening laptops or textbooks, students' cognitive engagement will be higher if they know that a lesson starts in a different way each time (Patston, 2021b). For example, a lesson could start with a statement, a question or an activity, thus generating an active rather than passive learning environment. This will promote student metacognition and increase productivity (Freeman et. al., 2014).

This will also help teachers and students build their creative competencies over time and realise that both can support and enable the development of knowledge and skills in any subject (Patston, 2021b). Rather than starting the lesson with a question from the teacher, a student may be pre-selected to ask a question. Students might swap notes from a previous class to compare understanding. A useful exercise to determine student levels of understanding is the traffic light exercise. Students with understanding of a particular concept sit in the 'green zone', those who are uncertain sit in the 'yellow zone' and those who do not understand sit in the 'red zone'. Green-zone students explain the concept to red-zone students, while the yellow-zone students observe. This encourages a social environment of psychological safety, an important ingredient in developing creativity, which we will discuss in the following section.

In a Year 10 mathematics class taught by a colleague of James', students were given a problem for homework they did not have the knowledge to solve individually. They were instructed not to use the internet for assistance but to go as far as they could on an individual basis and then stop. When they arrived at the lesson the next day, they were put into groups and asked to collaboratively solve the problem. This ensured that the lesson started with a certain level of intensity.

PSYCHOLOGICAL SAFETY

The social environment should also include acceptance, tolerance and meaningful, non-punitive feedback (Cropley, 2001; Holinger & Kaufman, 2018). The term *psychological safety*, although more prevalent in business literature, refers to an individual or group's perceptions of the consequences of risk-taking (Frazier et al., 2017). Psychological safety can be translated into teacher–student friendly language using words such as *safe* or *trusting space* for feedback.

Teachers need to build an atmosphere of trust to facilitate better information exchange and knowledge sharing (Carmeli, Sheaffer et al., 2013; Gong et al., 2012). Psychological safety has a demonstrated positive influence in terms of creativity (Carmeli, Reiter-Palmon & Ziv, 2010), as those who feel a sense of psychological safety are more likely to take greater intellectual risks (Edmondson & Mogelof, 2016). This is another reason why it is important to dispel students' fear of failure by building a sense of freedom in the classroom. Recent evidence from adult education has demonstrated that unless students feel a sense of psychological safety, their ability to take risks, have freedom to experiment with ideas and be creative may be compromised (O'Donovan & McAuliffe, 2020).

The following example demonstrates the importance of psychological safety in the classroom, particularly when discussing contentious issues.

CREATIVE ACTIONS

Religious education, secondary, Norway

WHAT THE TEACHER FOUND

> *The learner must dare to leave ingrained beliefs and try to see the world and phenomena from new perspectives. In that sense, the learner needs to feel safe to venture to meet new and unfamiliar perspectives.* (Flensner & Von der Lippe, 2019, p. 286)

Component of creativity	Facet(s) of creativity	Teaching with or for creativity
Environment	Psychological safety	For
Attitudes and attributes	Intellectual risk-taking	With
Attitudes and attributes	Multiple perspectives	With

PURPOSE OF LESSON: SUBJECT KNOWLEDGE OR SKILLS

The purpose of this lesson was for students to build knowledge about and understanding of the term *political correctness* when discussing religion, and to learn the skill of respectful listening, by discussing controversial matters in an informed and respectful manner.

PURPOSE OF THE LESSON: TEACHING WITH OR FOR CREATIVITY

In terms of creativity, the purpose of this lesson was for students to build an understanding of the concept of psychological safety – that views can be freely expressed without receiving negative or aggressive responses – by listening to the opinions of their peers which may be beyond their current narrow experiential view.

The second purpose was for students to build their intellectual risk-taking by offering opinions to the class which may be considered risky by themselves or by their peers.

REFERENCE
Flensner, K. K., & Von der Lippe, M. (2019). Being safe from what and safe for whom? A critical discussion of the conceptual metaphor of 'safe space'. *Intercultural Education*, *30*(3), 275–288. https://doi.org/10.1080/14675986.2019.1540102

ACCESS

ACTIVE LISTENING

Teachers can have a tendency to talk too much (Walsh, 2002). Active listening is an acquired skill and essential for developing a creative learning environment (Beghetto, 2009). Students are more likely to express their creative ideas if they believe that their teacher is listening and engaged (Black & Wiliam, 1998). Similarly, students want their peers to listen to them and hear their ideas, particularly when undertaking group work (Mueller & Fleming, 2001). In peer-to-peer conversations, students who articulate their understandings and are more receptive to peer feedback often feel more confident sharing and discussing ideas without their teachers' input (Boud et al., 2001). This type of active listening not only enhances student engagement but also promotes the concept of safe risk-taking in the creative process (Beghetto, 2009).

FEEDBACK

The same is true of constructive feedback (Brookhart, 2010). Feedback can be controlling or informal, and people expecting controlling feedback are more likely to be cautious and worried about what others think – not an ideal set-up for creativity (Wang et al., 2017). Negative feedback given poorly may also have a deleterious effect on creativity, with students less likely to share non-standard ideas (Svensson, 2015). It is important that students are given constructive, timely feedback on their creative process to encourage student autonomy and lead them to the next phase of their creative processes (Fairweather & Cramond, 2010).

Feedback can be given in many ways: verbally, visually or written, formally or informally. By modelling best practice, students will eventually develop the capacity to provide self-feedback to improve. Feedback should always be task specific, focus on elements the student can control and require more effort from the student than the teacher (Wiliam, 2012). When giving feedback teachers must demonstrate clear, honest communication, value individual contributions and set clear goals.

One of the most powerful forms of feedback, if used correctly, is peer-to-peer feedback (Davies et al., 2013; Karwowski, 2015). Building a classroom environment in which feedback is valued and integrated can greatly aid the development of creativity, as well as improve academic outcomes (Double et al., 2020; Tseng & Tsai, 2007). In terms of building the social environment of creativity, the language and tone used by teachers when giving feedback is critical to its success. Teachers can build a socially supportive environment of creativity by using words such as *perseverance* and *tolerance* so students understand that it takes time to mature and generate ideas, and by promoting more questions and fewer answers so students become reflective and independent thinkers.

In the creative social environment, it is essential for students to have a positive view of the process of iteration, known in some subjects as drafting or prototyping. The term *failure* may have pejorative implications for teachers, students and parents (Loscalzo, 2014). Teachers need to clearly articulate the benefits of iteration, verbally and through modelling behaviour, and explain the value of learning from mistakes and failures.

Similarly, appropriate use of the word *critical* is essential if learning environments are to support, rather than inhibit, creativity. The term needs to be used in the context of constructive feedback, rather than as negative criticism. This may involve encouraging and guiding the student to seek additional information, rather than simply observing that the work was not of a sufficient standard. Fear of failure needs to be dispelled during iterative processual learning. However, this type of change at the system level takes a long time. In the meantime, teachers can be supportive of the process of iteration, using language appropriate to the context. We will discuss the process of iteration in Chapter 5.

CONSTRAINTS

As mentioned previously, creativity sometimes needs constraints to be effective. The next two sections describe three of the constraints that teachers may explore when building creative competencies in their students.

TIME

Given creativity is a set of teachable knowledges, skills and attitudes, it is important that appropriate time is allocated in the classroom for creative tasks (Ritter & Mostert, 2017). Flexibility in time can be helpful in optimising the creative environment (Burnard et al., 2006). This does not mean that creative tasks require excessive amounts of time. In fact, a limited amount of time can have a positive influence on evaluating creativity (Baer & Oldham, 2006). Effective time management by students also has a positive impact on creativity (Britton & Tesser, 1991; Zampetakis et al., 2010). There can clearly be tensions between having too much time and not enough time (Beghetto, 2016). As with most examples in this book, the best way to see how much time gets the best results is through trial and error.

The following example found that students sketching under time constraints had less time to ruminate on negative self-talk about their sketching skills.

THE CREATIVE PLACE

Art, lower secondary, New Zealand

WHAT THE TEACHER FOUND

> *They noted a flexible approach to time within a planned supportive environment to encourage risk taking towards a creative response. They introduced influences to enhance the design physical space, to evoke creative thought through imagery (within the theme) and music* (McGlashan, 2018, p. 378)

Component of creativity	Facet(s) of creativity	Teaching with or for creativity
Environment	Constraints	With
Environment	Psychological safety	With
Process	Generating ideas	For

PURPOSE OF LESSON: SUBJECT KNOWLEDGE OR SKILLS

The purpose of this lesson was for students to build skills in rapid sketching by drawing a sketch of each other in one minute, followed by sketching three different objects for three minutes each. Rapid thinking sketching communicates information about shape, form and narrative through a lively interaction rather than a rigid process and is best experienced prior to students being introduced to existing works either by designers, artists or other students.

PURPOSE OF THE LESSON: TEACHING WITH OR FOR CREATIVITY

In terms of creativity, the purpose of this lesson was for students to build an understanding that creativity can happen effectively with constraints by sketching under time constraints. Another purpose was for students to improve their idea generating process by not allowing critical thoughts to occur during the sketching process since there is no time for students to overwork, criticise or sanitise initial ideas. The final purpose was for students to increase their sense of psychological safety and reduce competition in the class by having students sketch each other in pairs without looking at the page.

REFERENCE

McGlashan, A. (2018). A pedagogic approach to enhance creative Ideation in classroom practice. *International Journal of Technology and Design Education, 28*(2), 377–393. https://doi.org/10.1007/s10798-017-9404-5

ACCESS

DIGITAL AFFORDANCES

Students are becoming increasingly reliant on digital technologies and the internet is frequently the first port of call for students looking for information. Students need to recognise when information is needed beyond their own personal experience and resources, and to evaluate the reliability and relative value of information. When digital technologies first appeared, it was believed they could aid the development of higher-order thinking skills, such as discernment and critical thinking (Hopson et al., 2014). Recent research is less optimistic and indicates that as students become more reliant on technology, their research skills are declining (Van de Oudeweetering & Voogt, 2018). It is essential that students build their research competencies throughout school to develop higher-order thinking skills and therefore be more creative. At times this will require explicit teaching in the classroom. Once the information has been found, students need the skills to evaluate the value of the source and its contents, and the skills to store and organise the information for retrieval and sharing. Given that creativity can only occur when a student has a certain level of knowledge and skills, there is a strong link between digital competency and creativity.

PERSONAL AFFORDANCES

However, creativity is not just based on knowledge gained from the internet. Given that creativity requires higher-order thinking skills, students need to develop a set of interpersonal as well as digital research competencies. Students should undertake a negotiated approach toward creative problem-solving. Firstly, they look to their own set of knowledge and skills – do they have what they need to solve the problem? If not, their second option should be reaching out to a peer, or peers (Allsopp, 1997).

In a Year 8 geography class taught by a colleague of David's, the topic was urban design in different countries (Patston, 2021b). The teacher asked students if they had been to any of the countries discussed, or seen them on television or online (Patston, 2021b). Those students who had been to the cities were able to describe in detail the problems they had witnessed such as waste disposal or overpopulation. These observations led the group to a more creative range of solutions to urban problems as they were able to draw upon real-world experience (Patston, 2021b).

Students may also think about their broader social network and the knowledge and skills of their parents or relatives. Finally, students may conduct online research under the supervision of their teacher as a means of developing both research and thinking skills (Tanggaard, 2014). By building this sequence (looking to self, looking to peers, looking to the extended network and then looking online), students develop a sense of confidence about their knowledge and skills and those of their classmates.

COLLABORATIVE CREATIVITY

Collaborative creativity skills need to be developed in addition to the individual attitudes and skills of creativity discussed across the book. It is essential for students to develop some metacognition (also called self-awareness or self-understanding) regarding their creative processes before building the attitudes and skills needed for collaborative creativity (Kaufman & Beghetto, 2013a). Self-awareness facilitates creative processes and outputs, and the combination of self and contextual knowledge is important when students are being creative (Silvia & O'Brien, 2004; Sternberg, 1998). When fostering self-awareness in the classroom, it is advisable for students to be given tasks that enable them to reflect on and develop their own creative capacities in addition to developing their group problem-solving skills through collaborative tasks. Students are capable of doing this, even at the primary level of schooling (Kaufman et al., 2015). Linking back to earlier in this chapter, teachers must use appropriate, useful and actionable feedback as well as exposure to experience as students build their creative competencies on an individual level, discussed further in Chapter 4.

The ultimate expression of the creative social environment is collaborative creativity. Creative collaboration has benefits beyond the organisation of students within the learning space; group work traverses both the organisational and social aspects of the learning environment (Aguilar & Pifarre Turmo, 2019). If individuals have strong levels of creative metacognition, they are more likely to contribute effectively to collaborative creative tasks (Hirst et al., 2009; Pirola-Merlo & Mann, 2004). Similar logic applies to group creativity; it should be time, task and context appropriate (Beghetto & Kaufman, 2014). Teachers need knowledge and skills to effectively use collaborative problem-solving in their classroom. Successful groups are often comprised of diverse people, such as people from different cultures with diverse interests and knowledge and a variety of life experiences (Chua, 2018; Pluut & Curşeu, 2013; Yap et al., 2005). Teachers can explore and use this diversity if it exists in their classes. Creativity-promoting environments also include groups that are supportive, trusting and receptive to new ideas, but also willing to constructively challenge each other's ideas. This is evident in both primary and secondary education (Harris & De Bruin, 2018; Kong et al., 2018).

WHAT IS COLLABORATION?

The OECD has a clear definition of collaboration which it uses in its PISA testing:

> **❝** *Collaborative problem-solving competency is the capacity of an individual to effectively engage in a process whereby two or more agents attempt to solve a problem by sharing the understanding and effort required to come to a solution and pooling their knowledge, skills and efforts to reach that solution.* **❞** *(OECD, 2013, p. 6)*

WHAT ARE ITS KEY ELEMENTS?

Successful collaboration must have:
- students with a common purpose working together to solve a problem
- clear accountability regarding the contributions each member makes to the task
- clarity about the different roles each member of the group has throughout the process
- students who work effectively and respectfully, valuing each member's contributions
- flexibility and willingness to compromise to achieve the common goal
- shared responsibility for both the process and the final outcome.

WHAT IS THE DIFFERENCE BETWEEN COLLABORATION, COOPERATION AND COORDINATION?

These three terms are distinct in relation to attitudes, behaviours and outcomes and refer to different stages of the creative process (Castañer & Oliveira, 2020).

Coordination is the process of determining which roles students will take during the creative process. For younger and inexperienced students this process is best completed by the teacher. It is fair to say that if students coordinate the groups, they are more likely to be based on friendships. A big part of psychosocial adolescent development is determining social place within a group. It can require careful and detailed justification from the teacher on why a particular combination of students has been selected to work together. Students also need to learn that they may not have a choice regarding group membership and need to learn to work with whoever is chosen. Once again, the sporting analogy works here. Students understand that a sports team is a random selection of people with a shared interest who need to work together for a common goal. It is worth mentioning that students tend to be quite forgiving on the sporting field, at least until their senior years. This spirit of empathy and understanding also needs to be a part of the collaborative process in their subject areas.

Cooperation is the beginning of the implementation of the goal and the processes involved around working together. It is predominantly concerned with each member performing the tasks according to their role.

Collaboration refers to the attitudes and behaviours needed for a coordinated group to effectively work together from both a practical and a social perspective. An effective collaborator is one who shows empathy for the perspective, attitudes and competencies of others throughout the process. This is demonstrated in the language used during the process as well as in the practical running of the process. This is the element with which students most frequently struggle. Some explicit instruction on appropriate language for feedback is often needed to help students.

WHY USE COLLABORATION?

For students thinking about life after high school, they need to know that collaboration is seen as a key competency in having a successful life, not just in the workplace. The social skills needed for effective collaboration are also needed in friendships, relationships and especially the home environment. In the workplace, social skills are increasingly in demand and attract a premium in terms of remuneration (Mo, 2017).

The following example demonstrates the efficacy of collaboration in mathematical problem-solving.

CREATIVE ACTIONS

Mathematics, lower secondary, Singapore

WHAT THE TEACHER FOUND

> *We suggest that teachers may do well in being more deliberate in designing for thinking spaces within formal learning time, and scaffolding students towards more strategic planning and reflection of their learning behaviours, processes and outcomes, not only as individuals but also, importantly, as collective teams.* (Tan, et al., 2018, p.5)

Component of creativity	Facet(s) of creativity	Teaching with or for creativity
Environment	Constraints	With
Environment	Psychological safety	With
Process	Collaborative critical thinking	For

PURPOSE OF LESSON: SUBJECT KNOWLEDGE OR SKILLS

The purpose of this lesson was for students to build skills in collaborative problem-solving in mathematics by combining individual information to solve a mathematical problem. Students were given partial information regarding a mathematical problem and combined their individual information with one other student. They then used their mathematical knowledge and skills as a pair to determine a collaborative solution to the problem.

PURPOSE OF THE LESSON: TEACHING WITH OR FOR CREATIVITY

In terms of creativity, the purpose of this lesson was for students to collaboratively and creatively problem-solve by having a dialogue and sharing information with their peers. The 'quantity of ideas produced during an argumentation process conducted within a group is positively associated with successful completion of creative problem-solving tasks' (Tan, et al. 2018, p. 97). The cognitive and social processes including 'formulation of problem solutions, collective identification of goals, evaluation of progress towards goals, creation of common ground, forging consensus and dealing with conflicts, differentiate successful and unsuccessful problem-solving in collaborative creativity' (Tan, et al. 2018, p. 98). Teachers indicated that the framework helped students to conceptualise their work within the full trajectory of creative production, offering touchstones along the route to keep them on track.

REFERENCE

Tan, J. P-L., Caleon, I., Ng, H. L., Poon, C. L., & Koh, E. (2018). *Collective creativity competencies and collaborative problem-solving outcomes: Insights from the dialogic interactions of Singapore student teams*. In E. Care, P. Griffin & M. Wilson (Eds.), *Assessment and teaching of 21st century skills: Research and applications* (pp. 95–118). Springer. https://doi.org/10.1007/978-3-319-65368-6_6

ACCESS

WHAT THE EVIDENCE SAYS ABOUT COLLABORATION

- Collaborative creativity normally gives higher quality in terms of the solution.
- Social negotiation is an important skill to develop.
- Work can be divided among team members, spreading the load.
- Students can bring a variety of knowledge, perspectives and experiences to solve the problem.
- Group members can stimulate and motivate each other, leading to enhanced creativity.
- Collaboration is useful in developing skills in conflict resolution. (Baruah & Paulus, 2019)

WHAT IS THE IDEAL GROUP SIZE FOR EFFECTIVE COLLABORATION?

The answer depends on the task – how many students need to be in a group to fill the roles and meet the goals? There is broad consensus in literature that large groups are less effective than small groups when it comes to collaboration, as more social factors come into play and it becomes more difficult for every member to contribute (Rannastu et. al., 2019; Saqr et al., 2019).

Putting students into pairs for collaboration can be effective, but student absence can compromise this. For groups bigger than a pair, a range between three and six appears optimal. We would suggest experimenting with different group sizes depending on the class, task and subject.

WHAT ARE THE KEY ROLES IN COLLABORATION?

The roles of collaborative creativity fall into two distinct areas: the procedural and the behavioural. Procedural roles essentially monitor the progress of the process. Someone needs to be responsible for keeping track of time. Someone needs to make sure that ideas are recorded, collected and categorised for selection. Meanwhile, behavioural roles monitor the actions and behaviours of the students. For example, someone needs to be responsible for maintaining relevant communication and ensuring that ideas are shared in a respectful manner. Someone needs to coordinate and support feedback, make decisions about when a phase of the process is complete and negotiate the format in which the solutions are presented.

These roles need to be covered whether the students are working in pairs or in a group of six (Dowell et al., 2020). When first learning about collaboration, students tend to choose roles they think suit them best or simply prefer. It is essential that, over the course of their learning journey, students experience all roles in the collaborative process. Assuming different roles and looking at things from a variety of perspectives will help build their creative competencies. At some point, as with all the creative competencies, there must be explicit teaching of these roles. Creating and running scenarios early in the collaborative process and providing modelling and feedback is more effective than just throwing students into a collaborative experience and hoping they will be able to accurately assess their competence. Collaborative problem-solving requires keeping the team organised – for example, by monitoring interactions and providing feedback to each other. Team members need to build interpersonal competencies that help them manage relationships within the team, such as encouraging participation and effective communication. With experience and structured feedback students will develop the ability to take others' perspectives and to consider alternative views of problem elements. We strongly advise either informal or formal formative assessment of collaboration competency (see Chapter 6 for discussion of assessment).

Once again, we stress that it is not up to one teacher to do all of this. Having a collaborative teaching approach regarding planning with colleagues, it is possible to share the load and for students to see the commonalities between learning areas.

WHAT ARE SOME OF THE OBSTACLES TO EFFECTIVE COLLABORATION?

There are a number of obstacles that may inhibit effective collaboration (Le et al., 2018).

- A lack of collaborative skills: These can be both behavioural and procedural. Students require scaffolding around the process before they can be expected to be proficient. For instance, explaining ideas clearly to group members can be a challenge for some students. Skills such respectful listening, not interrupting and accepting new perspectives might take some time to develop.
- Challenges in monitoring: Teachers also need experience and skills as facilitators. Ensuring that every student in every group is on task and on time, and monitoring behavioural issues, can be an issue. By modelling these behaviours in the instructional phase, teachers should expect that students' skills will improve. Documenting evidence by using waypoints or tickets to demonstrate progress is one method to achieve this.
- Personality: Students may not be aware of the amount and manner in which they contribute to the group. It must be made clear in the instructional phase that dominant personalities may need to temper themselves, and that the group needs to give space, time and psychological safety for introverts to express themselves.
- Competence status: All students hold self-beliefs when it comes to their perceived confidence or competence in a subject. Students who believe they lack subject knowledge or skills may be reluctant to contribute. Under these circumstances, it is tactical to use silent brainstorming or brainwriting when generating or selecting ideas.
- Equal contribution: If there is one thing that frustrates students, it is peers who do not participate or contribute their share. This can be managed by the teacher during the process or reflected in assessments of the process by including peer-to-peer observations and feedback.
- Friendship: While students like working with their friends, this can cause some complications. In a practical sense, students may spend more time discussing friendship issues and less time being on task. From a social perspective, students may be less willing to criticise their friend's ideas.

In summary, when contemplating collaboration as a creative pedagogic approach, careful consideration must be given by the teacher to the groups in terms of not only subject knowledge and skills but also personality and social skills (Barron, 2003). Whenever using collaboration, students need to be introduced to some of the opportunities and obstacles. By role-playing examples of the obstacles and how to overcome them, teachers can build the collaborative competency of their students. Group collaboration is a skilled activity, which requires instruction, practice and feedback (Carmeli et al., 2013).

Throughout the book we stress the importance of understanding the value of iteration and failure. Our journey to this point has clearly shown us the importance of both. In workshops or classes on collaboration, we are often surprised by how much assumed and erroneous knowledge there is by both teachers and students regarding the collaborative process. There can be assumptions that students know how to collaborate (and understand all the concepts we have discussed so far) and, therefore, do not need any explicit instruction. There is also the myth that students are fully functioning and competent independent learners before they leave high school. This lack of understanding can lead to poor results when undertaking the collaborative process. The following example illustrates the point.

CREATIVE COLLABORATION IN A STEM WORKSHOP

Several years ago, David was conducting a creativity in STEM workshop with a group of lower secondary students. He made several significant errors in the planning and execution of the workshop, which led to less than satisfactory results.

The first error was the planning of the scope and outcomes of the workshop itself, by overestimating what was achievable within the proposed time frame. Normal classes had been collapsed and students were focusing on this project for three days. It was assumed that the students would have some competency in each stage of the creative process, from idea generation to idea recording, critical thinking skills and the idea selection process, and finally the presentation phase. It was also assumed that if they didn't have these skills, they would pick them up along the way.

A two-page document outlined the content of the workshop, the creative process step-by-step and a few dot points about effective collaboration. Those materials were clearly not enough. It was also presumed that by selecting the groups randomly, there would be a levelling of any issues regarding subject knowledge and skills, or personalities, attitudes and collaborative skills. The supervising teachers also assumed that students had the digital research capacities to find solutions to their problem online. It soon became clear that all presumptions were incorrect to some extent. With failure and inconsistency at each stage, the cumulative results were less than satisfactory. Probably the greatest disappointment was that students were very frustrated at the end of the process.

CREATIVE ACTIONS

As mentioned previously, the most important step to begin with is to teach about creativity. We will now take you through how this STEM project should have been run.

STEP 1: INTRODUCE THE CONCEPT – WHAT DO STUDENTS ALREADY KNOW?

As previously mentioned, the attitudes and skills of collaboration need to be developed incrementally over time. In our view it is better to focus on one or two aspects at a time and build from there. The best type of teaching is to start from the students' point of understanding by asking where they feel they already collaborate.

Working in groups has a number of benefits that need to be explained to students. Tim often uses the metaphor of the sporting team. For anyone to play a team sport they need a combination of physical skills, game knowledge and social competency to work together. Most students recall their first attempts at teamwork in a sporting context. Over time they build capacities and understand the importance of each member performing their role (not everyone can be a scorer, some need to defend). The same is true of collaborative creativity. Effective collaboration requires two key elements for success, group construction and the necessary attitudes and skills. An effective way to demonstrate this to students is through a simple role-based problem-solving game.

STEP 2: COLLABORATING AND REFLECTING

If students are novices in collaboration, a simple role-based problem-solving game can be used to stimulate their thinking. There are many simple games, often in the STEM area, that can be used to expose students to a more academic form of collaboration than a traditional game. The following example is but one game format designed for adolescents that can be played using a variety of rules and constraints.

> *Divide your group into sets of two to four people. Give each set two newspaper sheets, one foot of tape, five paper clips, one foot of string and a pair of scissors. Give each group 15 minutes to build the tallest tower. Measure each tower to determine who built the tallest one. You can also have the groups describe their approach to building their tower and what they learned about working together.* (SMILE, n.d., p. 4)

Variations of this example can include using particular types of materials and constraints to illustrate various elements of the collaborative process in creativity. To demonstrate how every member of a team needs to contribute, instruction may be given that everybody in the group needs to add one construction element. Elements may be added or subtracted from the listed materials for students to repeat the experiment and see what has changed.

Once students have had a brief introduction and taken time to reflect on the attitude and behaviour elements needed to solve the problem, and how successful each of these elements were, it is time for more explicit instruction of the terminology, the attitudes and the behaviours needed for effective collaboration in creativity. Examples of such attitudes and behaviours may include building a shared understanding within the group, collectively contributing to the problem-solving process, and regulating one's personal behaviour throughout the process (Scoular et al., 2020).

The following is an excellent example of collaboration in preference to cooperation in practice. This example introduces students to collaboration using the computer game Minecraft (Baek & Touati, 2020).

CREATIVE ACTIONS

Science, technology, engineering, art and mathematics (STEAM) and design, upper primary and lower secondary, South Korea

WHAT THE TEACHER FOUND

"Collaborative game-based learning, which involves synchronous communication, symmetry of roles, and collective problem-solving tasks may create better conditions for higher group performance than cooperative learning where students work interdependently." (Baek & Touati, 2020, p. 21)

Component of creativity	Facet(s) of creativity	Teaching with or for creativity
Environment	Collaboration	For
Process	Problem-solving	For

PURPOSE OF LESSON: SUBJECT KNOWLEDGE OR SKILLS

The purpose of this lesson was for students to build their research competencies by using the digital game Minecraft to design two houses, one using tiles and the other using straw. This lesson combined the subjects of art and engineering to design housing that is functional and stable.

PURPOSE OF THE LESSON: TEACHING WITH OR FOR CREATIVITY

In terms of creativity, the purpose of this lesson was for students to learn the difference between cooperation and collaboration, and the different individual responsibilities in a collaborative project, in a digital environment. The second purpose was for students to build their problem-solving skills by using iteration in the design process.

REFERENCE

Baek, Y., & Touati, A. (2020). Comparing collaborative and cooperative gameplay for academic and gaming achievements. *Journal of Educational Computing Research*, 57(8), 2110–2140. https://doi.org/10.1177/0735633118825385

ACCESS

CONCLUSION

Both the social and physical environments can have a significant impact on the development of creative competencies in students. It is also clear from the evidence that students need explicit teaching of the facets and components of creativity and exposure and experience with all of these. Finally, it is essential for students to have either structured feedback and or formative assessment of their evolving creative competencies.

CHAPTER 4

THE CREATIVE PERSON: WHAT ARE THE KEY ATTITUDES AND ATTRIBUTES OF CREATIVITY?

Referred to as the person in the 4Ps (as discussed in Chapter 1), this factor focuses on the personal attributes and attitudes of students in the creative process. For a student to develop their creative capacities, certain psychological attributes are desirable (Ivcevic & Mayer, 2006; Kaufman, 2016). The following factors have been shown to be important for teachers to consider when teaching with and for creativity. Some of these are attitudes that teachers can support in the classroom if positive and try to shift if negative, while others can be more explicitly taught in the classroom. You will notice that many of these attitudes and attributes have certain things in common, as they sometimes relate to, and at other times are dependent on, each other. In our view, as with all the other facets of creativity, we believe that the easiest way to develop these attitudes and attributes is to begin by teaching them separately and explicitly before starting to integrate through experiential practice.

ATTITUDES OF CREATIVITY

CREATIVE SELF-BELIEFS

Both teachers and students hold beliefs about themselves regarding their creative identity. Three key self-beliefs contribute to a person's overall creative identity, each playing a key role in determining whether a person will engage with or avoid creative performance opportunities, sustain effort when faced with challenges and, ultimately, demonstrate higher levels of creative achievement. *Creative self-concept* refers to general beliefs about one's creative abilities – 'I am a creative person' or 'I am not a creative person'. *Creative metacognition* is based on 'a combination of creative self-knowledge (knowing one's own creative strengths and limitations, both within a domain and as a general trait) and contextual knowledge (knowing when, where, how, and why to be creative)' (Kaufman & Beghetto, 2013b, p. 160). *Creative self-efficacy* refers to how confident someone feels to creatively perform a particular task – 'I do or do not have the knowledge and skills to creatively solve this mathematics problem.'

CREATIVE ACTIONS

We hope this book will allow teachers to reflect on their perceptions of their own creativity and use information in this section to help students develop their creative self-concept in a positive way. As with any form of self-belief, teachers have a strong influence on students' creative self-perception (Gralewski & Karwowski, 2016).

CREATIVE IDENTITY IN TEACHERS

Teachers can improve the creative identity of their students, but teachers who do not believe they are creative can find it challenging to build creative competencies in their students (Cropley & Patston, 2019). Some studies in creativity reported that although teachers say they liked having creativity in their classrooms, they did not like the associated qualities of creativity, such as questioning and challenging, expressing opinions, responding playfully and so on, when they were manifested in their students (Gralewski & Karwowski, 2016; Westby & Dawson, 1995). For some teachers, these may challenge their implicit belief systems – those who do not believe that they are themselves creative may find it difficult to observe creativity in others (Patston et al., 2018). The anecdotal reports of teachers criticising and crushing student potential across subjects are legendary (Amabile, 1998). Such negative feedback can lead to creative mortification, in which the student loses the desire to be creative (Beghetto, 2014).

However, more recent studies have reported that many teachers believe that creativity is essential, universal and unexceptional, and that teachers enjoy building the creative attitudes and attributes of their students, encouraging them to think more deeply and to challenge conventional thinking (Cropley et al., 2019; Karwowski et al., 2020).

CREATIVE IDENTITY IN STUDENTS

An important part of a student's development is how they develop their creative self-beliefs. If a student does not believe that they have the capacity to be creative, they are less likely to be creative. Creative self-concept may be generalised but is usually domain or subject specific (Beghetto, Kaufman, & Baxter, 2011; Kaufman & Baer, 2004).

Introducing the concept of creative identity from the students' perspective is a good way to start. Having introduced the topic of creative identity, students can discuss the areas in which they feel more or less creative. Teachers can then turn the conversation to discussing how competent the students feel in their particular subject. At this point it is appropriate to reinforce the link between knowledge, skills and creativity. Clarity of language and definitions is essential in this stage. Discussing creativity in non-specific terms can lead to confusion if students are asked to apply creativity in something such as their presentations (Ong & Nie, 2016) – 'Just do something creative' is not a helpful instruction.

Creative self-beliefs are based on two things: feelings and experience. If students feel that they are able to demonstrate competence at each stage of the creative process, can observe positive development in their peers, feel a sense of psychological safety when asking questions, and receive supportive and useful feedback from their teachers, they are less likely to experience negative feelings or anxiety and be more comfortable with risk-taking (Newman, Tse, & Schwartz, 2018). There is also evidence that if students are trained in peer-to-peer feedback, this too can support creative self-efficacy (Liu et al., 2016). As students gain knowledge and skills in creativity through problem-solving in a variety of subjects, their creative self-concept, creative metacognition and creative self-efficacy will improve.

The following examples demonstrate some of the factors that can impact self-efficacy in students, and how creative self-efficacy is linked to both creativity and subject knowledge and skills concurrently. In the first example, students reported high levels of self-efficacy in the design process, but a lack of experience with psychomotor skills in constructing a mobile phone stand inhibited their creative self-efficacy in product production. In the second example, teachers explored the link between subject knowledge and subject creativity and creative self-efficacy by building student skills in problem-posing.

CREATIVE ACTIONS

e4.1

Engineering and design, lower secondary, Taiwan

WHAT THE TEACHER FOUND

"While most students can generate ideas, they need guidance to implement them." (Huang et al., 2020, p. 9)

Component of creativity	Facet(s) of creativity	Teaching with or for creativity
Creative person	Creative self-efficacy	For
Creative process	Divergent thinking – fluency, flexibility and originality	For
Creative process	Idea generation to product creation	For
Evaluating creativity	Assessing divergent thinking	For

PURPOSE OF LESSON: SUBJECT KNOWLEDGE OR SKILLS

The purpose of this lesson was for students to develop skills associated with engineering and design by creating two products – a stand for a mobile phone and an elastic car. Students were required to use a combination of creative thinking and psychomotor skills to take the products from design to creation.

PURPOSE OF THE LESSON: TEACHING WITH OR FOR CREATIVITY

In terms of creativity, the purpose of this lesson was for students to improve their creative self-efficacy when designing and constructing an object by using the process of trial, repetition, refinement, consolidation and mastery in the design and construction process. Students were assessed on their divergent thinking in terms of fluency, flexibility and originality when designing a product, and if they thought differently about the creative self-efficacy in the design process, compared to their creative self-efficacy in the product creation process.

REFERENCE

Huang, N.-T., Chang, Y.-S., & Chou, C.-H. (2020). Effects of creative thinking, psychomotor skills, and creative self-efficacy on engineering design creativity. *Thinking Skills and Creativity, 37*, Article 100695. https://www.sciencedirect.com/science/article/abs/pii/S1871187120301693

ACCESS

THE CREATIVE PERSON

e4.2

Mathematics, upper primary, United States

WHAT THE TEACHER FOUND

❝*We concluded that mathematical crative self-efficacy and mathematical creative ability as first-level factors together constituted a second-order model named mathematical creativity*❞ *(Bicer et al., 2020, p. 476)*

Component of creativity	Facet(s) of creativity	Teaching with or for creativity
Creative person	Creative self-efficacy	For
Creative process	Problem-posing	For
Creative process	Divergent thinking	For
Evaluating creativity	Assessing divergent thinking	For

PURPOSE OF LESSON: SUBJECT KNOWLEDGE OR SKILLS

The purpose of this lesson was for students to build problem-posing and mathematical skills by examining provided solutions to questions on algebra, graphs, addition, multiplication, subtraction and division and generating a range of problems that could lead to the provided solutions.

PURPOSE OF THE LESSON: TEACHING WITH OR FOR CREATIVITY

In terms of creativity, the purpose of this lesson was for students to improve their creative self-efficacy, mathematical creativity and problem-posing skills by learning that creativity is a combination of cognitive factors, subject knowledge and creative process. Students were assessed on their divergent thinking in terms of fluency, flexibility and originality when posing problems.

REFERENCE

Bicer, A., Lee, Y., Perihan, C., Capraro, M. M., & Capraro, R. M. (2020). Considering mathematical creative self-efficacy with problem posing as a measure of mathematical creativity. *Educational Studies in Mathematics*, 105(3), 457–485. https://doi.org/10.1007/s10649-020-09995-8

ACCESS

OPENNESS TO NEW EXPERIENCES, OPENNESS TO INTELLECT

One of the measures most frequently associated with creativity is openness, one of the big five personality traits (DeYoung, 2015; Goldberg, 1992). The big five personality traits model is one of the most established and recognised approaches to describe and measure individual differences in personality, and includes openness to experience, conscientiousness, extraversion, agreeableness and neuroticism (Costa & McRae, 1992), with openness having the strongest influence on creativity (Mammadov, 2021). There is a considerable body of literature highlighting the link between openness to new experience and creativity (Feist, 1998; Silvia et al., 2009; Tan et al., 2019), particularly in the arts (Kaufman et al., 2016; Oleynick et al., 2017), and some involving school-aged students (Ivcevic & Brackett, 2015; Shi et al., 2016). While there is a genetic component to these personality traits, in openness genetics accounts only for 21 per cent of variability, with the remainder being accounted for by environmental impacts including the home and schooling (Power & Pluess, 2015). Teachers can have very powerful impact on personality traits students develop during their schooling.

Openness to new experience is usually discussed from two perspectives. One is the tendency to engage with aesthetic and sensory information (in both perception and imagination), by being open to new experiences, including seeking out sensations or risks, travelling, trying new foods or enjoying nature (DeYoung, 2014; DeYoung et al., 2007). The other is openness to intellect, which is the tendency toward engagement with abstract and intellectual information. It is possible to find individuals who are high in openness to new aesthetic experiences, but not intellectual experiences, or who are high in openness to intellect, but not openness to new experiences. Students who are open notice and appreciate novel, complex and unusual information in a variety of everyday experiences, are more likely to generate new and useful ideas, and are more comfortable with divergent thinking than those who have a low level of openness (Oleynick et al., 2017; Puente-Diaz et al., 2022). Those with high levels of openness to new experience have been shown to release higher levels of dopamine when engaged in divergent thinking (Käckenmester et al., 2019)

These qualities are highly desirable in terms of creativity, not limiting students to rote-like answers to convergent responses, but allowing a breadth and variety of possibilities to be considered. It is a creative attitude which teachers need to develop if they are to enhance their students' creative capacities.

ATTITUDES OF AN OPEN TEACHER

In terms of teachers, their openness to trialling new methods of pedagogic practice appears to be dependent on their personality, their self-efficacy as a teacher, the school climate created by the principal and their relationship with colleagues (Johnson et al., 2017). Students are more likely to feel more comfortable with openness to new experience if it has been modelled by the teacher (Cents-Boonstra et al., 2021). Open teachers exhibit higher levels of support of in-class creativity, for example, such teachers foster intellectual curiosity and imagination in their students (Kaya, 2021). Students whose teachers demonstrate openness in the classroom achieve higher scores on creativity tests (Şahin, 2020).

Teachers can demonstrate openness in their classroom through explicit and implicit behaviours. For example, explicitly asking students for feedback and ways lessons could be improved enhances relationships with students and builds a sense of psychological safety in the classroom, as we discussed in Chapter 2. Being open to student ideas and suggestions and showing a positive attitude are other qualities of an open teacher (Azer, 2005). Admitting to students that you are trying new things in the classroom and taking intellectual risks is another way of demonstrating openness.

INTRODUCING OPENNESS IN THE CLASSROOM

There are many ways that teachers can introduce the importance of openness to new experience in the classroom. When first introducing the idea, relating it to students' preferences in music or food can lead to an interesting discussion (this is also a useful way to introduce the concept of intercultural understanding in creativity, which we will discuss later in this chapter). What new music styles or foods have the students tried recently? Did anyone try something that required a high level of openness to new experience, either in terms of style or instrumentation in music, or the ingredients or the way a food was prepared?

Openness to new experience is also clearly connected to risk-taking. What is the difference between trying a new sport and a new way of solving a problem? A simple example is to ask if three or four students can explain a concept or solve a problem in different ways. One student might be asked to explain verbally, another to write on the board using only words, and a third to integrate text and diagrams. As an extension activity, students might be asked to research online and find some other ways of explaining this concept or solving the problem. It is then up to the students to determine which explanation or method suits them best individually. Having done this exercise it is worthwhile reminding students that they can try creative ways of note-taking, summarising and presenting information in their independent learning. We cover this in more detail in Chapter 8.

Another highly effective method is adaptive teaching, which is gaining traction through online tutoring courses. Students tend to treat course materials in a linear fashion and often skip over topics or tasks they find difficult. This can result in significant holes or gaps in their learning that may only be revealed in an assessment task. In a recent study, students who learned a topic by going to the answers in the back of the book and then finding the question that referred to that answer had lower overall test results (Lempinen, 2020). Adaptive learning requires students to demonstrate competency before moving to the next level. In adaptive learning, new and different examples are given rather than repeating the same question and asking the student to do it again. Openness to solving a range of problems, rather than one problem multiple times, also develops cognitive flexibility. Cognitive flexibility involves being responsive to incoming information in a flexible manner, and through flexible interaction with the environment, learning can occur more effectively. There is a positive relationship between openness, cognitive flexibility and creativity (Chen et al., 2022).

Another method to increase openness to new experience is via the sports coaching approach of nonlinear pedagogy (Galatti et al., 2019). Students accept that, within the environment of playing sport, there are many problems that need to be solved in quick succession. By exploring the variables around the problem, students improve their overall game literacy. In sport, it is possible to reduce the speed, distance and variety of trajectories the ball may travel, decrease the number of opponents or player density or enlarge the goals and playing area. These constraints can be varied over different timescales to allow players to become more flexible and adaptable. The same methodology can be applied to subjects in the classroom. Teachers can present students with different elements of a problem, or elements in a different order, to encourage students to think more deeply and to see relationships between problems by being more open-minded.

Openness to new experience in students is also strongly tied to other attitudes and attributes such as curiosity, engagement and motivation. This is particularly salient with the closing and reopening of many schools around the globe due to COVID-19. Teachers and students have needed to be more adaptive with their teaching and learning. A study conducted during COVID-19 examined two schools who experienced lockdown and found that students who were open to new ways of learning reported higher levels of engagement and enjoyment in their subjects (Patston, Kennedy et al., 2021).

INTELLECTUAL CURIOSITY

Being open to intellect can lead to students developing intellectual curiosity. This encompasses seeking information beyond the parameters of a prescribed task and knowledge, and embracing uncertainty, that makes intellectual curiosity a good fit with creativity (Kashdan & Silvia, 2009). The concept of curiosity, with its primary features of recognising and searching for new knowledge and experiences, has long been associated with personality factors related to creativity (Kashdan et al., 2013). As with each of the other factors in creativity, it is possible for teachers to develop students' intellectual curiosity through teaching, and they are expected to do so in some places such as the United Kingdom (Dann, 2013; Department of Education, 2014).

It is always preferable to introduce concepts such as intellectual curiosity by example and then articulate the benefits. Everyone is curious about something. For example, this book has three authors: one is curious about musical theatre and knows pretty much all there is to know about Stephen Sondheim; one is curious about building their fitness through stationary rowing (to the extent that they hold a world record); and the third is curious about how many different types of wine there are in the world and how they taste. Asking students what they are curious about and why is a good way to start the discussion and introduce the concept (Post & van der Molen, 2018).

There is a considerable and building body of knowledge that indicates that intellectual curiosity has several important and tangible benefits. Students with higher levels of curiosity do better in standardised tests, and have higher levels of wellbeing and self-compassion (Bluth et al., 2018; Jovanović & Brdaric, 2012; Kashdan & Yuen, 2007; Shah et al., 2018). Curiosity also deepens learning and information transfer (Lamnina & Chase, 2019). In adulthood, curious people are more creative and socially adaptable (Kashdan et al., 2013; von Stumm et al., 2011).

An effective way to promote curiosity is to build competency in asking open-ended questions. A simple example is to ask students 'What questions do you have?' rather than asking 'Do you have any questions?' Questioning techniques like this can be used to build both curiosity and to deepen learning (Jirout et al., 2018). The Harvard Graduate School of Education has developed a program of effective questioning called the Right Question Institute (https://rightquestion.org/education/). The aim of this program is to assist students in developing better questions, thus promoting curiosity, creativity and deeper learning. It is also possible for teachers to assess curiosity as it develops (Tor & Gordon, 2020). This will be discussed in detail in Chapter 6.

CREATIVE ACTIONS

History, secondary, United States

WHAT THE TEACHER FOUND

"Students ... are learning how to inquire, how to 'think in questions'. They are honing their speaking and listening skills, their problem-solving skills. ... Not only are students developing essential proficiencies, such as creativity, critical thinking, communication, and collaboration, they are also engaging more deeply in the content being taught in the classroom." (Minigan & Beer, 2017, p. 131)

Component of creativity	Facet(s) of creativity	Teaching with or for creativity
Creative person	Intellectual curiosity	For
Creative process	Open-ended questioning	With
Creative environment	Collaboration	For
Evaluating creativity	Multiple solutions to a problem	For

PURPOSE OF LESSON: SUBJECT KNOWLEDGE OR SKILLS

The purpose of this lesson was for students to develop their historical skills by reading a quote from President Abraham Lincoln and generating questions based on that quote. Students also developed their historical skills by assessing a cartoon of President Lincoln freeing the slaves and generating questions based on the cartoon.

PURPOSE OF THE LESSON: TEACHING WITH OR FOR CREATIVITY

In terms of creativity, the purpose of this lesson was for students to build their open-ended questioning skills and intellectual curiosity by asking questions after receiving information in a variety of formats, then directing the conversation. Students demonstrated their intellectual curiosity by exploring both possible causes and effects of the events which they were studying. In the process of sharing their intellectual curiosity through collaboration, students developed a deeper understanding of the content.

REFERENCE
Minigan, A. P., & Beer, J. (2017). Inquiring minds: Using the question formulation technique to activate student curiosity. *The New England Journal of History, 74*(1), 114–136.

ACCESS

INTELLECTUAL RISK-TAKING

When people talk about risk-taking, they predominantly discuss risks associated with health and safety, recreation, ethics and social behaviour (Tyagi et al., 2017). In the educational creativity literature, the key facet related specifically to creativity is intellectual risk-taking, related to the learning continuum of Vygotsky's zones of proximal development (Vygotsky, 1980). Intellectual risk-taking is an influential link in the relationship between creative confidence and creative behaviour (Beghetto et al., 2021). For adolescents in particular, expressing ideas that may be contrary or different to the social norm, is a form of risk-taking. Students who take intellectual risks share ideas with peers and ask questions of the teacher, at the risk of being incorrect, making mistakes or looking or feeling foolish. As risk-taking can involve sharing tentative or uncertain ideas, asking questions and having a willingness to try, students need a certain level of confidence to be creative (Beghetto, 2009). This may be intellectual confidence in terms of subject knowledge, the confidence to offer new or unusual ideas because of psychological safety, or social confidence as the student trusts their classmates.

The demonstration of risk-taking can begin with the teacher considering how to teach with creativity. Showing students that teachers take risks, for example, in explaining to them how topics can be taught in new ways, can make it clear to them that they are in a psychologically safe environment. Teachers can also demonstrate risk-taking in their creative process. For example, teachers might show students some draft attempts to draw a cat. Why is one draft better than another?

Another strategy is to talk about risk. Beginning with a general conversation about the role risk plays in our lives and asking students for specific examples is a good way to introduce the concept. Risk-taking can also be explored in an implicit manner, as in the following example.

CREATIVE ACTIONS

Art, secondary, Saudi Arabia

WHAT THE TEACHER FOUND

❝*The proper setup of an art classroom display is important for stimulating students by encouraging imagination, exploration, analysis, information gathering and new experiences, all of which can enhance their risk-taking ability and develop their critical and creative thinking skills.*❞ (Alawad, 2012, p. 4443)

Component of creativity	Facet(s) of creativity	Teaching with or for creativity
Creative environment	Changing the physical learning environment	For
Creative person	Intellectual risk-taking	For
Creative person	Motivation	For
Creative process	Critical thinking	For

PURPOSE OF LESSON: SUBJECT KNOWLEDGE OR SKILLS

The purpose of this lesson was for students to develop their artistic skills and understanding by describing how they used particular tools in creating an artwork and how the artwork specifically related to elements of the curriculum. Students were asked to justify their artistic thinking before beginning to create an artwork. The second purpose of this lesson was for the teacher to determine if an alteration of the physical environment of the art classroom, by more frequently changing the artwork on display, changed student learning behaviours and improved academic outcomes.

PURPOSE OF THE LESSON: TEACHING WITH OR FOR CREATIVITY

In terms of creativity, the purpose of this lesson was for students to build their intellectual risk-taking when constructing and drafting artworks by examining a variety of student artwork from different year levels on display, rather than just outstanding examples. The second purpose of the lesson was for students to build their engagement by having displays used for a limited amount of time before being replaced. Students who clearly articulated the topic, the tools, and how the curriculum related to their work before constructing the piece were shown to have artworks with higher levels of creativity.

REFERENCE
Alawad, A. (2012). How to influence students' risk-taking behaviour in order to enhance their creative and critical thinking processes. *Life Science Journal*, 9, 4483–4443. http://www.lifesciencesite.com/lsj/life0904/669_12384life0904_4438_4443.pdf

ACCESS

Students could also be exposed to the concept of risk in the assessment process. This approach involves giving students the autonomy to choose from a range of questions which have different values. For example, in a Year 9 language lesson students were given one mark by answering a question from the teacher with a gesture, such as a nod or shake of the head, and two marks for a single word verbal response. A response including words from an existing list of vocabulary was worth three marks, and a response using words outside the prescribed list was worth five marks. Students were given five questions in total and allowed to select the level of response they chose to give.

A similar approach was taken in a senior mathematics class. In a twenty-minute class test, students could answer twenty multiple choice questions worth one mark each, or six mathematical problems worth four marks each, or a combination. For the longer mathematical problems, students were also given a mark for demonstrating each step of the process to a solution and a bonus mark for trying to explain why they could not get a particular part of the problem-solving correct. The teacher had been successfully using this method for a couple of years. They found it particularly effective with senior students. The idea that students could be rewarded for demonstrating a lack of understanding was initially met with some confusion and resistance. However, as students became more articulate at explaining where they were lost with a particular concept, they found that the teacher was able to offer them much more specific support in closing the gaps in their knowledge.

ENTHUSIASM

ENTHUSIASM IN TEACHERS

Enthusiasm is a key characteristic of an effective teacher and also a predictor of student learning behaviour, emotional states, motivation and academic success (Peng, 2021). Teachers who are enthusiastic about teaching are more likely to create classrooms perceived by students as offering high levels of active learning support. This can also act as a buffer against students developing a declining interest in a subject (Lazarides et al., 2019). As with openness, curiosity and motivation, teacher enthusiasm is demonstrated by positive emotional signals and behaviours (Keller et al., 2018).

It is important for the students' creative process that teachers demonstrate authentic enthusiasm. One way to demonstrate enthusiasm is to explain to students why a teacher is enthusiastic about the subjects they teach and how that enthusiasm developed. Another is to explain the practical uses and relevance of the topic being taught. Teachers can also model enthusiasm by demonstrating openness to and acceptance of ideas generated by the students. These strategies might seem simple but can have a profound effect on a student's subject interest and motivation.

ENTHUSIASM IN STUDENTS

For students, enthusiasm is also a key part of the process of development from extrinsic to intrinsic motivation (Vandercammen et al., 2014). Enthusiasm can be inhibited by elements such as a lack of trust, frustration or the perception of insufficient support. Enthusiastic students work at a higher level of cognition, and they are also more intellectually curious, have more flexible cognition and are, therefore, more creative (Bledow et al., 2013).

PLAYFULNESS

The term *play* is difficult to define as it is highly contextual (Russ & Wallace, 2013). However, the processes of play are an integral part of discovering creativity. This can involve both early attempts at the creative process and finding meaning as well as enjoyment in problem-solving and can also include early attempts at collaboration.

In terms of creativity, the term *playfulness* refers to the dispositional aspect of play, combining spontaneous experimentation of ideas with collaboration (Barnett, 1990). The flexibility of play contributes to creative cognitions and the process of play has been demonstrated to enhance the creative process of problem-solving in school-age children (Chang, 2013; Chylińska & Gut, 2020; Lieberman, 1977; Russ & Lee, 2021; Taylor & Rogers, 2001). There are many different types of play. There is the type of recreational play students participate in during breaks in the school day, which may or may not have formal rules, as students often create their own rules unique to their context.

As students develop into high school, play is normally associated with sport or the arts rather than traditional academic subjects. In these subjects, teachers might choose to refer to activities as experimental, or develop a game to build understanding of a particular concept or skill. Play-based learning has been successfully integrated into STEM education in schools (Fleer, 2019).

In physical education classes, a creative way to encourage play is to ask students to look at the rules of a game and modify one with a particular outcome in mind. The modifications could be the size of the game space, the number of players in a team, the equipment used, the parts of the body used to play the game – there is a nearly infinite number of possibilities. This strategy can be particularly effective with student groups who have mixed experience and ability. In addition to the playful aspect, students can be encouraged to modify roles according to individual needs of team members, demonstrating both perspective and empathy (Sliwa et al., 2017).

Other spaces in which adolescents accept play as part of learning are the drama and music classrooms, particularly in improvisation. The purpose of play in these contexts is also a form of problem-solving, looking for new solutions through iteration. In English foreign language teaching and other humanities subjects, one method of solving problems is through role-play. This gives students more creative ways of expressing their understanding and exploring ideas from multiple perspectives (Samsibar & Naro, 2018).

ROLE-PLAY

Role-play can be used in subjects such as history, for example, holding a mock United Nations summit, to illustrate real-world problems and how difficult they can be to solve. This form of play does require more active monitoring from the teacher when students are first trialling it. The physical and social environments must include psychological safety and respectful relationships. As with most types of problem-solving, students will also need to be given a set of constraints for the creative process to be effective (see Chapter 5). Playfulness and discovery can also lead to anger and conflict, which must be managed (Taylor, 2018).

In mathematics and the sciences, play is normally referred to as experimentation. Asking students to demonstrate their subject knowledge and skills, as well as their creative competencies, by applying these experimentally in a real-world setting can enhance engagement, stimulate greater risk-taking and develop more effective collaboration skills. This type of problem-solving also demonstrates to students that the knowledge and skills they are gaining are relevant and useful.

In a middle years' design class, students were asked to look at the geometric shapes in clothing, for example, triangles as lapels on jackets, to determine if any of the geometric properties of shapes altered in three-dimensional fabric and how this needed to be accounted for when designing and making a piece of clothing. Students also needed to discover how to make seams parallel for clothing to hang properly on the body. Role-playing real-world scenarios can also be used in the sciences, as in the following example.

CREATIVE ACTIONS

Chemistry, secondary, Malaysia

WHAT THE TEACHER FOUND

> *The scenario allowed the participants ... to role-play as inspectors to conduct different types of experiments, for example, detection of blood, fingerprint and hidden message, to acquire certain scientific knowledge (e.g., polymerization, catalysis and pH indicators) ... active learning was advocated that the participating students took ownership of the activity, requiring them to take certain actions to explore and acquire the knowledge to be taught.* (Ng et al., 2019, p. 2921)

Component of creativity	Facet(s) of creativity	Teaching with or for creativity
Creative person	Playfulness through role-play	With
Creative person	Intellectual curiosity	For
Creative environment	Collaboration	For
Evaluating creativity	Multiple solutions to a problem	For

PURPOSE OF LESSON: SUBJECT KNOWLEDGE OR SKILLS

The purpose of this lesson was for students to build scientific knowledge and skills, for example, polymerisation, catalysis and pH indicators, by conducting different types of experiments at a constructed crime scene, for example, detection of blood, fingerprints and hidden messages. The second purpose of the lesson was for students to develop their problem-solving and questioning skills by exploring a real-world scenario, of which they could take ownership, and explore independently.

PURPOSE OF THE LESSON: TEACHING WITH OR FOR CREATIVITY

In terms of creativity, the purpose of this project was for students to explore playfulness in learning by taking specific roles when analysing evidence from the crime scene. The second purpose was for students to build their intellectual curiosity by trying to determine what was the appropriate test to use with the evidence provided. The final purpose was for students to build their collaboration skills by working together to find a solution to the problem

REFERENCE

Ng, Y. F., Chan, K. K., Lei, H., Mok, P., & Leung, S. (2019). Pedagogy and innovation in science education: A case study of an experiential learning science undergraduate course. *The European Journal of Social & Behavioural Sciences, 25*(2), 2910–2926. https://doi.org/10.15405/ejsbs.254.

ACCESS

THE CREATIVE PERSON

DIGITAL PLAY

With the advent of digital tools and social media, play has evolved to include gaming. However, there are many digital tools that can be used in education for role-playing and problem-solving. Possible advantages of gaming are higher motivation and increased engagement. Possible disadvantages can be a lack of student concentration, inappropriate choice of games, and unfamiliarity, unwillingness or anxiety around games among teachers. As with every element of creativity the right tool is needed for the right task in the right context. The following example explores the use of Kahoot!.

CREATIVE ACTIONS

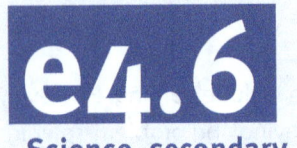

Science, secondary, Taiwan

WHAT THE TEACHER FOUND

"Kahoot! Helped the high performing group focus on their own learning processes, concentrate, and immediately adjust their misconceptions of the content. For the progressing group of students, they thought that Kahoot! improved the learning atmosphere in class, which helped them complete the assessment tasks. For the low performing group of students, they commented that Kahoot! prompted the teachers to provide timely feedback, which helped them clarify their misconceptions of the content." (Lee, 2019, p. 222)

Component of creativity	Facet(s) of creativity	Teaching with or for creativity
Creative person	Playfulness using Kahoot!	With
Creative environment	Independent problem-solving	For
Evaluating creativity	Formative assessment	With

PURPOSE OF LESSON: SUBJECT KNOWLEDGE OR SKILLS

The purpose of the lesson was for students to build their science knowledge around the structural properties of the Earth using a digital tool as a type of formative assessment to support student learning.

The second purpose of this lesson was for the teacher to assess the efficacy of student learning by asking questions such as 'Does using a digital form of formative assessment improve student academic outcomes in an end of unit test compared to a summative assessment using oral questions?' and 'Does immediate feedback on a number of formative tests improve motivation and academic outcomes?'

PURPOSE OF THE LESSON: TEACHING WITH OR FOR CREATIVITY

In terms of creativity, the purpose of this lesson was for students to develop their playfulness by using the digital tool Kahoot!. Students were encouraged to use the tool at any stage in the unit of work to check their understanding. It was proposed that frequent formative assessment would enhance student focus, concentration, engagement and motivation.

REFERENCE
Lee, C.-C., Hao, Y., Lee, K. S., Sim, S. C., & Huang, C.-C. (2019). Investigation of the effects of an online instant response system on students in a middle school of a rural area. *Computers in Human Behavior*, 95, 217–223. https://doi.org/10.1016/j.chb.2018.11.034

ACCESS

MOTIVATION

Motivation used to be seen in black and white terms: students were either motivated or they were not. An understanding then developed that there is a journey from extrinsic motivation to intrinsic motivation. More recently the term *self-determined motivation*, based on the work of Ryan and Deci (2020), has been explored in the field of education (Scales et al., 2020). As students experience a range of subjects and develop new knowledge and skills, they also develop motivation (Symonds et al., 2019). However, it can still be difficult to identify the exact moment when motivation shifts from extrinsic to intrinsic. The study of motivation is a field all its own, so in this section we will only focus on the aspects of teacher and student motivation that have an impact on creativity.

MOTIVATION IN TEACHERS

Motivation is a key component of education that is strongly influenced by teachers (Vero & Puka, 2017). Motivation shares common factors with openness and playfulness, in that teachers can demonstrate motivation through their emotions as well as their actions. A comprehensive study with a large sample of teachers and students identified a range of motivating and demotivating behaviours demonstrated by teachers (Cents-Boomstra, 2021). Twenty-three motivating teaching behaviours and sixteen demotivating behaviours were identified, which fell into a range of categories. Some motivating behaviours related to teachers who offered students autonomy, for example, choice in how they responded to or answered questions as well as some autonomy in the lesson content. There is a clear link between students' perceived autonomy in the classroom and their level of motivation (Guo, 2018). Students were more motivated by teachers who gave clear and concise instructions, took student suggestions seriously and gave positive verbal as well as written feedback. They were also motivated by teachers who physically approached them in discussions rather than merely talking from the front of the room. Teachers who used conditional language, inviting student responses using words such as *may* rather than *must*, were found to be motivating as were teachers who helped students to overcome failures and frustrations. Each of these behaviours has also been found to enhance creativity in students (Cropley, 1997; Şahin, 2021)

The demotivating behaviours related both to actions – controlling teaching, exercising power, interrupting students, demanding respect and being disorganised – and negative attitudes – favouritism, not paying attention to student suggestions, and general disregard for students. Fortunately, the study also reported that demotivating behaviours were far less frequent in this sample than the motivating behaviours.

MOTIVATION IN STUDENTS

There is a significant body of research exploring the links between creativity and motivation (Amabile & Pratt, 2016; Auger & Woodman, 2016; Csikszentmihalyi & Wolfe, 2014). Those who are intrinsically motivated have strong engagement in tasks and some sort of personal investment. Intrinsic motivation in a subject has been positively correlated with creativity (Beghetto & Kaufman, 2014). However, under some circumstances extrinsic motivation may have a negative impact on creativity as it focuses on results rather than process (Hennessey, 2019). There are many types of extrinsic motivation including both social and material rewards (Xue et. al., 2020). Lack of motivation may be reflected in student actions, through low engagement or even disengagement in lessons, and may demand a high level of motivational skills from their teachers (Şahin, 2021). The following offers an example of how student motivation can be developed in environmental science.

THE CREATIVE PERSON

Environmental science, primary, Hong Kong

WHAT THE TEACHER FOUND:

> *M-learning (Mobile technology learning) has been regarded as a promising tactic of motivating today's children to actively participate in school activities. This paper offers educational researchers and instructional designers new insights into employing Mobile-learning in outdoor contexts, in particular, shedding light on designing and implementing fieldtrip-based learning in natural landscapes.* (Jong, 2020, p. 13)

Component of creativity	Facet(s) of creativity	Teaching with or for creativity
Creative person	Motivation	For
Creative environment	External physical environment combined with a digital environment	For
Evaluating creativity	A digital presentation	For

PURPOSE OF LESSON: SUBJECT KNOWLEDGE OR SKILLS

The purpose of this lesson was for students to develop an awareness of and knowledge about the environment, cultivate the attributes that form the basis of environmental citizenship and develop skills for supporting environmental protection by taking students to an external physical environment and conducting inquiry-based learning with real environmental problems.

PURPOSE OF THE LESSON: TEACHING WITH OR FOR CREATIVITY

In terms of creativity, the purpose of this project was for students to increase their motivation in terms of perceived relevance, paying attention for longer in tasks, confidence in knowledge and skills acquisition, and satisfaction with their learning, by engaging with M-learning – the employment of mobile technology and devices, as well as other technologies (for example, web and multimedia), to support the course of learning and teaching. Working simultaneously in the digital and real environment increased both student motivation and knowledge retention.

REFERENCE

Jong, M. S.-Y. (2020). Promoting elementary pupils' learning motivation in environmental education with mobile inquiry-oriented ambience-aware fieldwork. *International Journal of Environmental Research and Public Health*, *17*(7), Article 2504. https://doi.org/10.3390/ijerph17072504

ACCESS

PERSISTENCE AND RESILIENCE

Persistence is the ability to make multiple attempts at a task. Resilience is the ability to face negative or adverse situations and emerge stronger from them. Persistence and resilience are both complex constructs that are dependent on a combination of personality and context (Fernández-Castillo et al., 2022). In terms of creativity, persistence is related to the process of iteration or prototyping, and resilience to a student's ability to continue working on a problem after setbacks or negative feedback.

To solve problems, particularly when generating ideas, it is essential that students develop their capacities for persistence and resilience (Baas et al., 2015). The creative process can be frustrating, with a number of options needing consideration before a viable solution is found. Students may experience perceptual and functional fixedness, which inhibits their ability to solve problems (Ritter & Mostert, 2017). Limited studies have demonstrated that students with higher levels of persistence and resilience demonstrate higher levels of original ideas and cognitive flexibility, which enhances creative capacity (Nijstad et al., 2010).

Both students and teachers need to be persistent and resilient in many aspects of life. An explicit introduction for students to discover the need for these two qualities may involve a discussion about when students have been persistent or resilient, or both. A teacher tried introducing this topic to sixteen-year-olds by giving examples of the teacher's persistence and resilience. This proved to be unsuccessful, with the students showing little interest. The teacher then flipped the lesson and asked students to write down samples from their own life experience and share if they were comfortable. Not all students chose to contribute, but after three or four students had discussed their experiences, the point was well-made, and they could then discuss persistence and resilience in the creative process. This example highlights the importance of relatedness to resilience, particularly in adolescents (Liu & Huang, 2021).

Persistence and resilience are most needed in the creative process during the idea generation and idea selection phase. In both collaborative and individual problem-solving, students without enough experience tend to land on the most popular idea very early in the process and stick to it no matter how unsuccessful or uncreative it may be. Persistence generates better ideas and improves the creative process (Lucas & Nordgren, 2015).

It is important for the teacher to question students to discover if a lack of persistence is due to a lack of confidence, a lack of effort, or a lack of collaborative or research competency. It is very important to be open with the students at this stage and to try to work it through with them. It is also possible for persistence and resilience to be included in the formative assessment of the creative process, both as a form of motivation and to demonstrate to students the importance of these qualities.

Persistence is also demonstrated to have an impact on creativity by neuroscience research. There are times when creativity requires persistence and times when it requires flexible thinking.

The flexibility pathway suggests stimulating creativity through a flexible switching between categories, approaches and sets while the persistence pathway leads to creativity through hard work, systematic and effortful exploration of possibilities, and in-depth exploration of just a few categories (Nijstad et al., 2010). It is important that students understand the difference between the two, as they often underestimate their capacity to be creative by being persistent.

It is of course also essential for teachers to have persistence and resilience in the classroom, particularly when trying some of the new pedagogic approaches described in this book (Rissanen et al., 2018; Wheatley, 2002). For students, building resilience enables them to rely on critical feedback as a valuable source of information for growth and to persist when solving problems. In Chapter 5 on the creative process, we discussed how feedback can encourage or inhibit student resilience.

There are several things teachers can do to foster perseverance and resilience in their students. As we discussed in Chapter 3, teachers must create conditions within the learning environment and the curriculum which foster student initiative, the exercise of autonomy and the expression of competence. The classroom needs social conditions that foster student persistence and resilience as part of knowledge and skills growth in a subject as well as in creativity.

Teachers also need to explicitly acknowledge that students have a range of extrinsic and intrinsic motivations, which may result in students exhibiting persistence and resilience in many ways. Finally, as we have discussed throughout the book, it is important that both teachers and students acknowledge that these steps are neither easy nor quickly acquired.

INDEPENDENCE

> *Autonomous learners are responsible, flexible, and curious; they see the need to learn, hold positive attitude towards learning, set their objectives, plan their learning, explore available learning opportunities and resources, use a variety of strategies, interact effectively with others, monitor their progress, reflect on and evaluate their learning, rationalize their actions, are aware of alternative learning strategies, are aware of their cognitive abilities and learning style, transfer what they have learned to wider contexts and, finally, appreciate that their efforts are crucial to progress in learning and behave accordingly.*
> (Pichugova et al., 2016, p. 2, https://doi.org/10.1051/shsconf/20162801081. Used with permission under Creative Commons Attribution License 4.0)

Education systems around the world are moving from a passive model of education, where students absorb and return information offered by teachers, to a more active learning model, in which students seek to deepen their understanding in a more proactive and independent way. We agree with this approach philosophically. Students do need explicit instruction in not only what to learn but *how* to learn.

Students need to build the attitude as well as the skills of independence. The focus of this next section is the models of pedagogy teachers can use to build independent learning skills in their students. Further discussion of independent strategies students can develop themselves to be more creative and successful learners occurs in Chapter 8.

Independence as an attitude is closely related to students having a sense of autonomy, which evidence shows has a strong impact on student engagement, self-efficacy, motivation and creativity (Han, 2021; Henriksen et al., 2018). For students to be creative, there are situations where they require some autonomy from prescribed processes and the freedom to work without the boundaries of pre-existing solutions, processes or biases. This is not to suggest that creativity requires complete autonomy and freedom – we have already discussed that there is ample evidence that creativity is much more effective with constraints (Kapoor & Kaufman, 2020; Tromp, 2022). It is, therefore, important for teachers to devise the appropriate response for each problem – freedom versus constraint, group versus individual, divergent versus convergent.

It is also fair to say that a key aim of school education should be to produce independent lifelong learners. As mentioned previously, school students are not genetically endowed as digital natives, nor can they be expected to be independent learners to the same level of university students. Independence must be taught, learned and earned. A common strategy used by teachers to build student autonomy is scaffolding. This involves gradually shifting the teacher's role from delivering information and skills to facilitating as students acquire information and skills. Students increasingly rely less on the teacher and more on themselves as learners. However, in terms of developing creative competencies it is important not to release the scaffolding too early. Teachers should always be involved in monitoring the learning of their students and maintain a mediating role regarding student knowledge and skills acquisition. Listening to learners' ideas, providing a variety of learning strategies, accepting student opinions, explaining how activities might be done differently, allowing student choice and talking in a collegial rather than didactic way, are all behaviours that encourage freedom of choice and increase student independence.

To deepen your understanding of building student independence, the next section will discuss significant trends in education that are impacting how teachers can build the attitudes and skills of independence in their students.

BLENDED LEARNING

An increasingly popular method is blended learning. Blended learning can refer to both the place and the modality of learning. It is a combination of face-to-face and online teaching. A useful definition for blended learning is:

> *Blended learning is a formal education program in which a student learns at least in part through online learning with some element of student control over time, place, path, and/or pace and at least in part at a supervised brick-and-mortar location away from home ... The modalities along each student's learning path within a course or subject are connected to provide an integrated learning experience.* (Christensen et al., 2013, p. 7)

It is claimed that blended learning fosters independence as it provides convenience, self-pacing, higher levels of engagement and improved academic outcomes. However, substantive empirically-based findings of efficacy at scale are yet to be developed (Poirier et al., 2019).

FLIPPED CLASSROOM

One example of blended learning is the flipped classroom. This method was originally designed by two chemistry teachers who were seeking a way for absent students to catch up with work they had missed (Begmann & Sams, 2014). In flipped learning, teachers prepare online materials and instructional videos for students to engage with outside of the classroom, generally watching before attending the lesson in person. This instructional method allows the students to pause and rewind the videos in an effort to understand the content independently. The teacher can then use their time differently in the class and operate as a facilitator, helping the students on an individual or small group basis. Thus, the students' independent learning is reinforced in a practical way in the classroom.

Flipped learning is gaining traction in developing nations where classroom resources may be limited but students have access to digital devices. Learners can review content repeatedly, stop and start as they need to and study on their own time and at their own pace. A recent meta-analysis of flipped learning reported that it is effective in providing structured active learning (Strelan et al., 2020). Students also believe that flipped learning makes them more independent learners (Vidergor & Ben-Amran, 2020). The following example shows teaching independence through flipped learning.

CREATIVE ACTIONS

Mathematics, secondary, Australia

WHAT THE TEACHER FOUND

> *Affordances of the flipped classroom approach mean that students have ongoing access to relevant resources that they can revisit, allowing them to develop competence and maintain a sense of autonomy over their learning ... I don't have to wait 12 hours when I'm stuck on a question for 12 hours not really knowing what to do.* (Muir, 2020, p. 82)

Component of creativity	Facet(s) of creativity	Teaching with or for creativity
Creative person	Student independence using flipped learning	With
Creative process	Multiple perspectives	For

PURPOSE OF LESSON: SUBJECT KNOWLEDGE OR SKILLS

The purpose of this lesson was for students to develop knowledge and skills in topics such as plane geometry, integration, differential calculus and probability, as well as calculating compound interests and understanding superannuation tables, by using the technique of flipped learning.

PURPOSE OF THE LESSON: TEACHING WITH OR FOR CREATIVITY

In terms of creativity, the purpose of this lesson was for students to build their independent learning, autonomy and competence by trying several learning approaches to determine which best suited them individually. The second purpose of this lesson was for students to improve their motivation by recognising the investment of the teacher's time in preparing the videos and content.

REFERENCE
Muir, T. (2020). Self-determination theory and the flipped classroom: A case study of a senior secondary mathematics class. *Mathematics Education Research Journal*, *33*, 569–587 https://doi.org/10.1007/s13394-020-00320-3

ACCESS

When using blended learning approaches, it is essential to consider purpose, context and audience. Research indicates that the preparedness, self-belief and digital and pedagogic competency of the teacher is more important than the competency of the students if flipped learning is to be effective (Chou et al., 2020). We will discuss how students can help themselves to become more effective independent learners in Chapter 8.

ATTRIBUTES OF CREATIVITY

PRE-EXISTING KNOWLEDGE AND SKILLS

It is commonly said that creativity does not occur in a vacuum; it requires a level of pre-existing domain and subject knowledge (Kaufman & Baer, 2004; Rietzschel et al., 2007). We have already stressed that creativity needs to be integrated into classroom practice and not treated as a separate subject, isolated from context. To build the creative capacity of students, the development of creative attitudes, attributes and skills must happen concurrently with the building of subject knowledge and skills. This next section explores how to weave together these elements.

We believe that the best way to develop creative competencies in students is to have a coordinated approach between subjects and year levels. By interleaving students' knowledge and reinforcing it in different subjects, they will become competent in all areas of creativity over their school journey. This may be a challenge, but it means the load is spread between teachers over time. It also demonstrates to the students that there is a unified purpose of education rather than a series of discrete silos which have no links. When introducing an element of creativity in the classroom, it is essential to explain to students how this is also supporting the development of their knowledge and skills in the subject. Remember, not every lesson has to contain an element of creativity. In fact, it is preferable that the learning of creative attitudes and skills is spread throughout the year.

For creativity to occur, students must look at what knowledge they currently have to solve a problem. It is important that teachers devise creative tasks appropriate to their students' level of knowledge and understanding. Asking a ten-year-old to paint in the style of Picasso may seem creative, but unless the student has some base knowledge or skills, the request is not creative nor likely to lead to a creative outcome. Given the importance of context when discussing creativity, knowledge is critical (Deng et al., 2016).

When working on building creative competencies in students, it is essential that teachers begin from their point of understanding. This may mean spending an amount of time on finding what exactly it is the students know about the topic (covered in Chapter 3). It is also vital both student and teacher understand where students are up to in terms of their creative competencies. For example, if brainstorming it is good for students to be reminded exactly what they are doing and how it should be done. As students build their knowledge and skills over time, more time can be spent on refining the process.

TOLERANCE FOR AMBIGUITY

Despite assertions that tolerance for ambiguity is an important part of being a creative person, the evidence for such assertions is, if you'll pardon the pun, ambiguous. There is also no dominant consensual definition as to what tolerance for ambiguity is – the terms *ambiguity* and *uncertainty* are often used interchangeably. Those with high tolerance for ambiguity are comfortable with ideas or solutions that may have unexpected or even illogical aspects, or perhaps insufficient information from which to draw a convergent conclusion. In terms of creativity, this is an asset as it allows solutions to come from unexpected or non-traditional sources (Zenasni et al., 2008). It is how a person interprets information, and responds cognitively, emotionally or behaviourally that determines their personal tolerance for ambiguity (McLain et al., 2015). Tolerance for ambiguity has two elements: the way information is presented and the way information is perceived. Information can be presented in ways that limit a student's ability to understand, such as by offering a multiplicity of causes of a problem, or the problem itself being ill-defined. Information could also be presented ambiguously, with conflicting, imprecise or missing information.

With the advent of social media and the increase of advertising language in students' lives, there are several ways the lens of advertising can be used to teach ambiguity. It can be through the use of images, text and even fonts. This type of critical thinking is essential for students in the modern world as students with a low tolerance for ambiguity are more likely to believe fake news and there is a constant stream of often conflicting information across online channels (Ianello et al., 2027). Tolerance for ambiguity can be taught in any subject as shown in the following examples.

e4.9

English as a foreign language, secondary, Jordan

WHAT THE TEACHER FOUND:

"When attempting to resolve an ambiguous sentence, several candidates compete with one another in the brain, the winning answer ... is the one (which) satisfies all constraints." (Almahameed, 2020, p. 257)

Component of creativity	Facet(s) of creativity	Teaching with or for creativity
Creative person	Tolerance for ambiguity	For
Creative person	Resilience	For
Evaluating creativity	Multiple solutions to a problem	For

PURPOSE OF LESSON: SUBJECT KNOWLEDGE OR SKILLS

The purpose of this lesson was for students to develop their English skills and comprehension by examining the structural ambiguities and ambiguous word meanings in the English language. Students were given four types of ambiguous sentences and asked to identify as many meanings as possible to develop their skills and assess if giving students the opportunity to translate a word or sentence in more than one way improves their skills in lexical and structural ambiguity.

PURPOSE OF THE LESSON: TEACHING WITH OR FOR CREATIVITY

In terms of creativity, the purpose of this lesson was for students to build a tolerance for ambiguity when studying languages by thinking more deeply and offering, and being offered, open-ended questions and responses. This also builds student tolerance and resilience.

REFERENCE

Almahameed, Y. S. (2020). Resolving lexical and structural ambiguity by Jordanian learners of English. *Journal of Critical Reviews*, 7(8), 2565–2573. http://www.jcreview.com/admin/Uploads/Files/61c9bc66423a74.09059604.pdf

ACCESS

CREATIVE ACTIONS

e4.10

Mathematics, secondary, Philippines

WHAT THE TEACHER FOUND

"The study aimed to determine if the deliberate use of clarified ambiguous problems is effective in developing mathematical problem-solving ability and positive attitude towards mathematics. Since solving some ambiguous problems requires new or unusual ideas, the study also aimed to determine if the students' creativity moderated the effects of the treatment on mathematical problem-solving ability and attitude."
(Sibbaluca, 2009, p. 77)

Component of creativity	Facet(s) of creativity	Teaching with or for creativity
Creative person	Tolerance for ambiguity	For
Evaluating creativity	Multiple solutions to a problem	For

PURPOSE OF LESSON: SUBJECT KNOWLEDGE OR SKILLS

The purpose of this lesson was for students to develop skills in the various methods of problem-solving and deepen their understanding of mathematical concepts, operations and processes by the use of clarified ambiguous problems.

PURPOSE OF THE LESSON: TEACHING WITH OR FOR CREATIVITY

In terms of creativity, the purpose of this lesson was for students to develop ambiguity tolerance to problem-solving, by using activities involving lateral thinking problems, riddles and analysis of impossible figures, where students must think outside the box. The ambiguous problems were given as a lesson motivation or warm-up activity, for individual work, pair work and group projects.

REFERENCE

Sibbaluca, L. M. (2009). Clarification of ambiguous problems: Effects on problem solving ability and attitude towards mathematics. *Alipato: A Journal of Basic Education*, 3(3), 76–87. https://journals.upd.edu.ph/index.php/ali/article/view/1758

ACCESS

INTERCULTURAL EXPERIENCE

In an increasingly connected world, education is becoming international. In many ways teaching a subject by building students' intercultural experience (known in many countries as multicultural experience) can be the most explicit type of openness to new experience, opening the door to how other cultures think, teach and learn.

Intercultural experience is associated with creativity (Ribeiro & Fleith, 2018). Multicultural adolescents (those whose parents are not from the dominant cultural background or are from two different cultural backgrounds) perform better in creativity tests than monocultural youth, and innovative, creative benefits have been found for business and entrepreneurship stemming from the formation of intercultural relationships (Chang et al., 2014; Lu et al., 2017). The greater the cultural difference between any two parents, the more creative their children (Cheng & Leung, 2013). Productive, creative groups often consist of people from diverse cultures with different experiences and interests (Chua, 2018; Pluut & Curşeu, 2013; Yap et al., 2005).

Globalisation has provided broader opportunities for people to have multicultural experiences (Leung et al., 2008). Being exposed to intercultural experience can enable creativity by offering new perspectives that require connecting diverse cultural ideas and concepts. Engaging in intercultural social relationships, immersive travel or living abroad can often engender a curiosity to probe and question underlying beliefs and assumptions as well as encourage openness and receptivity to new ideas (Lu et al., 2017; Maddux & Galinsky, 2009). Similarly, grappling with divergent ideas can also help disconnect from recurrent patterns of thinking and behaviours (Cheng & Leung, 2013). Indeed, when people think back on time spent in, and with, other cultures, those moments of reflection also help inspire creativity (Lee et al., 2012). It is worth noting here that people who are low in openness may be less creative if they travel.

The creative development of American musical theatre in the 1920s is a prime example of intercultural creativity. At a time of increasing nationalist and isolationist sentiment, a number of Jewish artists, often emigres from the Russian pogroms, became exposed to African American jazz music. Highly influenced by jazz and its cultural associations, Jewish and African American artists formed an alliance and re-imagined the shape and style of musical theatre, through which they promoted a more open and diverse vision of the United States (Hecht, 2011).

When introducing the concept of intercultural perspectives on problem-solving, two areas of students' lives come to mind: food and music (Ricardo-Barreto et al., 2022). In cities around the world there is increasing diversity in the food and restaurant culture. Discussion can begin with students reflecting on their experiences with a range of cuisines, looking at how different cultures combine ingredients and processes to generate an outcome. Contemporary music is another area in which students may have frequent exposure to intercultural products. How is the same style of music expressed across different cultures? How is language used in songs across different cultures? In the following example, students combine language and music learning to explore song lyrics to build their understanding of the English language.

CREATIVE ACTIONS

English as a second language (ESL), upper primary and lower secondary, Ecuador

WHAT THE TEACHER FOUND

> *Teachers can implement this strategy based on music activities to have a positive attitude in their learners, create an enjoyable environment in the class, animate learners to be more committed to the task activities, and make a connection between amusement and learning.* (Serrano-Espinoza & Argudo-Serrano, 2022, p. 507)

Component of creativity	Facet(s) of creativity	Teaching with or for creativity
Creative environment	Social – using songs to teach language	With
Attitudes and attributes	Motivation and playfulness	For
Creative process	Intercultural understanding	For

PURPOSE OF LESSON: SUBJECT KNOWLEDGE OR SKILLS

The purpose of this lesson was for students to build knowledge in subject content and skills in English as a second language by listening to songs. The second purpose of the lesson was for students to build knowledge and understanding around the importance of knowing English in a globalised world by exploring the way vocabulary, pronunciation, grammar and syntax differed in songs in a foreign language.

PURPOSE OF THE LESSON: TEACHING WITH OR FOR CREATIVITY

In terms of creativity, the purpose of this lesson was to increase student motivation for students to learn more effectively and retain more knowledge and skills, by using songs rather than standard text to teach linguistic concepts. The second purpose was for students to learn how to be playful by using a range of songs to illustrate varying cultural and linguistic values. This enhanced student subject engagement and motivation.

REFERENCE

Serrano-Espinoza, J. J., & Argudo-Serrano, J. C. (2022). A strategy based on music activities to promote motivation in a public school. *CIENCIAMATRIA*, 8(1), 490–512. https://doi.org/10.35381/cm.v8i1.687

ACCESS

THE CREATIVE PERSON

Exploring creativity through intercultural problem-solving can also give students a deeper understanding of the affordances and constraints of other cultures. Students can gain an understanding of First Nations cultures while also engaging in creativity. For example, Australian First Nations cultures did not have a formal written language. How did they retain and transfer knowledge and skills? How did they know which foods were available across the year and where they were located? The following gives an example of how this can be explored in the classroom.

Geography, secondary, Australia

WHAT THE TEACHER FOUND:

" For at least 60,000 years our First Nations people have been using social, medical, ecological and STEM creativity to solve problems. It was their creativity and adaptability that enabled them to flourish throughout the Australian continent for millennia."
(Naputa et al., 2019)

Component of creativity	Facet(s) of creativity	Teaching with or for creativity
Creative person	Intercultural understanding	With
Creative process	Critical thinking	For

PURPOSE OF LESSON: SUBJECT KNOWLEDGE OR SKILLS

The purpose of this lesson was for students to develop their understanding of First Nations cultures and build their geography skills, specifically on the night sky and food availability, by engaging with First Nations Dreamtime stories. The second purpose of this lesson was for students to develop their understanding of First Nations cultures by discussing how First Nations peoples communicated time of year, direction and distance without timepieces or written language.

PURPOSE OF THE LESSON: TEACHING WITH OR FOR CREATIVITY

In terms of creativity, the purpose of this lesson was for students to build intercultural understanding and critical thinking by looking at problems from multiple perspectives.

REFERENCE

Naputa, G., Patston, T., & Patston, G. (2019). *Aboriginal sky figures: Your guide to finding the sky figures in the stars, based on Aboriginal dreamtime stories.* https://www.creativeactions.com.au/indigenous-creativty-workshops
NOTE: Aboriginal and Torres Strait Islanders are warned that this document contains images, voices and music of deceased persons.

ACCESS

CREATIVE ACTIONS

Looking at problem-solving and creativity from other perspectives and cultures will increase not only students' subject knowledge but also their creative abilities. In recent years there has been a move towards a more unified approach in the teaching of STEM education. This is frequently presented as a problem-based project. In a project observed by one of the authors, middle school students were presented with the problem of how the Rapa Nui statues were moved from the quarry to their final position overlooking the sea. The students were presented with four different potential scenarios:

1. The statues were dragged using ropes. (How did they make ropes?)
2. The statues were rolled using ropes and rollers. (How did they make ropes and rollers?)
3. The statues were put in place by aliens. (Where is the evidence?)
4. Native Rapa Nui peoples once said that the statues walked into position. (How would this be possible?)

Some students who focused on the engineering challenges involved in moving the statues neglected to research the trees and vegetation that grew on the island. Others discarded scenario four as they believed it would be impossible – this overtly literal reading of a question is a common problem across year levels. (There is, in fact, a readily accessible and easily searchable video of a Rapa Nui person demonstrating how the statues walked, but students who regarded this scenario as impossible did not even search for it).

When introducing algorithmic thinking to high school students it can be interesting to explore how cultures historically did mathematics. The following example shows multiple options and could easily be transferred to history classes exploring particular periods of time and cultures.

e4.13

Mathematics, secondary, United States

WHAT THE TEACHER FOUND

"Here are some reasons why teachers should teach and use alternative algorithms in their classrooms: 1. Alternative algorithms accommodate different learning styles. 2. Alternative algorithms demonstrate that there IS more than just one way to solve a problem. 3. Alternative algorithms are fun! 4. Alternative algorithms provide a means so that we can appreciate the efforts of other people in other times and places." (Fischer & Davis, 2005, p. 1).

Component of creativity	Facet(s) of creativity	Teaching with or for creativity
Creative person	Intercultural understanding	With
Creative process	Critical thinking	For

PURPOSE OF LESSON: SUBJECT KNOWLEDGE OR SKILLS

The purpose of this lesson was for students to develop their mathematical skills by examining a range of algorithmic thinking strategies from around the world in addition, subtraction, multiplication and division.

PURPOSE OF THE LESSON: TEACHING WITH OR FOR CREATIVITY

In terms of creativity, the purpose of this lesson was for students to develop intercultural understanding, critical thinking skills and creative algorithmic methods by examining alternative algorithms from different periods of history and different cultures.

REFERENCE

Fischer, J. F. & Davis, J. F (2005). *Algorithms: Through the ages and around the world.* Texas University Press. https://citeseerx.ist.psu.edu/viewdoc/download?doi=10.1.1.615.6775&rep=rep1&type=pdf

ACCESS

CONCLUSIONS

There are many attitudes and attributes that contribute to the development of creativity in students and teachers, but everyone has the capacity to be creative to some degree. To get there requires the right physical and social environment, a good understanding of the creative processes and the appropriate attitudes and attributes. This journey is illustrated in the following fictional story about a student who goes from mini-c to Big-C creativity and the attitudes and attributes of their creative journey. It is important to note that, as with most elements of education, the work that happens in schools is foundational, dealing predominantly with mini-c and little-c creativity with students and Pro-c creativity as an educator.

At the mini-c level, someone creates something new and meaningful to them (Patston, 2019). It might not be exceptional, revolutionary or creative to others, but the creation generates interest and excitement in the individual. An example might be a drawing a student brings home from school. Positive feedback from their teacher or their classmates inspires them to bring it home and show their parents. In terms of attitudes and attributes the student shows some playfulness by doing the work and some basic creative self-belief. Their classmates, teachers and parents have shown some openness to the work and expressed enthusiasm for what the student has done.

The little-c level is the next level of creativity, with the introduction of knowledge and skills acquisition in the creative process combined with ongoing feedback from others (Patston, 2019). For example, the parents put the drawing on the refrigerator to show that they value it. To encourage their child, they give them a sketchbook and make some positive suggestions about how to further explore and improve their skills. The action and the feedback build their child's creative self-efficacy. Times goes on and the student chooses art as an elective when they reach high school, building on their pre-existing knowledge and skills. They begin to receive explicit instruction and assessed feedback, which improves their persistence and resilience. The person giving these instructions, the student's art teacher, is at the Pro-c level.

After a number of years of teaching, and gaining experience in a variety of pedagogic approaches, teachers are able to operate at the Pro-c level of creativity. In this example, the art teacher uses a variety of instructional strategies to build both the student's knowledge and skills and their creative capacity as an artist (Patston, 2019). The student is exposed to a variety of artists from different times and cultures, building intercultural understanding and their tolerance for ambiguity. The teacher uses Pro-c levels of creative pedagogies to introduce the student to types of deliberate practice and increasingly professional levels of feedback. This feedback includes acknowledgement that their work is sufficiently new and novel, helping to maintain the student's intrinsic motivation and creative self-efficacy. The student builds independence and autonomy in their artistic style and has an increasingly high level of creative self-concept. They begin to develop their identity as an artist. This identity is then further fostered by Pro-c educators at the tertiary and professional level.

The Big-C level of creativity (which we discussed in Chapter 2 is what many people mean when they say *creativity*) is the rarefied air of the very few (Patston, 2019). To take this example to a conclusion, the student becomes one of the greatest artists of all time. A century after their death, their work is still discussed by experts because their creativity took art to new forms of expression.

The majority of us operate at the mini-c and little-c level with our hobbies, recreational pursuits and activities (Patston, 2019). While they give us fulfilment and pleasure and we enjoy building skills and knowledge over time, we are not generally participating in them at a professional level. However, some people operate at Pro-c level in more than one area.

CHAPTER 5

THE CREATIVE PROCESS: FROM GENERATING IDEAS TO PRESENTING SOLUTIONS

When most people think of creativity, they think of the creative process of problem-solving – the *how* of creativity. We describe this as the engine room of creativity, and like any engine it requires a series of moving parts, both cognitive and procedural, working together to be efficient and effective. The origin of many popular problem-solving techniques lies in the components identified by J. P. Guilford and Alex Osborn in the 1950s. Guilford introduced the elements of divergent thinking: fluency (the number of ideas generated), flexibility (the variety of ideas generated) and originality (how original these ideas are compared to others of similar age and experience; Guilford, 1950). Recent research with school-age students shows that each of these three elements influences overall creativity in slightly different ways (Kaufman et al., 2021).

Guilford's concept of the appropriate use of divergent and convergent thinking in the creative process remains a cornerstone of creativity (Khairunnisa et al., 2022). The processes surrounding idea generation have occupied a large part of creativity literature, with the importance of divergent and convergent thinking skills holding centre stage. Convergent thinking focuses on coming up with single solution and is needed at the beginning and the end of the creative process. Divergent thinking seeks multiple perspectives and multiple possible answers to questions and problems and is used in the idea generation phase (Kim & Pierce, 2013). For example, tests and exams often require one solution, so students often focus on convergent thinking, whereas an essay or research assignment might require two or multiple possible solutions, which engages divergent thinking in the creative process (Baer, 2014). According to Sternberg (1987), 'Virtually no problems can be solved by single processes or thoughts in isolation, so one must learn to combine these processes in a way that gets things done effectively' (p. 253). Guilford also stressed the importance of cognitive capacity in problem-solving, with those having more knowledge and skills in a particular subject area or domain being more creative as they have a richer pool from which to draw.

The Osborn model (1953) focuses on the elements of the creative process, involving both divergent and convergent thinking. Originally a three-step process, consisting of fact-finding,

CREATIVE ACTIONS

idea-finding and solution-finding, it is now more commonly expressed as the following steps: facilitation, imagining the future, finding the questions, generating ideas, crafting solutions, exploring acceptance, then creating an action plan. There is now an enormous variety of problem-solving frameworks and models with their origins in Osborn's creative problem-solving techniques (Baruah & Paulis, 2019; Ward et al., 2004).

Essentially, problem-solving is a rigorous set of cognitive and behavioural skills practically applied to the creative process. These can be taught and learned. We stress here that it is not always necessary to go through the complete creative process all the time. Students spend the whole of their schooling gradually building competencies in numeracy and literacy; the same should be true of their creative competencies. When teaching about and for creativity it is worth breaking the creative process up into individual components and trialling them in small chunks. Over time students can build up to using the complete problem-solving process. This chapter will look at a range of thinking and practical skills of the creative process. Our experience has shown that using the whole process, particularly with complex problems in high school, is ineffective if students don't have the skills and experience to successfully negotiate each part of the process. We offer an example later in this chapter.

The components of process we suggest you follow are based on evidence from Guilford and Osborn and the body of research that has followed, using contemporary and clear language. This table offers teachers and students concrete practical advice on how they need to think and what they need to do when solving problems. We stress that these individual skills should be developed independently at first, before being combined into a complete problem-solving process. The table is an overview, with the detailed components discussed further in the following sections.

Table 5.1: The creative process

	Understand the problem	Generate ideas	Evaluate ideas	Develop the final solution	Validate the final solution
Stage	Understanding pre-existing knowledge and skills Convergent thinking	Using idea generation tools Divergent thinking	Using critical thinking skills Convergent thinking and divergent thinking	Convergent thinking	Convergent thinking
Example of thinking skill	Read questions effectively Ask open-ended questions Break down into sub-problems	Select methods of recording ideas Select methods of summarising ideas Select methods of generating ideas	Trialling, prototyping and testing	Testing for effectiveness	Checking against criteria

UNDERSTAND THE PROBLEM

When beginning the creative process with students, it is essential that they have some explicit instruction on how to read questions effectively and how to break questions down into smaller or sub-problems (teaching about creativity). It may be useful to ask some open-ended questions to help the students with their thinking. These might include: What does this problem really involve? What knowledge and skills do you already have that might help you solve this problem? Where might you need to do further research? How can you break the problem down into smaller pieces to ensure that you develop the best solution? Once these questions have been clarified it is time to select the methods you will use to record and generate ideas. Note that this is not the end of understanding the problem – as you generate ideas and look for ways to select the best ones, it may be necessary to ask some further questions.

It may be easy to think that understanding the problem is merely asking the question which needs to be solved, but as we have seen problems are rarely simple. It can involve generating sub-problems about a concept, topic or idea, and can also involve the re-formulation or re-framing of a problem during the course of solving it (Silver & Cai, 1993). Students can do this even from the mini- or little-c perspective, as discussed in Chapter 4. If the big picture problem is the task created by the teacher for the student to answer, the process of addressing this larger problem can lead to many more specific questions the student may ask. They may think 'Where do I start?' or 'What is the actual problem that needs to be solved?', thereby setting off a cycle of individual or sub-problem posing (Reiter-Palmon & Robinson, 2009). You can see the key thinking skill required at this stage is convergent thinking – students need to clearly define the problem which they need to solve.

GENERATING IDEAS

Generating ideas lies at the very heart of the creative process. In terms of the thinking skills required, idea generation is the divergent thinking phase, where students try to come up with as many ideas as possible to solve the given problem. However, the ideas need to be recorded and organised in some way for students to move to the next phase of idea evaluation. Organising, categorising and summarising ideas are very important skills for students to develop to effectively manage the ideas they have generated (Gerlach & Brem, 2017). At the early stages of students developing their creativity we would recommend that the teacher decides how ideas are recorded and summarised in terms of the format. As students become more confident with a variety of formats, they may then choose how they record, summarise and categorise their ideas. We begin this section with a range of suggested methods (it is beyond the scope of this book to cover every single possible method but we hope that these suggestions will encourage you to explore a range of possibilities). Having decided the format of recording and categorisation, the teacher can then discuss the various possible methods of idea generation which may be used.

METHODS OF RECORDING IDEAS

For ideas to be clearly articulated they must be recorded during the idea generation phase (van der Lugt, 2003). This is relevant for all contexts but particularly so in school settings, where it can be difficult to collate diverse student ideas and opinions (Ritchhart et al., 2011). By having some mechanism of recording, students are able to see all of their ideas, compare them, reflect on them and commence the convergent thinking process of idea selection. Methods of recording can have a significant impact on effective problem-solving, with variety being a key to success (Isaksen & Gaulin, 2005; Offner et al., 1996). As with all aspects of the creative process, it is essential to use the appropriate tool for the appropriate task. It is important to consider the stage of development of the student, the purpose for using a particular recording tool and the context in which the tool is used. There are many methods of recording ideas during the creative process. As students experience a variety of recording methods, they will come to understand the method, or methods, that best support their creativity. In this section, we will divide the strategies into categories – written, spoken, pictorial, combinatorial, and the analogue and digital versions of these.

WRITTEN STRATEGIES

Where would the creative process be today without sticky notes? There are even whole books written about them (Christensen & Klokmose, 2019; Straker, 1997). Researchers are now analysing whether analogue or digital sticky notes are more effective in the idea generation phase of the creative process (Jensen et al., 2018). Certainly, they are inexpensive, come in a variety of colours for organising into different categories and don't take up a lot of space. They have become the go-to tool for recording ideas. One possible drawback is that students' handwriting needs to be sufficiently neat for others to read. Another is that they are quite small and cannot contain a lot of written information. They can be easy to misplace, especially when working with younger children, and are a one-use tool.

In terms of the content when writing down ideas, you might ask students to write keywords, bullet points or complete sentences. They can then sort these by using a coloured highlighter to put the ideas into various categories. Writing ideas down is a relatively time efficient process as it is briefer than discussing everything that gets written down. It is also possible for students to write down their ideas anonymously before being collected and collated. This encourages and allows shy or introverted students to contribute and enables students to put down more unique ideas which they may fear proposing if they can be identified (see section on psychological safety in Chapter 3). This method also prevents the more confident or outgoing students from dominating the ideas.

Each of these points also apply to digital sticky notes. There are many online versions that can be selected. Digital versions do not suffer the problem of incoherent writing but still have some limitations in terms of size and single use.

SPOKEN STRATEGIES

It is also possible to record verbal ideas during the creative process. Sometimes, if there are high levels of trust within a group, conversations can stimulate thinking and provoke new and interesting ideas. If having a verbal discussion is the method chosen, there are three ways the ideas can be recorded. Students can write down the ideas once they have been shared, a scribe can be appointed from within the group to put the ideas up in a common space, or a recording can be made and transcribed at another time. The third method may seem time-consuming, but listening back may capture richer ideas, especially when working with smaller children who tend to talk over one another. The same can be true when appointing a scribe. James often asks two students to share the task. He calls one the recorder, whose job it is to write down what they hear, and the other the butterfly catcher, whose job it is to pay attention to the ideas that may be spoken quickly or quietly but are still important. They ensure that these ideas are captured by the scribe.

Whenever possible, all students should be encouraged and given the opportunity to actively contribute to the creative process (see the sections on psychological safety in Chapter 3 and on attitudes and attributes of creativity in Chapter 4). One method is to put numbered sticks into a cup and have the students take them out. This determines the order in which they present their ideas. Other strategies can be to follow the order of student birthdays or other techniques involving random selection.

PICTORIAL STRATEGIES

Not everybody likes to communicate using words; some prefer images, symbols, graphs or pictures. There are occasions when the visualisation of a problem is a very effective way for students to understand the problem, its variables and its complexities. This strategy is often used in mathematics. A young student may understand what an apple is but not understand that it can be categorised as a piece of fruit, or even more abstractly, as a type of food. The same issue occurs in high school when students are presented with algebra. Having a concrete visualisation that shows that X, Y and Z are real numbers or objects can help students to understand the concepts that underlie algebra.

Symbols and images can also be used in the idea selection phase of the creative process when categorising ideas. Colour-coding or using a simple image such as a pie chart can assist students in looking at where their ideas have been generated.

COMBINATORIAL STRATEGIES

There are times when it is better to use words and images in the creative process. These combined strategies, using pictures or structured images, are particularly useful in the categorisation of ideas stage. The very best strategies show not only the categories of ideas but also the interrelationship between ideas. These require a higher cognitive load from the students and therefore result in deeper learning of the ideas and concepts.

MIND MAPPING

One of the most popular tools to capture ideas and explore relationships used in the creative process is mind mapping (Buzan & Buzan, 1995). The advantages of mind mapping include having a free, rather than prescriptive, structure and format. There are no limits on the ideas and links that can be made, although students do need to be given constraints in this regard. As a form of collaboratively building a clear representation of the categories of ideas, mind mapping is an excellent tool. Mind mapping has been used successfully in building creative skills in students in a broad range of subjects from around the world, not only as a recording tool also but in students' skills in critical thinking (Polat & Aydin, 2020).

THE CREATIVE PROCESS

Science, primary, Holland

WHAT THE TEACHER FOUND

> *All teachers were able to use mind mapping as a collective platform for linking student questions to the core curriculum ... classroom mind maps can be useful platforms to exchange and visualize new knowledge.* (Stokhof et al., 2020, p. 218–219)

Component of creativity	Facet(s) of creativity	Teaching with or for creativity
Process	Idea recording tools such as mind maps	With and for
Process	Idea generation tools such as small group brainstorming	For
Attitudes and attributes	Intellectual curiosity	For

PURPOSE OF LESSON: SUBJECT KNOWLEDGE OR SKILLS

The purpose of this lesson was for students to learn the key concepts, categories and ideas in the topic of water by exploring the interaction between numerous variables in the topic.

PURPOSE OF THE LESSON: TEACHING WITH OR FOR CREATIVITY

In terms of creativity, the purpose of this lesson was for students to improve their intellectual curiosity and learn about idea generation and idea recording by using idea recording tools to explore categories of ideas and simple relationships between them. Students improved their skills in recording ideas and use of questioning techniques by participating in small group brainstorming to generate ideas and recording them on a mind map. Students also built their intellectual curiosity by seeking to add branches to the mind map through research and group discussion, as shown in the following diagram.

REFERENCE

Stokhof, H., de Vries, B., Bastiaens, T., & Martens, R. (2020). Using mind maps to make student questioning effective: Learning outcomes of a principle-based scenario for teacher guidance. *Research in Science Education*, 50, 203–225. https://doi.org/10.1007/s11165-017-9686-3

ACCESS

CREATIVE ACTIONS

Figure 5.1: The Catcher in the Rye *mind map*

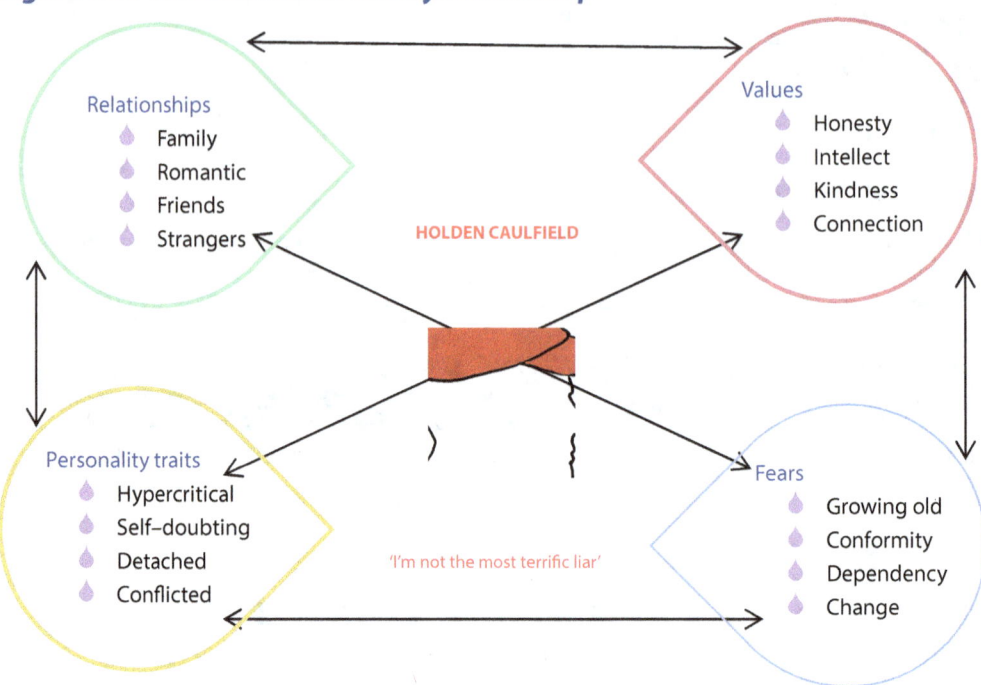

SOURCE: A. Patston (personal communication, August 7, 2022)

One disadvantage of mind mapping is that the types of links being made are limited to simple associations. They are an excellent way to present categorised ideas but do not show the relationships between them. The absence of clear links between ideas is an obvious constraint. Mind maps can also become crowded and hard to read.

CONCEPT MAPPING

One tool that does show the relationships between ideas is concept mapping, first used in schools in science education (Novak, 1990). Unlike mind mapping, concept mapping is more structured and less pictorial in nature. The aim of concept mapping is not to generate spontaneously associated elements but to outline relationships between ideas. It is a relational device and, therefore, very valuable when looking at possible consequences of using ideas that have been generated. As all educators know, linking concepts is a key part of the learning journey for students. A concept map has a tree structure with branches and sub-branches (primary, secondary and tertiary ideas). It is also very useful when moving from the divergent to the convergent stage of idea selection. Simple concept maps can be used in primary school and more complex versions can be used in high school. In the senior years of high school concept maps can be used to identify missing components of knowledge that students need to fill with research. While there are digital versions of concept mapping, it is generally simpler for these to be drawn by hand.

THE CREATIVE PROCESS

English, secondary, Taiwan

WHAT THE TEACHER FOUND

"Concept mapping activity improved students' critical thinking because it allowed students to think critically about meanings, propositions, and relationships among concepts. However, training must be provided ahead of time, especially for students who are not used to specifying the nature of the relationships between concepts in concept maps." (Tseng, 2020, p. 255)

Component of creativity	Facet(s) of creativity	Teaching with or for creativity
Process	Idea recording tools such as concept maps	With and for
Process	Idea evaluation and critical thinking	For

PURPOSE OF LESSON: SUBJECT KNOWLEDGE OR SKILLS

The purpose of this lesson was for students to develop their English knowledge and skills by reading an English language text, identifying the key concepts and constructing an essay outlining the relationships between these concepts.

PURPOSE OF THE LESSON: TEACHING WITH OR FOR CREATIVITY

In terms of creativity, the purpose of this lesson was for students to build critical thinking and idea evaluation skills by recording ideas using concept maps to explore categories of concepts and complex relationships between ideas. Group 1 filled in an existing map and Group 2 built their own concept map from scratch. Group 2 found it more satisfying and educationally beneficial to create their own concept map, as they built core skills, such as interpretation, analysis, explanation, inference and evaluation

REFERENCE

Tseng, S.-S. (2020). Using concept mapping activities to enhance students' critical thinking skills at a high school in Taiwan. *The Asia-Pacific Education Researcher, 29,* 249–256. https://doi.org/10.1007/s40299-019-00474-0

ACCESS

CREATIVE ACTIONS

ARGUMENT MAPPING

Argument mapping can be a very powerful tool if used effectively during the creative process. Argument maps are particularly useful in the idea selection phase of the creative process, as students provide evidence for the effectiveness of the ideas they have generated. Students can add supportive claims or objections to the ideas generated. Argument mapping clarifies thinking, stimulates critical thinking and improves students' abilities to argue their case using a combination of verbal and graphic representations. As with concept mapping it is useful when moving from the divergent to the convergent phase of the creative process. It is an excellent tool for the senior years of high school where students are often required to defend propositions in a range of subjects. Argument mapping also has a clear role when looking at larger problems, such as the real-world problems behind project-based learning (Lidåker, 2019). From the teacher's point of view, argument mapping requires fairly detailed instruction and modelling before students can use it effectively, as in the following example.

THE CREATIVE PROCESS

Native tongue (Finnish), secondary, Finland

WHAT THE TEACHER FOUND

> *Argument diagrams ... provided the students with a tool for reflecting on their previous debate and earlier knowledge. The use of several conceptual tools together with versatile working methods to support students' learning probably also increase students' motivation and promote their active involvement in studies.*
> (Marttunen & Laurinen, 2007, p. 123)

Component of creativity	Facet(s) of creativity	Teaching with or for creativity
Process	Idea recording tools such as argument maps	For
Process	Idea evaluation and critical thinking	For
Process	Iteration and drafting	For
Attitudes and attributes	Accessing pre-existing knowledge	For
Environment	Collaboration	For

PURPOSE OF LESSON: SUBJECT KNOWLEDGE OR SKILLS

The purpose of this lesson was for students to develop their comprehension and analytical skills by reading a text in Finnish, identifying the key arguments and points of view relating to a topic (for example, should we use genetically modified crops?), presenting their understanding of the various arguments and outlining the relationships between these arguments.

PURPOSE OF THE LESSON: TEACHING WITH OR FOR CREATIVITY

In terms of creativity, the purpose of this lesson was for students to build their critical thinking, evaluation and collaboration skills by using argument maps to record ideas and explore categories of concepts and complex relationships between points of view. Students constructed an individual argument map based on their pre-existing knowledge, then second and third collaborative iterations of an argument map based on new information. Students used their critical thinking skills to evaluate the proposed arguments and their collaborative skills in creating the second iteration, before returning to the next iteration of their individual argument maps.

REFERENCE

Marttunen, M., & Laurinen, L. (2007). Collaborative learning through chat discussions and argument diagrams in secondary school. *Journal of Research on Technology in Education*, 40(1), 109–126. https://doi.org/10.1080/15391523.2007.10782500

ACCESS

CREATIVE ACTIONS

FISHBONE DIAGRAMS

One final graphic organiser has its place in the creative process as students move from idea generation to idea selection. The Ishikawa or fishbone diagram, also known as a cause-and-effect diagram, is useful as a screening tool for ideas when moving students towards making final decisions regarding ideas implementation. They can also be very useful for identifying the causes of a problem, which can help students to identify possible solutions. Any subject that explores cause and effect can benefit from the use of a fishbone diagram, as shown in the following example.

Figure 5.2: Example of a fishbone diagram

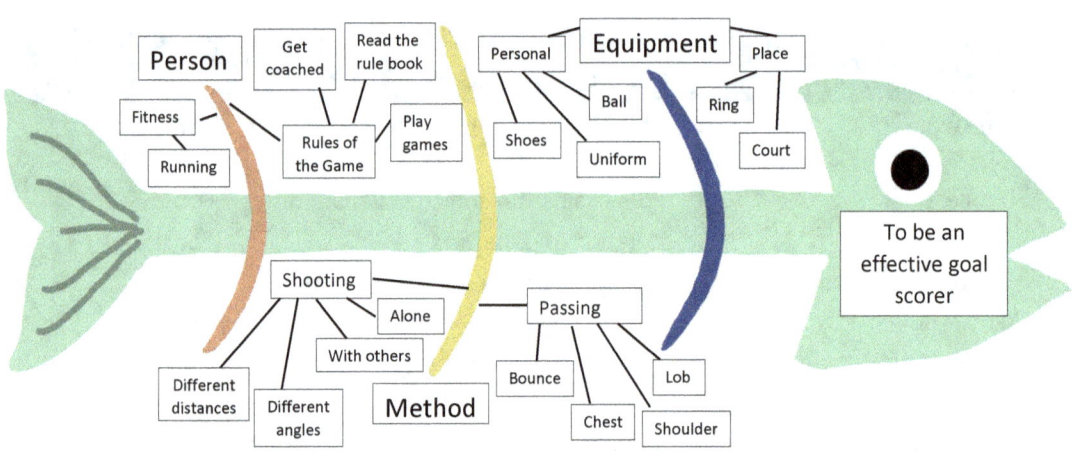

SOURCE: E. Patston (personal communication, August 7, 2022)

THE CREATIVE PROCESS

e5.4
Biology, secondary, Indonesia

WHAT THE TEACHER FOUND

"Fishbone Diagrams assists the students in clarifying and organizing the relationship between concepts and ideas; helps the students focus on the materials; facilitates the students in doing brainstorming of the possible causes of a problem; aids the students in solving a problem, making decision or action, and helping the students enhance memory skill and understanding; and guides the students in communicating their thinking process in either spoken or written form." (Priyadi & Suyanto, 2019, p. 6)

Component of creativity	Facet(s) of creativity	Teaching with or for creativity
Process	Idea recording tools using the fishbone diagram	For
Process	Idea evaluation, critical thinking and synthesising ideas	For
Attitudes and attributes	Accessing pre-existing knowledge	For
Environment	Collaboration	For

PURPOSE OF LESSON: SUBJECT KNOWLEDGE OR SKILLS

The purpose of this lesson was for students to develop an understanding of possible causes and effects of environmental change in biology by exploring pre-existing knowledge then building on this knowledge through research and collaboration.

PURPOSE OF THE LESSON: TEACHING WITH OR FOR CREATIVITY

In terms of creativity, the purpose of this lesson was for students to build their critical thinking, evaluation and collaboration skills by using a fishbone diagram as a tool to record ideas and explore cause and effect relationships between variables. Students constructed an individual fishbone diagram, based on their pre-existing knowledge, then created collaborative iterations of fishbone diagrams based on new information and peer feedback. The skills students developed included finding, identifying and analysing the root causes that related to the materials

REFERENCE

Priyadi, A. A., & Suyanto, S. (2019, July 12–13). The effectiveness of problem based learning in biology with fishbone diagram on critical thinking skill of senior high school students. *Journal of Physics: Conference Series, 1397*, Article 012047. https://iopscience.iop.org/article/10.1088/1742-6596/1397/1/012047

ACCESS

SUMMARISING AND CATEGORISING IDEAS

To make the creative process a little clearer for students, they need to be made aware of the importance of summarising and categorising ideas. Categories can be selected when choosing the strategy that ideas will be recorded. You can develop some categorising templates or students may select the categories as they develop their competencies. At the most basic level, similar ideas can be colour-coded and then compared to refine further.

With older students more sophisticated categorisation is possible, and weighting can be given to different categories (for example, in business subjects where possible solutions have to be costed). There are a number of options to consider, therefore these need to be discussed early in the process. For example, ideas might be classified for which criteria the idea addresses, or if they have a theme in common. As suggested in relation to idea generation, this might be done publicly or privately by members of the group (we would strongly advise trying both strategies, as social influences on students can sometimes inhibit them contributing in a creative manner). Classifying ideas during the idea generation process has been demonstrated to produce more novel ideas of higher quality (Kirjavainen & Hölttä-Otto, 2019).

METHODS OF GENERATING IDEAS

Having decided the format in which ideas will be recorded, summarised and classified, the next thing to consider is which idea generation tool or tools will be used to encourage and facilitate students to think divergently. When generating ideas, two key factors warrant consideration – the technique chosen and its purpose. A prevalent myth in creativity is that ideas occur spontaneously (Weisberg, 2020). As discussed previously, creativity is context dependent and builds on knowledge and skills. Therefore, the tools chosen must fit the context and purpose and reflect the development of the students. For example, in the early years of schooling, students may require the problem and method to be clearly articulated with only the solution unknown. However, as they develop knowledge and skills in the subject domain and in idea generation, they require less information and can make creative choices (Shiever & Maker, 1991). A method such as analogous thinking may appear to be relatively sophisticated but has been shown to be effective in students in third grade (Aiamy & Haghani, 2012).

The following selection of idea generation tools will offer both analogue and digital techniques and discuss which are most appropriate for particular contexts. To develop your creative competencies as a teacher and that of your students, it would be useful to try a variety of techniques over time. You will also notice that idea generation requires other components of creativity, including the students' attitudes and attributes and the environment in which the creative process occurs. You can refer to these in the appropriate chapters.

Many creative tools, such as SCAMPER and design thinking or de Bono's six thinking hats, are all derived from Guilford's original model of divergent thinking. Most either do not deal exclusively with the idea generation phase or include it within a more holistic approach to the problem-solving process. It is our view that by developing competency in each facet of the creative process, learners will become more adept in their overall creativity.

The whole point of idea generation is exactly that – to generate as many original (within the specific context) ideas in different categories as possible. This is essentially a cognitive process, with students using their pre-existing knowledge, or knowledge gained from research, in thinking about the problem. But how many ideas do you need? What is the relationship between the number of ideas generated and their quality? This question has been explored by creativity researchers for over sixty years (Reinig & Briggs, 2008). There is consensus that two things limit the quality of ideas: how much pre-existing knowledge the idea generators have, or if the information about the task has been previously discussed; and how much cognitive stamina the students have. It is for this reason that there are essentially two different methods of idea generation that build divergent thinking skills. The first involves asking students what ideas they have from their pre-existing knowledge and skills. The second is to engage students in research to develop their knowledge, which then provides them with new ideas they hadn't previously considered. Either way, classroom experience shows that it is better to offer a finite amount of time to generate ideas and to aim for a certain number. These constraints are known to improve the quality of the creative process. While it can be exciting to generate a large number of ideas, they are usually not of the highest quality. As students become more experienced, as with any developing skill, the quality of idea generation will improve.

BRAINSTORMING

Probably the most well-known idea generation tool is brainstorming, developed by Osborn in the late 1930s and refined in the 1950s. The basic idea is to generate as many ideas as possible, without any critical observation or evaluation, over a set period of time. Interestingly, the term originally used the component of the word *storming* as a verb: 'Brainstorm means using the brain to storm a creative problem and to do so "in commando fashion, each stormer audaciously attacking the same objective"' (Osborn, 1948, p. 265). Osborn's original version of brainstorming, around which hundreds of books and websites have been created, contained four principles. We have slightly rephrased these for a contemporary school audience. As you will see these also contain some of the other facets of creativity discussed in the book (in italics for your reference).

1. When brainstorming there should be no evaluation or criticism of ideas (*maintaining an environment of psychological safety*). The focus is on generating, not justifying ideas. (*This justification occurs in the idea evaluation phase.*)
2. Students are encouraged to suggest the most outrageous solutions they can think of, on the assumption that these may contain some elements of truth that can be built on in the idea evaluation phase.

3. As many ideas as can be thought of are spoken or written down, depending on the method of recording, in the belief that quantity will lead to quality. The brainstorming session only moves into the idea evaluation phase after the group has exhausted the supply of ideas.
4. The aim is to build on, integrate and develop ideas that have been presented in the session. Students can suggest variations, combinations or improvements of previous ideas in this phase (Pfeiffer, 1998).

Brainstorming can be conducted individually or in groups (Ritter & Mostert, 2018). There is some contention as to whether individual or group brainstorming is more effective. Some studies have shown that individual brainstorming produces more, and often better, ideas than group brainstorming while other studies report better quality of ideas come from group brainstorming (Ma et al., 2021; Ritter & Mostert, 2018). These inconsistencies reflect the many different ways in which brainstorming can be conducted. It is of course possible that generating ideas in a group after generating ideas individually may have a beneficial effect on the quality of the ideas generated (Yuan et al., 2022). We will discuss some of the most commonly used brainstorming techniques, and their benefits and disadvantages, in the following section.

Brainstorming can be done manually, using pens, paper, sticky notes and other tools, or using a digital format – there are many digital versions online. We note that digital brainstorming can eliminate 'many of the problems of standard brainstorming, including production blocking and evaluation apprehension. A perceived advantage of this format is that all ideas can be archived electronically in their original form, and then retrieved later for further thought and discussion' (Chandra Sekhar & Lidiya, 2012, p. 115; Gobron, 2021).

INDIVIDUAL BRAINSTORMING BENEFITS

Students doing individual brainstorming tend to be more focused and less distracted than those doing group brainstorming. Individual brainstorming can also be effective at stopping one of the greatest inhibitors of creativity: 'self-criticism or negative self-talk' (Pfeiffer, 1998, p. 4). Students often tend to 'criticise themselves, their thoughts, and their actions far more than they praise themselves' (Pfeiffer, 1998, p. 4). 'Because the brainstorming process encourages the continual production of [uncensored and imaginative] ideas, it can be an effective exercise in creativity (Pfeiffer, 1998, p. 4). In terms of how teachers can assist with this process, the focus should be on building an environment of psychological safety and stressing the emphasis on idea quantity. Individual brainstorming is also more successful if students are given some autonomy in how they record their ideas.

INDIVIDUAL BRAINSTORMING DISADVANTAGES

Individual brainstorming is limited by the amount knowledge each individual has and how good they are at generating ideas. Individual brainstorming may also be limited by the personal characteristics of the student (see Chapter 4). Students lacking motivation, intellectual curiosity and creative self-efficacy may find the process difficult.

BRAINSTORMING IN GROUPS

There are a range of strategies students can use when brainstorming in groups. Group brainstorming introduces factors such as the size of the group and the personality types within the group. These need to be considered carefully when group brainstorming.

When doing a group brainstorming session, it is essential to allocate roles to each member of the group. In younger students this should be done by the teacher, while older students may make the allocations themselves. Each group needs to have a scribe to collate ideas and a timekeeper to keep students on track. To account for both introverted and extroverted personalities, teachers may choose the order in which each member of the group makes a contribution, or that every member of the group must generate at least one or two ideas.

OPEN BRAINSTORMING

In terms of the social environment, there are different ways brainstorming can be conducted. One way is for people to articulate their ideas to the group as they record them. The benefit of this is that people in the group know what others are thinking and over time the idea generation process will slow down, but everybody knows the ideas that have been generated by the group. It can give a group a strong sense of achievement when they realise they have a great deal of knowledge and skills to share. Another benefit of this approach is that it increases the cognitive load of the students as they hear and see the ideas that have been generated and try to find something new to suggest. A drawback is that shy or introverted students may be reluctant to make their suggestion in front of the group. Others might be wary of looking foolish in front of their classmates, despite instructions not to judge ideas when they are presented.

SILENT BRAINSTORMING AND THE 6–3–5 METHOD

One possible solution is silent brainstorming or brainwriting. In this approach students generate ideas in silence and only share them at the end of a set amount of time. You may find either of these approaches effective, depending on the group and the problem you are dealing with. An example of this is the 6–3–5 method. The 6–3–5 method, where students brainwrite individually before sharing ideas with classmates, has been shown to generate ideas of better quality (Litcanu et al., 2015). In each round, six people write down three ideas each within five minutes. After the first round, everyone swaps their piece of paper with someone else, reads it and then writes down three more ideas. These can be new ideas or can build on the ideas that have already been shared. Through discussion and iteration students select one final idea.

A third possibility is a combination of the two. You may start with brainstorming and at a certain time move to silent brainstorming. This will give you the best of both processes.

CREATIVE ACTIONS

English as a foreign language, secondary, Indonesia

WHAT THE TEACHER FOUND

"The teacher tells the students the rules of doing 6–3–5 Brain Writing. The students are not allowed to talk while writing the ideas. The ideas can be a phrase. It is better for the students to write the ideas short enough because the time is limited." (Sari & Fitrawati, 2018, p. 534)

Component of creativity	Facet(s) of creativity	Teaching with or for creativity
Process	Idea generation and brainwriting	For
Attitudes and attributes	Multiple perspectives	For
Environment	Collaboration and sharing ideas	For

PURPOSE OF LESSON: SUBJECT KNOWLEDGE OR SKILLS

The purpose of this lesson was for students to build skills in observing and analysing points of view by watching a video recording in English. Students then wrote an analytical exposition of the text in English. Students developed more fluency in their written English and demonstrated a higher level of usage than if they were required to give a spoken response.

PURPOSE OF THE LESSON: TEACHING WITH OR FOR CREATIVITY

In terms of creativity, the purpose of this lesson was for students to build their individual and collaborative skills, idea generation skills, and understanding through differing perspectives by using brainwriting and the 6–3–5 method.

REFERENCE

Sari, E. K., & Fitrawati, F. (2018). Using 6-3-5 Brainwriting in helping senior high school students doing brainstorming in writing process. *Journal of English Language Teaching, 7*(3). 531–537. http://ejournal.unp.ac.id/index.php/jelt/article/view/101115

ACCESS

NOMINAL GROUP TECHNIQUE

This method, combining both open and silent brainstorming, is designed to give all students the opportunity to contribute (Chandra Sekhar & Lidiya, 2012). First, students anonymously record their ideas (Chandra Sekhar & Lidiya, 2012). The ideas are then collected and the group votes on each idea. The vote can be public, for example, by a show of hands, or anonymous, via an onlune poll or ballot box. This process is called distillation (Chandra Sekhar & Lidiya, 2012).

After distillation, 'the top ranked ideas may be sent back to the group or to subgroups for further brainstorming' (Chandra Sekhar & Lidiya, 2012, p. 115). This technique has been shown to greatly improve the quality of ideas in groups (Rietzschel et al., 2006).

GROUP PASSING TECHNIQUE

This strategy can be a very effective tool in the building of ideas during the problem-solving process. In this technique, an idea is built on as it is passed from individual to individual around a group. This gives individuals an opportunity to build ideas without interruption. Once the piece of paper returns to its original owner the next phase of evaluation of ideas takes place. This technique may appear time-consuming but it does give individuals, in particular introverts, an opportunity to think more deeply about the problem without fear of negative criticism.

DIRECTED BRAINSTORMING

This is another method designed to protect individual anonymity and for students to appreciate the full diversity of ideas generated by a group. In this technique, which can be done manually or digitally, participants are given one question to answer on one piece of paper, or electronic form. The responses are then randomly swapped throughout the group. In this round participants are asked to improve on the idea they have received. This round can be repeated multiple times or until the ideas are fully formed. This is an excellent strategy to demonstrate to students the variety of ideas which can be generated within a group and also to prevent them being fixed on a very narrow range of ideas when trying to solve a problem.

GUIDED BRAINSTORMING

A guided brainstorming session is constrained by perspective and time. This type of brainstorming aims to reduce cause for conflict and shortens conversations, while stimulating critical and creative thinking in a supportive environment (Chandra Sekhar & Lidiya, 2012). This strategy uses a group mind map, on which students are asked to make contributions from different perspectives, for example on topics like the different reasons countries go to war. The ideas must be generated and recorded on the mind map within a specific and limited amount of time. Adopting different perspectives is also part of the methodology of Synectics and de Bono's six thinking hats.

DISADVANTAGES OF GROUP BRAINSTORMING

Groups bring with them multiple personalities. As students develop their skills in group brainstorming, they will need to learn the skills of collaboration, cooperation and negotiation as discussed in Chapter 3. Two flaws in group work can be social loafing and unfair marking (Lin, 2019). *Social loafing* refers to the phenomenon that people spend less effort in group work than individual work when problem-solving. *Unfair marking* refers to assessment, which students worry will not reflect each individual's contribution to the group. One of the common methods to address the issues in group work is to perform self and peer assessment among students (see

Chapter 6). Group work might also cause issues such as peer pressure to conform, friendship groups taking sides when it comes to contributing ideas, some students dominating discussions while other students contributing little or less than their fair share, students being distracted by too many ideas, or only accepting ideas expressed by the majority (Shirvani & Porkar, 2021). There is also likely to be an uneven distribution of motivation as well as ability across members of a group and can be time-consuming compared with individual work.

DISADVANTAGES OF BRAINSTORMING

While brainstorming is very popular, its efficacy is coming into question (Runco, 2019). For all kinds of reasons, from social to knowledge and skills, brainstorming sometimes simply does not present very good ideas. There are times when students just need a little bit more guidance in their quest to generate ideas. There is no question that well-structured processes lead to better outcomes.

There is a variety of prompts or constraints that students can be offered when being asked to generate ideas. These guide the idea generation process without giving students concrete suggestions. The simplest of these prompts, sometimes called *six good men* (probably *people* in modern times), uses open-ended questioning to elicit a greater range of ideas from students. The prompts are who, what, when, where, how and why? (Vernon & Hocking, 2014). Another constraint, as mentioned previously, is the time given to this phase. Too little time can put students under pressure and reduce the number of ideas. Too much time can result in the groups becoming restless and bored.

SYNECTICS

Another type of tool for idea generation is Synectics, otherwise known as analogous or metaphorical thinking, developed by Gordon in the 1960s. In this method there are three types of analogous thinking. In personal analogy, the thinker identifies with the problem, or at least a component of the problem, and can imagine or role-play the problem to understand that particular view. In symbolic analogy, there is also identification but with phrases, images and objects. Ideally two words are put together that appear to be incompatible in meaning but give an insight into the problem. For example, how can we do 'dry washing'? In fantasy analogy, real-world constraints are released, and the thinker can consider how the situation would be if the impossible were possible. A core idea of Synectics is the idea of 'making the strange familiar', for example, how is a fish's heart like a swimming pool? and 'making the familiar strange', for example, considering 'What would Harry Potter do?'

THE CREATIVE PROCESS

e5.6
Mathematics, secondary, Pakistan

WHAT THE TEACHER FOUND

"Use of everyday familiar analogies increased interest and motivation level of the students of the experimental group and contributed to their high achievement and better understanding of abstract concepts of mathematics." (Khan & Mahmood, 2018, p. 193)

Component of creativity	Facet(s) of creativity	Teaching with or for creativity
Process	Critical thinking and analogous thinking	For
Attitudes and attributes	Tolerance for ambiguity	For
Environment	Collaboration	For

PURPOSE OF LESSON: SUBJECT KNOWLEDGE OR SKILLS

The purpose of this lesson was for students to develop an understanding of abstract concepts in mathematics knowledge and skills in the topics of sets, polynomials and fundamentals of geometry.

PURPOSE OF THE LESSON: TEACHING WITH OR FOR CREATIVITY

In terms of creativity, the purpose of this lesson was for students to build their tolerance for ambiguity and analogous thinking by giving examples of experiences with mathematical concepts from their personal lives. The control group completed exercises from the textbook without training in analogous thinking while the experimental group received explicit instruction and had group discussions on the analogies they developed.

REFERENCE
Khan, A. A., & Mahmood, N. (2018). Effect of synectics model of teaching in enhancing students' understanding of abstract concepts of mathematics. *Pakistan Journal of Distance and Online Learning*, 4(1), 185–198. https://files.eric.ed.gov/fulltext/EJ1267261.pdf

ACCESS

DISADVANTAGES OF SYNECTICS AND ANALOGOUS THINKING

Synectics does require a certain amount of explicit teaching of the model, including discussions of what constitutes analogous thinking. It is also true that not all idea generation requires analogous thinking and that synectics may not be the appropriate tool (Gazizov et al., 2018). Teachers need to be very conscious that students have the level of cognitive development required to attempt such an idea generation strategy. Students may also find it difficult to break down old associative connections when being introduced to this tool.

DIFFERENT PERSPECTIVES – DE BONO'S SIX THINKING HATS

As discussed in guided brainstorming, one useful tool in idea generation is challenging assumptions by looking at things from different perspectives. This method is employed by some of De Bono's (1985) six thinking hats: four of the hats can be used by asking students to generate ideas from a particular perspective, via data or facts, emotions and feelings, caution and risks, or optimism. A similar approach is used in commerce or business subjects, where students are asked to generate ideas from the perspective of a customer, a manufacturer, or an advertising team. Another creative competency in use is intercultural understanding when seeking a variety of perspectives. A simple example of this would be to explore the language of advertising across a range of countries. A question might be, 'Is the same type of language used when advertising a particular car?'

Another, simpler type of prompt is imagination prompts, also known as provocations, such as 'Imagine if …' or 'Why or why not?'. This method encourages students to look at idea generation from a different perspective. This can also work as an idea generation conversation. The first person says, 'What if …?' and the second person says 'And then we …' This conversation can continue around the room.

SCAMPER

One method used frequently in primary school idea generation, but less often in secondary schools, is SCAMPER. This tool can be used individually or within a group setting and is an acronym for a set of actions that should be applied to the problem: substitute; combine; adapt; modify, magnify or minimise; put to other uses; eliminate; and reverse or rearrange (Eberle, 1997). SCAMPER is frequently used in business for product development, but can be used in many subjects, including the sciences and humanities. It is in many ways similar to de Bono's six thinking hats, in that it asks students to look at solutions from a variety of different perspectives (Toraman & Altun, 2013).

An effective way to introduce the technique of SCAMPER to students is to give practical examples from the real world. An example of *substitute* could be touch screens replacing keyboards on digital devices. An example of *combine* could be a Swiss army knife, or another item that brings many tools together into one. An example of *adapt* could be the development of a multivitamin tablet instead of a single vitamin tablet. An example of *modify* could be putting reflective paint on the road to show the middle of the road at night. An example of *put to other uses* could be phones that can now be used as cameras, as computers, for playing games and for playing media. An example of *eliminate* could be soft drinks that don't contain sugar. An example of *reverse or rearrange* could be the standing desk.

This example table was used by Tim with primary students in biology. Students were asked to demonstrate creativity by looking at how animals use their senses and suggesting new opportunities for the human body. Notice the open-ended questions generated using this technique.

Table 5.2: The SCAMPER model in the classroom

SCAMPER category	Action	Possible questions
Substitute	Substituting a familiar part of their body for something else	What if I substituted my left hand with my nose? How would I smell differently if my nose was the size of my hand? What could I do if my left hand was on my face?
Combine	Make something new by combining body parts or senses	What if I had tastebuds in my feet like a butterfly?
Adapt	Identify parts of our body which could be adapted to change how we live	What animal's sense do I wish I could have? Do I want 24 eyes like a box jellyfish? How would that help me? What might be more difficult to do?
Modify, magnify or minimise	Making body parts or senses work in an unusual or different way by increasing, decreasing, or changing	What would happen if I had eight legs like an octopus, or my head was the size of an apple?
Put to other uses	How might you put the body part to another use?	What if I used my ears for echo location like a bat or a dolphin? Would it make hide and seek easier?
Eliminate	What might happen if you eliminated parts of your body?	What if we didn't have bones? How would we move around?
Rearrange or reverse	What if our body were rearranged?	What if our head was in the middle of our body? What are some positives and negatives?

ADVANTAGES OF SCAMPER

This tool can be applied to generate new ideas or to modify ideas that have already been generated, manipulating them to generate a new suite of ideas for consideration. It could also be used purely as an introductory idea generation tool to build students' skills in this area, without necessarily going on to complete the rest of the problem-solving phase. This method is relatively simple and straightforward to teach and is helpful in showing students how to overcome blocks in their idea generation process by manipulating ideas.

While the SCAMPER technique is more frequently used when designing products to solve problems, it can also be used in science, English and design subjects (Ozyaprak, 2016).

DISADVANTAGES OF SCAMPER

In using this tool, students may come up with impractical or impossible ideas. It is essential that the teacher establishes an environment of psychological safety and makes it clear to students that, as with brainstorming, as many ideas as possible need to be put forward before any feedback is given. It is imperative that students develop the skill of respectful listening when using this type of tool. Students with high levels of anxiety or perfectionism may feel overwhelmed with the range of choices SCAMPER offers (Apriliani et al., 2016). In these circumstances it is better to ask students to perhaps perform one or two aspects of this tool to gain confidence.

e5.7

English, upper secondary, Palestine

WHAT THE TEACHER FOUND

"Using SCAMPER strategy is more effective than the traditional method in developing the students' vocabulary achievement skills … using SCAMPER strategy is very effective in the achievement of tenth graders' motivation." (Jouda, 2019, p. 103–104)

Component of creativity	Facet(s) of creativity	Teaching with or for creativity
Process	Idea generation with the SCAMPER tool to manipulate ideas	For
Attitudes and attributes	Using pre-existing knowledge	For
Attitudes and attributes	Multiple perspectives	For

PURPOSE OF LESSON: SUBJECT KNOWLEDGE OR SKILLS

The purpose of this lesson was for students to improve their competency in the English language by examining synonyms, word families, adjectives and construction of new words and by manipulating words to make new sense and meanings. These manipulations develop both grammatical and usage skills as well as broadening vocabulary.

PURPOSE OF THE LESSON: TEACHING WITH OR FOR CREATIVITY

In terms of creativity, the purpose of this lesson was for students to build idea generation skills by using the SCAMPER tool to manipulate pre-existing knowledge, constructs and ideas to provide information from a variety of new perspectives.

REFERENCE

Jouda, A. A. (2019). The impact of SCAMPER strategy on developing English vocabulary learning, accomplishment motivation and retention for tenth graders in Gaza Governorate [Doctoral dissertation, The Islamic University of Gaza]. https://library.iugaza.edu.ps/thesis/126912.pdf

ACCESS

CREATIVE ACTIONS

EVALUATING IDEAS

The creative process consists of a series of stages (de Buisonje et al., 2017). Although it is essential to generate enough ideas to solve a problem, it is also necessary to discuss and refine the most promising ideas by critically analysing and evaluating the suggestions. This shift of focus from the divergent phase, where the number of ideas is important, to the convergent phase, where only relevant and useful ideas are selected, is critical to effective problem-solving (Rietzschel et al., 2010).

Just as there is a variety of idea generation tools, there is also a variety of idea evaluation tools (Leopoldino et al., 2016). When brainstorming, there is no filtering or analysis of ideas until enough ideas have been generated (Aiamy & Haghani, 2012). When using idea recording tools such as concept mapping or fishbone diagrams, it becomes apparent earlier if ideas are worth pursuing. There are some practical processes and strategies involved in idea selection, as well as some cognitive skills and social skills when doing collaborative problem-solving. Ideas need to be processed, evaluated and selected as efficiently as possible. As with the rest of the creative process, choosing the appropriate tool according to task, purpose and context is essential.

A very simple tool for idea evaluation is the basic balancing idea of pros versus cons. Younger students can use the image of a seesaw to observe which ideas ultimately carry the most weight. Ideas can also be categorised using concept or argument mapping as described previously. Seeing connections visually can help students to select the most appropriate ideas. Another form of visualisation is a decision tree, where the consequences of any idea can be followed through to implementation. It is also possible for students to notate the reason for selecting a particular idea using this method. Using decision trees in the classroom at a simple level can also be an excellent introduction to algorithmic thinking. In primary school this could be presented as a choose your own adventure story.

Evaluating ideas requires cognitive, attitudinal and organisational skills. A sophisticated template for idea categorisation and evaluation is the decision matrix. The decision matrix aims to objectively identify the most suitable and practical solutions for a problem.

THE CREATIVE PROCESS

Science and STEM, lower secondary, United States

WHAT THE TEACHER FOUND

"Students saw the value of the decision matrix tool not only in addressing problems in science and engineering but also in their daily lives outside of the classroom ... Another benefit was that the matrices helped students be objective and data-focused when making decisions." (Gonczi et al., 2017, p. 14–15)

Component of creativity	Facet(s) of creativity	Teaching with or for creativity
Process	Idea evaluation using a decision matrix	For
Attitudes and attributes	Using pre-existing knowledge	For
Attitudes and attributes	Multiple perspectives	For

PURPOSE OF LESSON: SUBJECT KNOWLEDGE OR SKILLS

The purpose of this lesson was for students to develop their understanding of ecosystem interactions and biodiversity by developing expertise in ecosystem interactions and developing recommendations for hypothetical state officials on how to best address the problem of an invasive species in their community's ecosystem. Students were required to define the criteria and constraints of a design problem with sufficient precision to ensure a successful solution, taking into account relevant scientific principles and potential impacts on people and the natural environment that may limit possible solutions.

PURPOSE OF THE LESSON: TEACHING WITH OR FOR CREATIVITY

In terms of creativity, the purpose of this lesson was for students to identify the multiple perspectives of the competing solutions and evaluate these by using a decision matrix as a tool to develop a systematic process and weighting system to determine how well they met the criteria and constraints of the problem.

REFERENCE

Gonczi, A. L., Bergman, B. G., Huntoon, J., Allen, R., McIntyre, B., Turner, S., Davis, J., & Handler, R. (2017). Decision matrices: Tools to enhance middle school engineering instruction. *Science Activities, 54*(1), 8–17. https://doi.org/10.1080/00368121.2016.1264922

ACCESS

CRITICAL THINKING

Critical thinking lies at the heart of the idea selection phase and is considered an important part of the creative process by many education systems around the world. Unfortunately, though used frequently in international curriculum documentation, there is no consensus on the definition of critical thinking among experts, scientists, educators, psychologists and philosophers (Lombardi et al., 2021; Patston, Kaufman et al., 2021). While this may appear problematic there are several key elements of critical thinking that are common between the various models and frameworks.

WHAT IS CRITICAL THINKING?

Critical thinking is a form of reflective judgement whereby students analyse, evaluate and select ideas from those generated through personal knowledge and experience, but also analyse and evaluate other thinkers' ideas and resources.

HOW DO STUDENTS DEMONSTRATE CRITICAL THINKING?

Students demonstrate critical thinking skills by:
- asking appropriate questions
- gathering and creatively sorting through relevant information
- relating new information to existing knowledge
- re-examining beliefs and assumptions
- reasoning logically
- drawing reliable and trustworthy conclusions. (UNESCO, 2013, p. 15)

By combining the what and the how, students will determine the best and most feasible plan to pursue. The critical thinking rubrics in Chapter 4 offer ways to observe and assess student critical thinking skills.

One relatively straightforward way of describing critical thinking to students is as informed decision-making – do they have enough evidence to make a selection about a particular idea or ideas? This combines two elements: sufficient knowledge of the problem and its proposed solutions to make a truly informed choice; and the ability to think logically and use multiple pieces of information to come to a conclusion. As students get older and their cognitive skills develop, critical thinking begins to involve a more sophisticated level of discernment. This is essential as we live in era of social media where fake news is always a risk, not only for our students but also for our community.

METHODS OF TEACHING CRITICAL THINKING

It is not the purpose of this book to cover all the pedagogic and philosophical approaches to teaching critical thinking (van Peppen et al., 2021). We will, however, offer some methods that have been used successfully in education. (You will note the frequent appearance of attitudes and attributes, which we discussed in more depth in Chapter 4).

THE CREATIVE PROCESS

CRITICAL THINKING IN PRIMARY SCHOOLS

As with the elements and aspects of creativity discussed in this book, the principles behind the critical thinking processes are the same, however, critical thinking varies between subjects, as the concept of knowledge varies. Willingham (2019) proposes that critical thinking has three criteria for how students demonstrate critical thinking and can be readily explained to primary students:

1. Your thinking is novel – that is, you aren't simply drawing a conclusion from a memory of a previous situation.
2. Your thinking is self-directed – that is, you aren't merely executing instructions given by someone else.
3. Your thinking is effective – that is, you respect certain conventions that make thinking more likely to yield useful conclusions. (Willingham, 2019, p. 3)

Table 5.3 from Lombardi et al. (2020, p. 9) illustrates how the various aspects of critical thinking can be taught in specific topic areas in a range of subjects at the primary level.

Table 5.3: Analysis of core skills of critical thinking through the syllabus

Core skills	Description	Syllabus
Interpretation	To foster the students' ability to distinguish between important information in a text and search for information autonomously using diverse written sources	Art Discovery of the world Ethics education Language 1 and 2 Music Religious education
	To help students recognise and decode a problem	Mathematics
	To understand and gather information about others' team strategies to reach a goal	Physical education
Analysis	To make connections with pre-existing knowledge	Art Discovery of the world Ethics education Language 1 and 2 Music Religious education
	To understand and compare information about different cultures To understand important information To select the knowledge needed to solve a problem To select the best strategy for a give problem	Be, think and act European Mathematics

continued …

CREATIVE ACTIONS

Core skills	Description	Syllabus
Inference	To express students' opinions, formulate hypotheses and make predictions	Art Discovery of the world Ethics education Language 1 and 2 Music Religious education
	To question and debate different options	Be, think and act European
	To improve cooperation and interactive exchanges between students To inquire from other students, pose key questions and generate ideas	ICT Mathematics
Evaluation	To draw conclusions	Art Discovery of the world Ethics education Language 1 and 2 Music Religious education
	To make informed decisions using the results of discussion and reasoning in a small group of students To make decisions in teams according to rules	Mathematics Physical education
Explanation	To ecnourage students to express the process they used to make their decisions and foster debates	Art Discovery of the world Ethics education Language 1 and 2 Music Religious education
	To improve students' learning strategies To encourage students to reason and think through how to describe, interpret and explain their thinking	ICT Mathematics

Core skills	Description	Syllabus
Self-regulation	To conduct daily assessments and self-assessments through a process that involves teachers' checking students' understanding and students' consistent involvement in learning revision pathways	Art Discovery of the world Ethics education Be, think and act European ICT Language 1 and 2 Mathematics Music Physical education Religious education

SOURCE: Lombardi et al., 2020, p. 9, https://doi.org/10.3390/educsci11090505. Used with permission under Creative Commons Attribution License 4.0.

CRITICAL THINKING IN SECONDARY SCHOOLS

In secondary schools there are a wide range of subjects taught by individual teachers. Willingham (2019) proposes that:

> *If students are to read as historians do, they need to learn specific skills like interpreting documents in light of their sources, corroborating them, and putting them in historical context. Notably, skilful reading is different in other disciplines. Scientists believe that the source of a document is irrelevant so long as it is trustworthy. And unlike historical documents, scientific documents are written in a consistent format. Learning to read like a scientist means, in part, learning the conventions of this format.* (p. 12)

He then proposes a four-step approach for high school teachers when it comes to building critical thinking skills in their students. This approach closely and clearly aligns with our approach to building all of the components and facets of creativity in students. The four steps are:

1. Teach and practice the element or elements of critical thinking that are required explicitly.
2. Tie this element or elements to the specific subject content that is required.
3. Carefully select the best sequence for the introduction of the skills to the students.
4. Decide which skills need to be reinforced, either within the unit of work or over a longer period of time. (Willingham, 2019)

Critical thinking should be taught concurrently with subject skills, as demonstrated in the following example.

CREATIVE ACTIONS

History, secondary, United States

WHAT THE TEACHER FOUND

❝ *By employing the lessons and activities delineated here, teachers will allow students to develop genuine historical and critical thinking skills … students with sound historical thinking skills are, by definition, sound critical thinkers and critical thinking is a crucial characteristic of competent citizens in a global, multicultural, and democratic society.* **❞** *(Waring & Robinson, 2010, p. 28)*

Component of creativity	Facet(s) of creativity	Teaching with or for creativity
Process	Critical thinking	For
Attitudes and attributes	Using pre-existing knowledge	For
Attitudes and attributes	Multiple perspectives	For

PURPOSE OF LESSON: SUBJECT KNOWLEDGE OR SKILLS

The purpose of this lesson was for students to develop their understanding of the role of historians, how they think and what attitudes and skills they need to be successful by understanding the term primary source through a range of historical resources including documents and photographs. The teacher attempted to bring history to life by asking students to imagine themselves positioned within a photo. Questions exploring the human senses, along with traditional journalistic inquiries, were employed as students were asked 'What does it smell like?' and 'What do you feel?' The second purpose of this lesson was for students to understand that history can be viewed from multiple perspectives.

PURPOSE OF THE LESSON: TEACHING WITH OR FOR CREATIVITY

In terms of creativity, the purpose of this lesson was for students to build critical thinking skills including analysis and inference and learn how to determine the credibility of information by developing the ability to view problems through multiple perspectives. Students developed these skills alongside their understanding of the content of the curriculum.

REFERENCE

Waring, S. M., & Robinson, K. S. (2010). Developing critical and historical thinking skills in middle grades social studies. *Middle School Journal*, 42(1), 22–28. https://doi.org/10.1080/0094 0771.2010.11461747

ACCESS

THE CREATIVE PROCESS

PRACTICAL TOOLS FOR EVALUATING IDEAS

Critical thinking skills may take some time to develop across a student's journey at school and require detailed and specific instruction tied to subject knowledge. However, there are some very simple and practical tools that can be used to evaluate ideas in the classroom, such as the CSDS (Creative Solution Diagnoses Scale; Cropley et al., 2011; Pantaleo, 2019).

Remember the overarching objective of evaluating ideas is to use convergent thinking to identify the proposed solution. At this stage the relevance, effectiveness and practicality of the ideas are more important than their novelty, but novel ideas still need to be considered carefully in order not to stifle creativity (Cropley, 2006).

In terms of the convergent thinking needed at this stage, the role of the teacher is once again critically important. Teachers can both actively and passively affect information processing and the final ideas selected by the students. Finding a balance between observation and intervention can be challenging (Seeber, 2019).

One useful tool is the ABC technique – a simple table that students can use to rank ideas in terms of how they meet three simple criteria.

Table 5.4: ABC technique table

Criteria	A Very	B Somewhat	C Not at all
How relevant is the idea to the problem?			
How effective is the proposed idea in solving the problem?			
Can the idea be implemented?			

Once students have filled in this tool, there may be some convergent thinking needed to rank the ideas. It may also be at this time that another round of divergent thinking is needed to determine if the ideas presented may in fact be modified, combined or improved in some way before moving to the next stage of the creative process. It is essential at this stage that students are provided with targeted, specific and useful feedback (Todd et al., 2022). We give examples of such feedback when discussing the CSDS in the next section – this is a more comprehensive evaluation tool.

The students then return to convergent thinking once more to make the final selection. If working in groups, it is also possible for this stage to be conducted anonymously to remove personality issues from the decision-making process (see Chapter 6 on peer-to-peer evaluation).

TRIALLING, PROTOTYPING AND TESTING

After using the appropriate thinking skills, idea recording and divergent and convergent thinking to complete the idea generation process, the next phase is evaluation by taking ideas from a concept to a tangible object. This practical application of trialling and testing ideas involves what is known as prototyping. A common view of prototyping is that it only applies to subjects such as marketing or engineering. However, it is possible to prototype and test a solution in many subjects, from mathematics (Painter, 2018), to senior chemistry (Pernaa L& Wiedmer 2020), to physics (Bunprom et al., 2021), to computer science (Miller, 2021) and music technology (May, 2020).

This stage can be difficult for students as they may struggle with the ability to see a product as a learning point when it fails or does not work the first time (Marks & Chase, 2019). When introducing the concepts of trialling, prototyping and testing, the initial explanation may only have three points:

1. Make mistakes and learn from them.
2. Go through cycles of making, testing and thinking.
3. It's okay to have a number of attempts.

RAPID PROTOTYPING

It is then worthwhile to introduce the process of rapid prototyping. Rapid prototyping consists of the development of incomplete or draft versions of possible problem solutions, or prototypes, and testing them in rapid succession to verify their effectiveness. By producing multiple iterations rather than one and emphasising the process of revision, formative evaluation and testing at the start of the physical stage of the idea evaluation process, a more effective final solution will emerge. It is preferable that only one variable is manipulated at a time and a record is taken of the strengths and areas for improvement of any prototype. When working with students, a supportive social environment of psychological safety is once again essential. Rapid prototyping also prevents students being paralysed by indecision or perfectionism. This has been used successfully in a range of subjects, including a senior engineering class in Mexico (Hernandez-de-Menendez et al., 2020) and in computer-aided product design in Switzerland (Schifferle & Kollegger, 2021).

The first stage of the trialling, testing and prototyping phase is to convert the idea into a tangible form. This can involve words, images or a preliminary model made out of paper or cardboard, or on a digital device. The following example brings together elements from this chapter and shows that this is an iterative process. Following this process the product can be submitted for assessment and evaluation (we discussed this in detail in Chapter 6).

THE CREATIVE PROCESS

MODELLING, DEMONSTRATION AND VALIDATION

One way to demonstrate this phase is through a simple demonstration of problem-solving which David has used successfully with school students, teachers and university students. Any problem should have a range of criteria against which solutions can be assessed. Note that in this example the criteria are novelty compared to the group, elegance of design and effectiveness in terms of distance flown. There are also weightings for each criteria.

THE PROBLEM

Make an original paper aeroplane from one sheet of A4 paper. You must submit three prototypes for this project.

SUCCESS CRITERIA RUBRIC

Table 5.4: Paper place success criteria rubric

Paper plane	Prototype 1	Prototype 2	Prototype 3
Novelty (How original is your design compared to the rest of the class?) 20% of mark			
Design (How elegant is your design? 30% of mark			
Effectiveness (How far did your design fly?) 50% of mark			
Total			

Here are three possible designs for the paper aeroplanes – how would you rate each one and which one do you think would fly the furthest?

DEVELOP THE FINAL SOLUTION

This is primarily a final check of effectiveness. Make any final changes to your solution to check effectiveness. Is there any way you can make your final design more original or more elegant than your three prototypes? Can you make any minor modifications to enable it to fly further?

VALIDATE THE FINAL SOLUTION

Before submission it is essential that students check that all elements of the process have been followed as well as they could have and that they are ready to submit their final product for assessment. Please note we have added a third column where students are asked to provide supporting evidence for each stage of the process. It is useful to have this reflection early in the instructional and learning stages of solution validation. It also demonstrates to students that these aspects are important.

There are two key questions to be asked:
- Does the product do what it is supposed to do?
- Have you met *all* the criteria?

Table 5.5: Final solution checklist

Final criteria checklist	Yes	Evidence to support
I reflected and chose the best idea based on the criteria.		
I created a quality and detailed prototype.		
I gave and received feedback from my peers and my teacher.		
I refined and tested my prototype based on this feedback.		
I built the final product based on all the criteria.		

PUTTING IT TOGETHER

Once students have experience with each of the facets of the creative solving process it is of course possible to put them all together. This example goes into considerable detail, but explains very clearly the progression from understanding the problem, to idea generation, evaluating ideas, developing and validating the final solution and incorporating both formative and summative assessments of both creative process and creative product. The specific language they use is appropriate to their context, but clearly uses the model we propose in this book.

Music, lower secondary, Canada

WHAT THE TEACHER FOUND

> *Teachers described supporting students with a variety of assessment responses, including (a) referencing a creative process framework, (b) guiding exploration, (c) promoting refining and revision, and (d) identifying next steps.*
> (Bolden & DeLuca, 2022, p. 378)

Component of creativity	Facet(s) of creativity	Teaching with or for creativity
Environment	Constraints	With
Environment	Psychological safety	With
Process	Problem-solving process	For

PURPOSE OF LESSON: SUBJECT KNOWLEDGE OR SKILLS

The purpose of this lesson was for students to build skills in music by composing sixteen parts of music within selected constraints. Students needed to incorporate a variety of note values including quarter notes, half notes and eight notes and have a time signature such as 4/4 time. The standard approach to this task would likely be logistical in nature, with students only required to meet certain criteria. This lesson challenged students to be more creative using the following process.

PURPOSE OF THE LESSON: TEACHING WITH OR FOR CREATIVITY

In terms of creativity, the purpose of this lesson was for students to build their problem-solving skills by using a suggested model of problem-solving and creation. The model describes a circular, cyclical process through eight stages: challenging and inspiring; imagining and generating; planning and focusing; exploring and experimenting; producing preliminary work; revising and refining; presenting, performing and sharing; and reflecting and evaluating. All stages are shown to interact with feedback (from peers and teacher) and reflection. Teachers indicated that the model helped students to conceptualise their work within the full trajectory of creative production, offering touchstones along the route to keep them on track.

REFERENCE

Bolden, B., DeLuca, C., Kukkonen, T., Roy, S., & Wearing, J. (2020). Assessment of creativity in K–12 education: A scoping review. *Review of education*, 8(2), 343–376. https://doi.org/10.1002/rev3.3188

ACCESS

CONCLUSION

As Molnár and Csapó (2018) reported from their findings involving over 4000 students from Years 3–12 in Hungary: '[These findings] highlight the importance of explicit enhancement of problem-solving skills and problem-solving strategies as a tool for knowledge acquisition in new contexts during and beyond school lessons' (p. 1).

We appreciate that this has been a very long and detailed chapter. However, there is consistent evidence that problem-solving in schools is inefficient and ineffective (Molnár & Csapó, 2018). Before we conclude this chapter, we reinforce that it is critically important students are given time to reflect on each stage of the creative process. It is far too common for students to only focus on elements that they think will be graded and to discard work the moment it has been completed.

CHAPTER 6

EVALUATING CREATIVITY: MEASURING AND ASSESSING THE COMPONENTS OF CREATIVITY

6

Creativity is increasingly considered an important knowledge and skill set students will need not just at school, but for lifelong learning to flourish in a twenty-first century workplace. The rise of artificial intelligence has changed the kinds of jobs available now and in the future. This means students need to know not just what to learn, but how to learn.

When it comes to evaluating creativity, people most commonly think of evaluating the results of the creative process. Any act of creativity requires both a purpose and an outcome, which we refer to as a product. The standard way of evaluating creative products is by rating them in terms of originality, relevance and usefulness (Runco & Jaeger, 2012). However, each component of the model of creativity – the environment, the person, the process and the product – and the facets that lie within each component, can also be reported on and assessed formatively or summatively. It is essential that any element of creativity be measurable within its context, such as subject discipline, age group and setting. It is possible to reflect on, discuss, analyse or measure any of the four components of creativity or the facets that lie within. It is up to the teacher to decide the appropriate time, scope and situation for any assessment. The teacher, within the context of their subject and needs, can determine the product of any facet of creativity, and consequently, how this is evaluated.

As we have stressed throughout the book, students should build their attitudes and skills across their school journey in a gradual way. In terms of evaluating facets of creativity, students need to incrementally build skills in reflecting on, giving feedback on, and evaluating their own creativity as well as that of their peers.

While there are examples of formative and summative assessment and creativity, and teacher, self and peer assessment in creativity, there are few studies in this area in school education (Bolden et al., 2020). Our approach throughout this book has been that teachers offer short, explicit, clear and targeted approaches to developing the components and facets of creativity in the classroom. In this chapter we provide evaluation, reporting and assessment strategies to support this type of approach in developing the creative capacity of students.

WHY EVALUATE CREATIVITY?

Schools tend to be outcome driven, with many countries around the world completing a student's education journey with some form of summative written exam that gives students a mark or grade used to enter the world of study or work after school. As a result, much schooling in the senior years is focused on test results. We note that summative assessments are also used as a means of assessing teacher performance as well as student accountability and consequently have a strong impact on both what is taught and how it is taught, so-called 'teaching to the test' (Hopfenbeck, 2019). There is currently a global movement toward more formative, or process-based, assessments that capture student development in attitudes, skills and competencies, both within and outside subjects (Thompson & Meer, 2021).

Formative assessment and feedback, now often called *assessment for learning*, has been shown to be highly effective in building students' academic competencies, creative competencies and the attitudes associated with creative competencies (Chan & Lam, 2010; Cizek et al., 2019; Klapwijk, 2017; Lucas, Claxton & Spencer, 2013). The OECD (2008) states:

> *Formative assessment – while not a 'silver bullet' that can solve all educational challenges – offers a powerful means for meeting goals for high-performance, high-equity of student outcomes, and for providing students with knowledge and skills for lifelong learning.* (p. 5)

WHO CAN EVALUATE CREATIVITY?

When it comes to evaluating the facets of creativity, who is capable of evaluation depends on which facet or component of creativity is involved. In terms of creative products, experts such as teachers, are often considered the ideal judges, although we will also demonstrate that with explicit instruction, practice and time, students can also develop some capacity in offering both feedback and assessment (Amabile, 1996; Kaufman & Baer, 2012).

Indeed, experienced teachers can clearly articulate high, medium and low levels of creative ideas in students of particular ages and stages in their subject area (van der Zanden, Meijer, et al., 2020). However, though most of the creativity work in schools is done at the mini-c or little-c level, with some explicit instruction students can develop their skills to understand the various facets of creativity and how they manifest in themselves and their classmates. They can then apply that knowledge and skills when giving feedback.

EVALUATION BY TEACHERS

Throughout the book we have stressed the importance of being highly specific, and not too ambitious, in terms of the amount of knowledge or skill being built in any particular lesson or unit when it comes to creativity. The same is true when it comes to the evaluation of any component or facet of creativity. Teachers must be very clear about the subject knowledge and skills being developed and the creativity knowledge and skills being built in tandem. Any type of evaluation should include both.

In addition to the formal learning outcomes and assessment requirements, informal formative feedback should be built into the unit plan. Students are familiar with being given summative feedback about a subject, particularly in the early years of high school, often looking for the mark or grade rather than the comments. They can be less familiar with being given formative feedback throughout the process of learning, but it is well worth introducing. This addition provides an excellent opportunity for the teacher to model the style of interaction they prefer in terms of formative feedback. For example, the unit planner could be laid out as a train journey, with the stations representing opportunities to stop and reflect. The authors' experience with workshops is that people tend to rush towards the final destination, without taking the opportunity to pause, digest and reflect before moving from one station to the next. It is not enough to say students should avoiding rushing; there need to be mechanisms in place to ensure that the reflective practice of learning is building creative competency for the students.

As discussed in Chapter 3, the creative environment is very important. We highlighted the importance of allocating an appropriate amount of time to building any element of creativity. One mechanism to achieve this is through a process of discrete stages. A useful tool to use is tickets, also known as exit slips. In many computer games it is not possible to move past a level until a problem has been solved successfully. The same is true of facets of the creative process. By teachers modelling a pause and reflect approach, students will understand that this is integral and essential to the creative process. In Chapter 3 we also stressed the need for psychological safety in the learning environment and how on occasion it is good for students to be able to ask a question anonymously.

The teacher needs to provide feedback that the stage of the ticket has been completed. (Tim has used cardboard tickets that need to be hole-punched or stamped before students can move to the next stage.) Tickets could also be a way for students to ask for assistance anonymously, by writing questions on the back as they pass it to the teacher (Johnson & King-Seers, 2020). An additional benefit for the teacher is that when they examine students' responses, they can determine which students need further clarification of ideas or concepts and observe how students perceive their learning is progressing.

EVALUATION BY STUDENTS

PEER-TO-PEER TEACHING

Students as teachers has proved to be an effective way of information transfer, building academic self-concept in students and introducing students to the skills of feedback and evaluation (Moliner & Alegre, 2020). Building some understanding of the attitudes and skills needed as a teacher can increase students' willingness to share information and questions as well as their confidence in sharing information, and informally evaluating responses. By using a model of reciprocal tutoring students can share the experience of being both teacher and learner with a partner.

CREATIVE ACTIONS

Mathematics, secondary, Spain

WHAT THE TEACHER FOUND

❝*The main conclusion that can be drawn from this study is that peer tutoring may be very beneficial for middle school students' mathematics self-concepts ... Also, from an organizational point of view, same-age and reciprocal tutoring is easier to implement, as it can take place within the same classroom of students.*❞ *(Moliner & Alegre, 2020, p. 11)*

Component of creativity	Facet(s) of creativity	Teaching with or for creativity
Creative person	Creative self-efficacy and subject self-efficacy	For
Creative person	Openness to new experience	For
Creative environment	Collaboration through peer-to-peer tutoring	For
Evaluating creativity	Assessing multiple ways to solve problems through peer-to-peer feedback	For

PURPOSE OF LESSON: SUBJECT KNOWLEDGE OR SKILLS

Year 7s worked on 'basic first-degree equations, calculated surfaces and volumes of regular prisms, used the Pythagoras' theorem, calculated basic statistical centralization parameters for both qualitative and quantitative variables, used Laplace's rule, and completed basic tree diagrams (p. 5).

Year 8s revised the prior year's course, and 'calculated compound probabilities, standard deviations and variances, first degree equations with fractions, second degree equations and surfaces, and volumes of irregular prisms' (p. 5).

Year 9s 'also refreshed previous content and worked with quartiles, percentiles, and box plots, developed advanced tree diagrams, applied Laplace's rule of succession, calculated complex surfaces and volumes, and solved third- and fourth-degree equations of direct solving (using Ruffini's rule and factorizing)' (p. 5).

PURPOSE OF THE LESSON: TEACHING WITH OR FOR CREATIVITY

In terms of creativity, the purpose of this lesson was for students to improve their creative self-efficacy and subject self-efficacy by exposing them to their peer's problem-solving strategies. Students were explicitly trained in peer-to-peer tutoring. 'Trying to find different ways to explain a content to a tutee' and offering feedback by 'valuing the different procedures used to solve a problem was highlighted. Respect and patience were defined as the basis of the interactions' (p. 7). Peer-to-peer tutoring sessions were no more than 25 minutes in any individual lesson.

> **REFERENCE**
> Wu, Y., & Schunn, C. D. (2020). The effects of providing and receiving peer feedback on writing performance and learning of secondary school students. *American Educational Research Journal*, 58(3), 492–526. https://doi.org/10.3102/0002831220945266

ACCESS

PEER-TO-PEER FEEDBACK AND EVALUATION

Students in high school are experiencing a complex set of developing psychological, emotional and physiological processes. Adults, who understand the value of peer-to-peer feedback and evaluation in the workplace, can still sometimes find honesty and openness difficult. For students, there are many social issues they need to explicitly or implicitly consider when evaluating a classmate. The best way to do this is to make it as practical and unemotional as possible, by building skills and removing scaffolds.

The reality of the classroom is that students spend more time speaking to each other than they do as individuals to the teacher. Knowing they can ask for and offer peer feedback can lessen student frustration as well as build confidence. They may also receive unique perspectives from their peers. Building their feedback literacy will also in turn lead to improved metacognition and autonomy (Banister, 2020). Before embarking on formal peer-to-peer evaluation it can be useful to trial simple peer-to-peer feedback in verbal or written form.

Given that students are more experienced and more comfortable with summative feedback, it is preferable to give feedback on final products such as essay assignments, mathematical solutions or scientific experiments, before introducing the subtleties of giving feedback on individual ideas. By the time students have built an understanding of feedback and evaluation (evaluation should never be given without some form of feedback) through teacher modelling, peer-to-peer feedback and improved self-evaluation, students will be more comfortable with evaluating individual ideas. As students become comfortable giving structured and useful feedback on final products, teachers can build creative competencies in providing feedback in the idea generation phase, and in the critical evaluation required to select ideas for iteration or prototyping. When students develop the understanding that critically evaluating an idea is the same as critically evaluating a paragraph of writing, they will feel more confident in the critical thinking aspect of creative competencies.

One method used by a teacher in a Year 10 religious studies class involved students swapping essay responses in pairs. Students were asked to provide three positive observations and three recommendations for improvement for their classmate's essay. This method proved very effective – all students gave some sort of feedback and there were some very insightful observations. This method builds confidence in student ability to critically evaluate the work of their peers, without having to allocate a grade. It also builds expectations for receiving constructive feedback from a classmate.

The second stage involved students asking their paired classmate to critically evaluate two or three aspects of the response. By indicating that they had some concerns or questions about their essay, an open and supportive dialogue was established between the students. Students also developed an awareness of what is timely, appropriate and effective feedback.

A more formal method for developing student competency in giving feedback is to use a rubric. This gives students structure and guidance in the process as well as providing modelling of appropriate language for feedback (Wu & Schunn, 2020). With time and experience, students can also be involved in the construction of rubrics.

EVALUATING CREATIVITY

English, secondary, United States

WHAT THE TEACHER FOUND:

> *The current findings reveal that peer reviewing not only helps secondary school students improve a draft but also enhances student learning, particularly, from the activities of providing comments and making revisions after receiving comments. Second, two learning paths have been identified as relevant to learning from peer feedback: learning by routine practice and learning by observation.* (Wu & Schunn, 2020, p. 519)

Component of creativity	Facet(s) of creativity	Teaching with or for creativity
Creative person	Creative self-efficacy and subject self-efficacy	For
Creative person	Openness to new experience	For
Creative environment	Collaboration and peer-to-peer feedback	For
Evaluating creativity	Peer-to-peer assessment	For

PURPOSE OF LESSON: SUBJECT KNOWLEDGE OR SKILLS

The purpose of this lesson was for students to develop their analytical skills and argument strategies by reading a one-page persuasive writing passage and then writing a well-developed essay analysing the rhetorical strategies used in the source passage. Students were required to describe what rhetorical strategies were used, support their descriptions and analysis of rhetorical strategies with evidence taken from the source text and talk about how the rhetorical strategies connected to the overall thesis.

PURPOSE OF THE LESSON: TEACHING WITH OR FOR CREATIVITY

In terms of creativity, the purpose of this project was for students to improve their creative problem-solving process, and analysis and feedback skills by submitting a first draft and then providing peer-to-peer feedback. Students submitted the first draft of the passage using an online assessment tool. Teachers explicitly trained the students in how to use this assessment tool for peer-to-peer feedback. Technical analysis of text is a relatively straightforward way of introducing students to the concepts of providing feedback which they will need in the problem-solving process. Students were required to give feedback as well as grades. The students who submitted the passage were then offered the opportunity to rewrite and resubmit based on the feedback given.

REFERENCE

Khan, A. A., & Mahmood, N. (2018). Effect of synectics model of teaching in enhancing students' understanding of abstract concepts of mathematics. *Pakistan Journal of Distance and Online Learning*, 4(1), 185–198.

ACCESS

CREATIVE ACTIONS

Building experience and skills in peer-to-peer teaching and giving feedback can then be applied to students developing skills in evaluation.

SELF-EVALUATION

Through their high school journey, students need to develop a sense of self-awareness regarding their strengths and areas for improvement. Self-evaluation can be quite challenging if students do not know the purpose and the context. Self-evaluation must be formative and lead to reflection and iteration. It should rarely be used as a summative tool (Andrade, 2019).

In the initial learning phases of self-assessment, it makes sense that students look at their final product and assess its strengths and areas for improvement. As students become more skilled, they should be able to self-reflect formatively on the processes involved in their learning. This is particularly important in terms of building creative competencies, not only those of idea generation and idea selection but also those of using appropriate attitudes and attributes of creativity. Parallel with evaluation is developing the skill of self-feedback, or justification of the ideas, that one has generated

Here is a simple self-reflection tool used by students in upper primary. The students were involved in loose parts play, using resources made up of different physical pieces that students used to create a range of products (Nüdel Kart, 2021). This reinforces the language we have used consistently throughout this book regarding all components of creativity. Note the open-ended response questions at the end. As presented, this table is quite comprehensive. It is possible to break it down into individual parts if you are working on sections of the problem-solving process individually.

Table 6.1: Student self-reflection on loose parts play problem-solving

Self-reflection points	All the time	Some of the time	None of the time
Environment			
I had all the resources I needed to show my ideas.			
I felt safe sharing my ideas with my classmates.			
I felt safe sharing my ideas with my teacher.			
I used specific knowledge and experience I already had to solve today's problems and challenges.			
Attitudes			
I was open to using many different pieces.			
I was curious about what each piece might do.			
I tried to use each piece in a different and creative way.			

EVALUATING CREATIVITY

Self-reflection points	All the time	Some of the time	None of the time
I enjoyed and worked hard for the whole session.			
I worked well with others in my group and gave them ideas.			
I talked to students in my group about how to make our ideas better.			
I was able to explain my ideas clearly to others.			
Problem-solving process	**More than 10**	**5 to 10**	**Less than 5**
How many ideas did I (or my group) come up with?			
How many different types of ideas did I (or my group) have?			
How many different models or prototypes did I (or my group) make?			
When I look at all the other models or prototypes in the class, how many original ideas did I (or my group) have?			

Overall creativity (Can be compared to other students, or if the project is replicated, how your creativity has changed)	I am at a high level	I am at a medium level	I am at a low level
I think I could improve my creativity by:			

SOURCE: Nüdel Kart (with the University of South Australia), 2021, p. 30–31. Used with permission.

WHEN SHOULD WE EVALUATE CREATIVITY?

Creativity needs to be evaluated according to purpose and context. We believe the best way to develop creative competencies is to teach about them first, preferably briefly and succinctly, while at the same time showing their relevance to building subject knowledge and skills. When you are building the basic principles of creativity in students, it is best to provide mini-feedback or mini-evaluation chunks along the journey. This method is of course not unique to building creative competencies – it is the process of teaching. We do not teach English in schools by starting with whole Shakespeare plays and working backwards to spelling and handwriting. We do not teach mathematics by starting with differential calculus and working our way back to addition and subtraction. We build creative competencies by building an understanding of the individual components and facets, and when, where, how and why they are needed. To paraphrase Karl Marx, we teach creativity according to students' ability and needs.

The purpose of evaluation is to provide students with an understanding of their understanding and provide them with feedback, either summative or formative. Any element of the creative process and its associated environments, attributes, attitudes and products can be evaluated.

HOW TO EVALUATE THE COMPONENTS AND FACETS OF CREATIVITY

One of the main focuses of this book is to show that creativity is best built incrementally. The same is true of evaluation. In the classroom there are many opportunities to offer informal verbal feedback or to write a quick observation on a student's piece of work. This section will focus on more formal and structured feedback, which provides evidence of student progress over time that can be referred to by both students and teachers. It is up to the teacher to decide if this feedback constitutes part of the grading for students in their subject. Each of our suggestions can be used by students as well as teachers, but please bear in mind that students will need some explicit instruction in how to use these most effectively.

At the systems level of education, education departments around the world have a variety of language which they use to describe either the attitudes and attributes of creativity, or the creative process. If this is the case, it is of course appropriate for teachers to use this language in their classroom. Unfortunately, these are often combined into topics such as critical and creative thinking which makes it more difficult to provide feedback on individual components or facets of creativity (VCAA, n.d.). The OECD has produced what it calls class-friendly assessment rubrics that assess both the creative process and creative products (OECD, 2019).

RUBRICS

You will notice from the examples later in this chapter that one of the most frequently used tools for assessment is rubrics. In researching this book we found many rubrics were either far too simplistic or far too complex to be used in a classroom. Rubrics must be both developmentally and task specific. There are three types of rubric, each with a different purpose, used in school education – holistic, analytic and single point.

HOLISTIC RUBRICS

A holistic rubric offers 'three to five levels of performance [and] a broad description of the characteristics that define each level (Gonzalez, 2014, para. 3). Labelling can be with numbers (such as 0 through 4), letters (such as A through E), or verbal descriptors (such as *poor* through to *good* or *excellent*; Gonzalez, 2014). Holistic rubrics do not take much time to prepare, are quick and easy to grade, and simple for students to use.

Table 6.2: Holistic rubric evaluating idea generation

Score	Description
4	The student generates a number of relevant and original ideas, showing a clear understanding of the problem.
3	The student generates a number of relevant ideas, showing some understanding of the problem.
2	The student generates some relevant and some irrelevant ideas, demonstrating partial understanding of the problem.
1	The student generates few or mostly irrelevant ideas, demonstrating minimal understanding of the problem.
0	No answer is given.

A key drawback of a holistic rubric is that it doesn't provide targeted feedback to students, only general observations (Gonzalez, 2014). They are useful for listing specific characteristics for each level, but there is only one mark, offering single feedback for one facet (Gonzalez, 2014). However, the purpose is to offer direct and immediate feedback on one specific facet, this may be a useful type of rubric under some circumstances.

ANALYTIC RUBRICS

An analytic rubric breaks down the components or facets into parts. An advantage of using analytic assessments is that they provide a more nuanced and detailed image of student performance. By judging the quality of different dimensions of student responses, both strengths and areas in need of improvement may be identified (Gonzalez, 2014). This facilitates formative assessment and specific feedback (Jonsson et al., 2021).

An analytic rubric might look like the following example table. This rubric has been significantly adapted from one used in physics and mathematics for teachers in Colombia (Salazar-Torres, Leal & Ortega, 2021). Teachers will of course use language appropriate for their particular class and subject. In this particular rubric, the term data extraction is used – a common term in senior mathematics and science. However, if this rubric were to be adapted for humanities subjects for example, it may use the term evidence instead.

Table 6.3: Analytic rubric for defining and understanding the problem facet of the creative process

Indicators	Excellent (4.6–5.0)	Outstanding (4.0–4.5)	Good (3.5–3.9)	Acceptable (3.0–3.4)	Poor < 3.0
Clarity of restatement of the problem in written or oral form in their own words	The student clearly defines the problem and outlines the necessary objectives in an efficient manner. The restated problem statement is relevant and consistent with the initial problem statement	The student defines the problem and outlines most of the necessary objectives. The restated problem statement is relevant or coherent with the initial problem statement	The student attempts to define the problem and outlines some of the necessary objectives. The restated problem is related to the reality of the initial problem statement.	The student attempts to define the problem and outlines few of the necessary objectives. The restated problem statement has some ambiguity or misses some important issues	The student defines the problem incorrectly or too narrowly, missing key information or including incorrect information. The restated problem statement is not relevant or coherent with the initial problem statement and shows lack of understand of the initial problem statement.

EVALUATING CREATIVITY

Indicators	Excellent (4.6–5.0)	Outstanding (4.0–4.5)	Good (3.5–3.9)	Acceptable (3.0–3.4)	Poor < 3.0
Identification, application and integration of existing knowledge	The student identifies all the components and data in the problem. The student effectively applies prior knowledge to the current problem. The student integrates new information to assist in the problem-solving process.	The student identifies relevant situations or unknown data in the problem. The student effectively applies some prior knowledge to the current problem. The student attempts to integrate new information to assist in the problem-solving process.	The student identifies some of the unknown situations in the problem. The student applies a small amount of prior knowledge to current problem. The student does not consistently use information effectively.	The student identifies very few situations or data not relevant to the problem. The student applies a limited amount of prior knowledge to current problem. The student does not use information effectively.	The student does not identify unknown situations or data in the problem. The student is unable to make connections to prior knowledge. The student is unable to review summaries of prior knowledge for useful information.
Data extraction from the presented problem statement	The student extracts all the data given in the problem statement.	The student extracts at least 80% of the data given in the problem statement.	The student extracts at least 70% of the data given in the problem statement.	The student extracts at least 60% of the data given in the problem statement.	The student extracts less than 50% of the data given in the problem statement.

SOURCE: Adapted from Salazar-Torres, Leal & Ortega, 2021, p. 3-4, https://iopscience.iop.org/article/10.1088/1742-6596/1981/1/012018. Used with permission under Creative Commons Attribution License 3.0.

Analytic rubrics, while comprehensive, take significant time to create. They must be specific to context and level of development, and use language which clearly delineates between the levels from poor to outstanding (Gonzalez, 2014). This level of detail can result an analytic rubric which is overly complex and unwieldy. Too much feedback can mean students may not actually read the whole document (Gonzalez, 2014). Hence, this type of rubric may be more suitable for the senior years of schooling. Another drawback is that while it identifies the strengths and weaknesses of a student's work, it does not provide any information on how a student can improve.

SINGLE-POINT RUBRICS

A single-point rubric is a lot like an analytic rubric, however it only describes meeting or not meeting the criteria. It provides evidence as to how the student meets or or does not meet the criteria and gives the student an opportunity to respond as to how they can better meet the criteria in the future. It is a useful tool students can use when explaining to each other components or aspects of the creative process or how they have demonstrated creative attitudes.

> *The single-point rubric has several advantages: it contains far less language than the analytic rubric, which means students are more likely to read it and it will take less time to create, while still providing rich detail about what's expected.* (Gonzalez, 2014, para. 21)

It also states the areas of concern and excellence as open-ended and, more importantly, gives the student an opportunity to immediately address any concerns in their own words. The following is an example of a single-point rubric for students to reflect on their use of intellectual curiosity (adapted from Fluckiger, 2010).

Table 6.4: Single-point rubric evaluating intellectual curiosity

How I will revise to better meet the criteria	Name of the criteria: Intellectual curiosity	Evidence to demonstrate meeting the criteria	Evidence to demonstrate exceeding the criteria
	The student sought to extend their understanding by questioning, trying new approaches or considering new ideas.		
	The student proposed ideas that might be seen as risky, silly or unusual, but that relate to the challenge or task and could lead to an effective solution.		

SOURCE: adapted from Fluckiger, 2010, p. 24. Used with permission.

The fact that single-point rubrics require more writing to complete, either on the part of the teacher or the student if they are used for self- or peer-reflection, may be considered a disadvantage (Gonzalez, 2014). This is especially true if a student has fallen short of mutliple criterias or areas of learning (Gonzalez, 2014). The given examples only includes guidance and descriptions of successful work without listing a grade.

HOW TO EVALUATE THE ATTITUDES AND ATTRIBUTES OF CREATIVITY

These attitudes and attributes do not need to be evaluated formally for every problem-solving situation. However, over their school journey students need to appreciate the need for these attitudes and attributes and be able to apply them. An amount of explicit instruction followed by a formative evaluation to check understanding is needed at some point. This is why we suggest a coordinated approach between members of a department or across the learning areas and subjects in a school. It would of course not be possible for one teacher to cover all these topics with each class in a year. Ideally a scope and sequence of development should be constructed at the management level of the school.

HOW TO EVALUATE THE PROCESSES OF CREATIVITY AND ITS FACETS

Students need to be capable at each stage of the creative process before joining the components together. It is not necessary to evaluate each stage of the process in the detailed manner that follows at all times. As students become more skilled, a simple acknowledgement or observation may be enough for students to continue to the next stage of the process.

When writing this book, we searched high and low for examples of rubrics that only dealt with individual elements of the creative process in some detail. It was disappointing to find that many of the rubrics we uncovered dealt with the creative process or the problem-solving process from beginning to end, without much focus on how the students had developed sufficient competencies in one part of the process before proceeding to the next. Consequently, we have gone into some detail in this area, as a generic rubric about problem-solving is insufficient for developing student competencies in all facets. We wish to stress here that we are not suggesting teachers go into the detail we have presented for every step of the creative process every time they do anything. However, the point remains that these competencies need to be explicitly taught and explicitly evaluated at some point in time, and we are offering the tools to do so.

We will presume here that students have been given a problem that needs solving and are going through the process beginning at the problem definition and idea generation phases.

We remind you of the five stages of the creative process used in Chapter 5 and offer some possible rubrics.

UNDERSTAND THE PROBLEM

The creative process begins with students understanding the problem. When evaluating this component, it should be a requirement that students demonstrate either verbally, visually or in written form their consideration of all the variables that need to be considered when solving the problem. A simple rubric might involve:

- At the most basic level, the student merely describes the problem.
- At the next level, the student identifies the elements of the problem if there are more than one.
- At the more sophisticated level, the student explains the significance of a problem or challenge and defines its limitations, guidelines or restrictions.

GENERATE IDEAS

The creative process continues with generating ideas (discussed in Chapter 5). There are many ways to evaluate the idea generation phase, dependent on the technique or tool being used. If part of the evaluation is that students have selected the idea generation tool, its appropriateness can be evaluated. When beginning this process, it is good to remind students of the following myths and to use open-ended questioning to stimulate students' cognitive activity.

THERE IS ONLY ONE TECHNIQUE TO COME UP WITH IDEAS

Just because a strategy has been successful in one context does not mean it will be successful in every context. Encourage students to list some techniques that might be suitable for generating ideas for this particular problem. Get them to justify their thinking and assess when and why they could use convergent or divergent thinking (see Chapter 5 for a reminder).

THE FIRST IDEA YOU COME UP WITH IS THE ONE YOU SHOULD USE

Ask students if they can think of some reasons why this may not be the case. Remind the students that idea generation is a divergent phase where the aim is to capture as much information as possible from the group or the individual.

In its most basic form students are asked to generate as many ideas as possible within a specific time frame. Evaluation is more sophisticated as there are multiple dimensions to consider: the fluency, flexibility and originality of ideas (Guilford, 1967). Fluency refers solely to the number of ideas generated. Even if multiple ideas share some similarity, they still count. Flexibility considers the number of categories in which the ideas fit. A student might have many different ideas (and so have high fluency), yet these ideas might cluster together into a couple of different categories, meaning the student may have a lower flexibility score. Finally, originality is how rare or uncommon the responses are compared to other students in the group or other groups in the class. The following is an example of teaching fluency, flexibility and originality.

EVALUATING CREATIVITY

Physics, secondary, Indonesia

WHAT THE TEACHER FOUND:

"It is very important to develop a proper physics instructional design that can develop scientific creativity, critical thinking and creative thinking skills." (Astutik & Mahardika, 2020, p. 1)

Component of creativity	Facet(s) of creativity	Teaching with or for creativity
Creative person	Divergent thinking – fluency, flexibility, originality and elaboration	For
Creative environment	Independent learning	For
Evaluating creativity	Assessment of divergent thinking skills	For

PURPOSE OF LESSON: SUBJECT KNOWLEDGE OR SKILLS

The purpose of this lesson was for students to understand the theory behind Newton's laws and applying these laws when solving problems, by using a range of pedagogic strategies. The second purpose of this lesson was for students to build their problem-solving skills by recognising, inferring, analysing, summarising, evaluating and solving problems. The assessment for each problem was based on providing a simple explanation (elementary clarification), building basic skills (basic support), summing up (inference), making further explanation (advanced clarification), and strategy and tactics (explanation). In addition, students were assessed on their divergent thinking skills.

PURPOSE OF THE LESSON: TEACHING WITH OR FOR CREATIVITY

In terms of creativity, the purpose of this lesson was for students to build their competencies in scientific creativity by developing the following set of creative skills: fluency (students can offer more than one answer for a problem; flexibility (students can provide different ways to solve a problem; originality (students can provide answers along with different solutions or new ideas with other students in solving problems; and elaboration (students take steps systematically in solving problems and can combine elements, principles and concepts that exist so as to become a unified whole).

REFERENCE

Astutik, S., & Mahardika, I. K. (2020). HOTS student worksheet to identification of scientific creativity skill, critical thinking skill and creative thinking skill in physics learning. *Journal of Physics: Conference Series*, *1465*, Article 012075. https://iopscience.iop.org/article/10.1088/1742-6596/1465/1/012075/pdf

ACCESS

CREATIVE ACTIONS

RECORDING AND SUMMARISING IDEAS

Evaluation of the method (or methods) of recording ideas is part of the idea generation phase. It can have two forms. If the method of recording ideas has been selected by the teacher, then before the students move onto the idea selection stage, they must demonstrate that they have recorded enough ideas correctly in the selected format. If the students are selecting the tools for recording ideas, then the suitability and efficacy of their selection can also be evaluated. Part of the evaluation should include students justifying their choice of tool.

As discussed in Chapter 5 there are a variety of tools that can be used to record ideas (Christensen & Abildgaard, 2021).

EVALUATING IDEAS

When evaluating the process of idea selection, purpose and context are key. It is the purpose of the idea selection phase to evaluate the range of ideas generated and converge on the best selected ideas (those that meet the defined evaluation criteria) to move to the next process of problem-solving. (If problem-solving in groups, there needs to be consensus that the best ideas have been selected.)

Do the students need to provide evidence of the stages of the critical thinking process which they undertook to select these ideas? Having categorised ideas, how did they then winnow down to the next stage? Which tools did they use to modify or expand any of the generated ideas? What criteria did they use to select the ideas? Did they need to make any assumptions?

The following table, used by David in an introductory STEM workshop, is best used gradually over a unit of learning for students to formatively understand their development as critical thinkers. Critical thinking capacities take time to develop. Each criterion must be considered according to the development of the students and used to develop an opportunity for further learning. This rubric uses language suitable for upper primary but could be modified according to context for high school students.

EVALUATING CREATIVITY

Table 6.5: Components of critical thinking for assessment

Component of critical thinking	Beginner	Developing	Competent
Organises and summarises the topic or problem	Does not organise or summarise information. Poor understanding of the components of the problem	Some attempt to organise or summarise information. Misses some key components of the problem	Good summarisation and categorisation of information. Key components clearly identified
Articulates assumptions and potential bias	No consideration of potential bias and assumptions	Some identification of potential bias and assumptions	Clear identification and understanding of potential bias and assumptions
Conducts research to broaden understanding of potential bias and misconceptions	No research conducted to support argument.	Informal research conducted with peers or online. Not all sources are credible	Research conducted using reliable resources
Analyses all forms of data, identifying the main point of a proposed argument or solution and the reasons that support an argument or solution	No analysis. Listing of solution, but no supporting reasons given	Some analysis and interpretation of data. Some identification of key argument and supporting reasons	Clear analysis and interpretation of data. Complete identification of key argument and supporting reasons
Evaluation of evidence to make a judgement	No evaluation of evidence, just personal opinion. Little understanding of alternative suggestions or perspectives	Some evaluation based on the credibility and logic of the evidence. Some understanding of alternative suggestions or perspectives	Clear evaluation of credibility and logic of evidence. Good understanding of alternative suggestions or perspectives

continued ...

CREATIVE ACTIONS

Component of critical thinking	Beginner	Developing	Competent
Inferring or drawing a conclusion based on evidence, and identifying if and what additional information is needed to decide between two possible solutions	Conclusion not based on evidence. No identification of further information required	Some inference from evidence drawing on implied and explicit information	Clear linking of claims to evidence, drawing on implied and explicit information
Reasoning and explanation, and presenting and justifying solutions.	Solution is presented with no justification or reasoning. No solution presented	Solution is presented with some attempt at justification or reasoning	Solution is presented with clear justification and reasoning
Reflection on the process and identification of strengths and opportunities for learning	No meaningful reflection	Some useful reflection and identification of strengths and opportunities for learning	Clear and detailed reflection and identification of strengths and opportunities for learning

The following critical thinking rubric could be used for middle or senior school problem-solving. It uses five criteria instead of seven. We suggest using the number and type of criteria needed according to task and context.

Table 6.6: Evaluating, analysing and/or synthesising relevant information to form an argument or reach a conclusion supported with evidence

Category	0	1	2	3	4	5
Evaluating		Minimally determined the relevance and reliability of information that might be used to support a conclusions or argument		Partially determined the relevance and reliability of information that might be used to support a conclusion or argument		Extensively determined the relevance and reliability of information that might be used to support a conclusion or argument

Category	0	1	2	3	4	5
Analysing		Inaccurately interpreted information to determine meaning and to extract relevant evidence		Interpreted information to determine meaning and to extract relevant evidence with some errors		Accurately interpreted information to determine meaning and to extract relevant evidence
Synthesising		Inaccurately connected or integrated information to support an argument or reach a conclusion		Connected or integrated infromation to support an argument or reach a conclusion with some errors		Accurately connected or integrated information to support an argument or reach a conclusion
Forming arguments (structure)		Made a claim and provided incomplete evidence to support it		Made a claim and provided partial evidence to support it		Made a claim and provided complete evidence to support it
Forming arguments (validity)		The claim, evidence and reasoning were minimally consistent with accepted disciplinary ideas and practices		The claim, evidence and reasoning were partially consistent with accepted disciplinary ideas and practices		The claim, evidence and reasoning were fully consistent with accepted disciplinary ideas and practices
Comments						

SOURCE: Reynders et al., 2020, p. 9, https://doi.org/10.1186/s40594-020-00208-5. Used with permission under Creative Commons Attribution License 4.0.

CREATIVE ACTIONS

STEM, secondary, United States

WHAT THE TEACHER FOUND

"Another instructor used the critical thinking rubric to assess their students' abilities to choose an instrument to perform a chemical analysis. According to the instructor, the students provided evidence of their critical thinking because "in their papers, they needed to justify their choice of instrument. This justification required them to evaluate information and synthesize a new understanding for this specific chemical analysis." (Reynders et al., 2020, p. 10)

Component of creativity	Facet(s) of creativity	Teaching with or for creativity
Creative person	Critical thinking	For
Creative environment	Independent learning	For
Evaluating creativity	Assessment of critical thinking skills	With

PURPOSE OF LESSON: SUBJECT KNOWLEDGE OR SKILLS

The purpose of the lesson was for students to develop information processing skills by applying these skills in problem-solving contexts through justifying their choice of the appropriate scientific instrument. The second purpose of the lesson was for teachers to understand students' information processing skills and critical thinking skills by assessing with rubrics.

PURPOSE OF THE LESSON: TEACHING WITH OR FOR CREATIVITY

In terms of creativity, the purpose of this lesson was for students to build their critical thinking skills – evaluating, analysing, synthesising, forming arguments in terms of the correct structure and forming arguments in terms of validity – by solving a scientific problem.

'It was observed that students [could] earn high scores for evaluating, analyzing and synthesizing, but still struggled to form arguments. This was particularly common in assessing problem sets in the physical chemistry course … Some students may be able to include all of the expected structural elements of their arguments but use faulty information or reasoning. Conversely, some students may be able to make scientifically valid claims but not necessarily support them with evidence. The two forming arguments categories are intended to accurately assess both of these scenarios' (Reynders et al., 2020, p. 9).

REFERENCE

Reynders, G., Lantz, J., Ruder, S. M., Stanford, C. L., & Cole, R. S. (2020). Rubrics to assess critical thinking and information processing in undergraduate STEM courses. *International Journal of STEM Education, 7*, Article 9. https://doi.org/10.1186/s40594-020-00208-5

ACCESS

EVALUATING CREATIVITY

The following rubric from a study by Croatian researchers has been modified to be suitable for students completing senior business studies. It clearly demonstrates a number of categories that can be considered using both open-ended and closed questions when solving a complex problem.

Business studies, secondary, Croatia

WHAT THE TEACHER FOUND:

"Contrary to expectations, the time required for the implementation of the valuation of ideas (via rubrics) is not longer than the time that would be spent on an "ad hoc" estimation, which encourages and promotes the practical adaptation and application of the method." (Stevanovic et al., 2015, p. 9)

Component of creativity	Facet(s) of creativity	Teaching with or for creativity
Creative person	Critical thinking	For
Creative process	Evaluating and selecting ideas	For
Evaluating creativity	Rubric for idea evaluation	For

PURPOSE OF LESSON: SUBJECT KNOWLEDGE OR SKILLS

The purpose of this lesson was for students to understand business idea evaluation by assessing the many variables and considerations, such as feasibility, market, value, usefulness and usability, when trying to develop a business idea.

PURPOSE OF THE LESSON: TEACHING WITH OR FOR CREATIVITY

In terms of creativity, the purpose of this lesson was for students to develop their critical thinking skills in idea selection and evaluation by using a structured approach. This is more effective when students have a clear picture of all the considerations for making a final decision when using a rubric which contains criteria against which the ideas can be assessed, and by assigning a weighting to each component.

REFERENCE

Stevanovic, M., Marjanović, D., & Štorga, M. (2015, July 27–30). A model of idea evaluation and selection for product innovation. In C. Weber, S. Husung, G. Cascini, M. Cantamessa, D. Marjanovic & F. Montagna (Eds.), *Proceedings of the 20th International Conference on Engineering Design* (ICED15; Vol. 8), Milan, Italy (pp. 193–202). The Design Society.

ACCESS

CREATIVE ACTIONS

Table 6.7: Attributes and guidelines for the assessment of customer value of ideas

Customer	Basic question	Value		
		1	5	9
Necessity	How users will evaluate the necessity of products based on the idea?	Users will negatively assess the need for the realisation of the idea.	Users will remain neutral towards the needs for the product based on the idea.	Users will strongly emphasise the necessity or products based on the idea.
Novelty	How will users evaluate the novelty the idea introduced?	Users will negatively evaluate the novelty the idea introduced.	Users will remain neutral towards the novelty the idea introduced.	Users will consider the novelty the idea introduced significant.
Usefulness	How will uses evaluate the usefulness the idea brought to the product?	Users will negatively evaluate the usefulness of a product based on the idea.	Users will remain neutral towards the usefulness of a product based on the idea.	Users will consider the usefulness significant.
Usability	How will users evaluate the usability of the product?	Users will negatively evaluate the usability of the product based on the idea.	Users will remain neutral towards the usability of the product based on the idea.	Users will consider the idea to bring a substantial increase in the usability of the product.

SOURCE: Stevanovic et al., 2015, p. 6. Used with permission.

DRAFTING AND PROTOTYPING TO DEVELOP THE FINAL SOLUTION OR PRODUCT

Essentially, this final stage of problem-solving involves the solutions or products proposed by the students. Our experience has shown that the drafting and prototyping phase is often done in a cursory manner. If done thoroughly and correctly, this phase is invaluable in building persistence and resilience in students as well as the skills of drafting and prototyping their solutions. It will also eventually occur to students that their final products are greatly improved by going through a process of iteration and prototyping.

VALIDATE THE FINAL SOLUTION OR PRODUCT

We would suggest that the students are given a rubric used to assess the final product, such as those following, and then compare are their draft or prototypes or their final solutions to the rubric to see how they have met the criteria.

EVALUATING THE PRODUCTS OF CREATIVITY

> *The fact that creativity research sits largely within the discipline of psychology means that it is no surprise that creativity assessment is dominated by those things that interest psychologists.* (Cropley, in press)

So far, we have focused on evaluating the process, the attitudes and the collaboration involved in creativity. They represent the most practical manifestation of creativity in individuals. A person may be motivated, willing to take risks, open to new experiences, adept at divergent thinking, and embedded in a supportive environment, but unless they can actually develop a creative product, their creativity may be nothing more than unfulfilled potential (Cropley, in press). The purpose of creativity is to have a useful outcome or solution. This may be an idea or a tangible product – it depends on the context. Whatever form the outcome takes, we need to know if it is, in fact, creative. In this section we will present a number of methods for measuring creative products. We have consistently argued that creativity is highly related to the subject or domain in which the students are solving problems but that some concepts are universal. Each has its use depending on the specific context.

Throughout the history of the science of creativity, there have been a number of attempts to devise methods and measures for assessing the value of creative products (Plucker et al., 2021; Yin et al., 2021). Most frequently cited measures are from the world of psychology and from the worlds of consumer product design, engineering and education (Amabile, 1979; Besemer & Treffiger, 1981; Besemer & O'Quinn, 1987; Cropley & Cropley, 2000; Cropley & Cropley, 2007; Horn & Salvendy, 2006; Reis & Renzulli, 1991; Taylor, 1975). However, the basic principle of creativity remains – creative products must be new or novel, relevant and useful. Owing to its well-validated properties and successful use in mathematics and English, we offer discussion on the consensual assessment technique (CAT; Amabile, 1982; Kaufman et al., 2021). This will be followed by the creative solution diagnosis scale (CSDS), which has also been validated, used in schools and trialled by Tim and David (Cropley et al., 2011; Pantaleo, 2019).

CONSENSUAL ASSESSMENT TECHNIQUE

The CAT is a straightforward and simple way of measuring creativity (Amabile, 1982, 1996). This technique is not a standardised rating of creativity, rather a comparison between a group of similar products, such as an essay, a mathematical equation or even a PowerPoint presentation. A product or response is creative when experts in the field agree that it is creative. Of course, there can be disagreement on particular products. However, when looked at collectively, experts will converge on some products being particularly creative, others being somewhat creative and so on. There are many different types of experts for any particular subject; for creative writing, for example, an expert might be a published writer, an editor, a literary critic or a writing or literature teacher.

In this case, teachers are experts. It is also possible to use the CAT as a teaching tool, asking students to comparatively rate their peers' products for creativity. James has used this tool extensively with students in senior school to develop their skills in offering feedback and assessments. Upper primary students can also use it to judge the creativity of work such as a poem or a drawing by comparing works in their class. We acknowledge that this tool is subjective, but it has demonstrated a high level of inter-rater reliability for many years across a large range of subject areas or domains (Barth & Stadtmann, 2021; Hickey et al., 2022). It is worth remembering that in the classroom we mostly work with little-c and mini-c creativity. Thus, assessing student work against adult outputs is not the purpose of school education, except perhaps for advanced musicians and athletes.

To apply the CAT, judges simply rate the creativity of given creative products on a six-point scale using their own subjective definition of creativity. In our study looking at mathematical creativity we asked students to use their creativity to generate an equation or a process which would lead to a particular product, such as the number eight (Kaufman et al., 2021). We then asked four judges, including students doing postgraduate studies in mathematics education and an experienced mathematics teacher, to use the CAT to rate the responses between one and six with one being highly creative and six being uncreative. The correlation between the judges was high. In addition, students who scored highly on the CAT in mathematics also tended to score highly in their final year examinations, thus strengthening its utility in schools.

However, the CAT is limited by its binary nature. Imagine a teacher encouraging students to come up with creative ideas for an essay. Each student shows the teacher a draft of their essay for feedback. If all the teacher said was, 'No, this isn't creative' or 'Yes, this is creative', there would be little for the student to learn and nothing they could do to change their creativity. Even giving feedback that the essay lacks novelty or is very effective but not very original probably isn't enough to drive specific changes and actions that develop the student's creativity. What the teacher needs is a rating scale that not only addresses the indicators that we know are important – novelty, usefulness, effectiveness and perhaps elegance in older students – but also allows the teacher to rate these in a way that the student can see the degree of novelty, or the degree of usefulness, and not just a binary, indication of these qualities.

CRITERIA-BASED RUBRICS FOR CREATIVE PRODUCTS

More detailed and sophisticated measures of student products are those that are criteria based. These begin to add criteria, such as ratings of novelty, relevance and usefulness, which add up to an overall score of creativity. However, in James' experience working with both primary and secondary students, these three terms can be difficult to explain. Consequently, we have reworked these terms to use those in the following rubric (modified from Dean et al., 2006).

Table 6.8: Criteria-based rubric evaluating the facets of creative products

Construct	Criteria	Range
Novelty	How new to the student is the way of expressing the solution?	1 (not at all new) – 3 (very new)
Thoroughness	Has the student followed all stages of the problem-solving process before arriving at their solution?	1 (Not at all) – 2 (sometimes) – 3 (yes)
Functionality	How well does the product work in practice?	1 (not at all) – 4 (functions very well)
Total		

SOURCE: adapted from *Identifying good ideas: Constructs and scales for idea evaluation* by Dean, D. L., Hender, J., Rodgers, T., & Santanen, E, © 2006. Used with permission from Association for Information Systems, Atlanta, GA; 404-413-7445; www.aisnet.org. All rights reserved.

As students get older you can introduce the terms *novelty, relevance, effectiveness, elegance* and *usefulness*. These are some useful introductory statements when acquainting students with this type of evaluation.

A thing is novel if it is a new or unusual example of that thing. If it is just an improvement on previous examples of that thing, then it is a little bit novel. You will recognise a high level of novelty in a product because the product or the solution is something never seen before, it is clearly a very different approach to solving the problem, or it's something that helps show how further improvement could be made.

A thing is relevant and effective if it does what it is supposed to do or solves the underlying problem. If it only does some of what it is supposed to do, then it is partly relevant and effective. If it does most of what it is supposed to do, then it is moderately relevant and effective. If it does everything it is supposed to do, then it is fully relevant and effective.

A thing is elegant if it is a complete and well-made example. If it is incomplete and poorly made, assembled or composed, it is not elegant.

CREATIVE ACTIONS

Such rubrics give students more detail on what specific elements of their products to work on, according to the criteria allocated by the teacher.

The creative solution diagnosis scale (CSDS) is an example of a useful criteria-based measure whose language can be adapted for schools (Cropley et al., 2011). The next rubric is for a senior high school level.

Table 6.9: Creative solution diagnosis scale

Criteria	Related Indicators Scale 0 = that does not apply to the product or solution to 4 = applies very much to the product or solution
Relevance and effectiveness (The product or solution solves the problem it is intended to solve)	The product or solution correctly applies widely accepted, conventional ideas and standard techniques – it's what you'd expect to see at this age or grade level. The product or solution does what it is supposed to do – it works, or it answers the question posed. The product or solution fits within any given constraints, such as number of words allowed, or materials permitted to be used.
Novelty (The product or solution helps you to understand the given problem or task in a new way)	The product or solution shows how the problem has been solved in a new way – it shows a new and unexpected way of solving the problem or answering the question. The product or solution offers a fundamentally new perspective on possible solutions to the problem or task – it makes you see the problem in a whole new light.
Elegance (The product or solution is well-executed)	The product or solution is skilfully executed and well-finished – it is a competent piece of work. The product or solution is neat and well done – it looks like a good piece of work. The product or solution is well-proportioned and nicely formed – it's attractive and graceful to look at, handle or read.

SOURCE: D. Cropley (personal communication, July 20, 2022)

Teachers need to be quite specific with their feedback when using such rubrics. For example, rather than say 'make it more creative' (which isn't terribly helpful), a teacher could say 'the novelty is generally very good, but the effectiveness of this idea is low' or 'It's well-constructed, but not really breaking any new ground'. The teacher can be more specific and concrete, for example, 'novelty is good, but the effectiveness needs to be strong. Therefore, go back and try to find a solution that is likely to work better, perhaps by looking for something a little more unconventional.'

EVALUATING COLLABORATION

Collaboration is frequently mentioned in the curriculum of countries around the world as one of the essential competencies of the twenty-first century for students to develop (Patston, Kaufman et al., 2021). In Chapter 3, we explored the difference between cooperation, coordination and collaboration and highlighted both the opportunities and the obstacles of effective collaboration in problem-solving. It was clear from the examples that teaching collaboration is a long-term task requiring specific and targeted teaching and learning. Taking time to build these incredibly important skills with students is essential. Each of the authors has had experiences working with others where there were plenty of creative ideas, some excellent critical thinking, and a lot of knowledge and experience but a lack of collaboration leading to poor evaluation of creativity. True collaboration is a combination of practical and social skills, both of which need to be evaluated.

Once again, we would recommend a combination of formative and summative feedback and evaluation. There are several rubrics that have been designed to evaluate and assess student collaboration. Many are extremely complex as they try to assess all the skills and attitudes in one rubric. Our belief is that teachers focus on one or two components or facets at a time, until students are ready to apply a number of attitudes and skills in a creative collaboration situation. The range of rubrics should give insight into some of the language that might be considered when designing a rubric of your own. Naturally, any rubric should be fit for purpose, subject, year level and the context.

One scaffolded approach towards building the attitudes and skills of collaboration was developed in Belgium by thirty-two European Ministries of Education (fcl.eun.org). We would recommend these stages be used as a means of introduction to collaboration, as students move from dependent to interdependent learning. These stages are:

1. Students are not required to work together in pairs or groups.
2. Students do work together but they do not have shared responsibility.
3. Students do have shared responsibility but they are not required to make substantive decisions together.
4. Students do have shared responsibility and they do make substantive decisions together about the content, process, or product of their work but their work is not interdependent.
5. Students do have shared responsibility and they do make substantive decisions together about the content, process, or product of their work and their work is interdependent.

CREATIVE ACTIONS

There are many rubrics to assess student collaboration available online (see Herro et al., 2017; Johnson et al., 1994). The following table includes most of the elements which are represented in such rubrics and was used by Tim in a Year 8 music class in an improvisation exercise.

Table 6.10: Rubric for observing the attitudes of collaboration

Attitudes of collaboration	Effectiveness 1 = Low, 2 = Medium, 3 = High
Shares their knowledge, opinions, ideas and skills	
Shares resources and materials	
Respects others' views and listens to their opinions	
Respectfully challenges the ideas and opinions of others	
Helps build group consensus by valuing and respecting others	
Stays focused on the task	
Makes compromises for the benefit of the group	
Builds on the thinking of others	
Understands and accepts their role in the group	

PISA promote a twelve-point matrix to evaluate and assess collaborative problem-solving in fifteen-year-olds. However, studies from Taiwan (Li & Liu, 2017), and Sweden (Nouri et al., 2017), in attempting to use the rubric, found no documented uses of the PISA 2015 collaborative problem-solving framework, and PISA's own description of the framework (OECD, 2013) lacks explanations of how the framework should be employed and how scoring should be done. It is our belief as authors that trying to combine an assessment of the social and practical elements of collaboration is extremely difficult to do. This rubric does not account for the quality or productivity of student conversations (Nouri et al., 2017). We would recommend focusing on one or two components and providing the evaluation on those before attempting to use the whole rubric as an assessment tool.

The evaluation of the attitudes and attributes of collaboration is extremely difficult if the teacher and students are trying to deal with too many individual components at once, at least while students are building an understanding of how these various elements come together. Another way to improve the evaluation of collaboration is for students to complete the same rubrics as the teachers, but from the perspective of evaluating their classmates and evaluating themselves. There are rubrics that have been designed purely for self-evaluation and peer-evaluation.

The following table is a basic rubric but serves as a good way to introduce students to the attitudes and skills needed by themselves and their peers when collaborating. We refer back to how to give targeted, specific and supportive feedback and the appropriate language and social environment for self and peer evaluations. The idea that the social and communication skills are as important as the practical skills in collaboration must be taken into account when teaching.

In the following example, adapted from Estell et al., (2016), grades are included as well as space for comments. Designed for peer-to peer assessment of collaboration in a Year 9 physics topic, the teacher has provided descriptors for elements that met the criteria and some possible responses have been written in as examples. Giving the students some autonomy in filling in the comments has proven a successful manner of keeping them or engaged in this process, though of course the final grades are at the discretion of the teacher (Ragupathi & Lee, 2020).

This table may look quite large and complex. We use it to illustrate the range of elements you can provide feedback on when it comes to collaboration. You may choose to use all of the table or only parts relevant to your context at a particular period of time and for a particular purpose. We have left cells blank for teachers to be able to insert their own, context appropriate language according to subject, task and age. Teachers can of course modify this to suit their own students and context.

Table 6.11: Peer review of collaboration in science project using single-point rubric

Teamwork constitutes behaviours that are under the control of individual team members (the effort they put into tasks, their manner of interacting with others and the quantity and quality of their contributions in team discussions). For each row, provide feedback by either circling the listed standard for proficiency or by writing constructive comments in the appropriate column.

Criteria	Grade 1 – Exceeding the criteria	Grade 2 – Meeting the criteria	Grade 3 – Below the criteria	Grade 4 – No evidence of the criteria	Comments
Team meeting facilitation	They did a very good job in coming up with the ideas for the application.	They engage team members in ways that encourage their contributions through constructive means.			

continued …

CREATIVE ACTIONS

Criteria	Grade 1 – Exceeding the criteria	Grade 2 – Meeting the criteria	Grade 3 – Below the criteria	Grade 4 – No evidence of the criteria	Comments
Team meeting contributions		They offered multiple ideas, solutions or courses of action that build on the ideas of others			
Completion of tasks	They always completed what they were assigned, and occasionally came with more done than what was asked of them.	They completed all assigned tasks by the deadline.			
Completeness of tasks	The work that was done greatly contributed toward the completion of the project.	The work accomplished is thorough, comprehensive and advances the project.			
Respectfulness		They treated team members respectfully by being polite and constructive in all forms of communication.			

Criteria	Grade 1 – Exceeding the criteria	Grade 2 – Meeting the criteria	Grade 3 – Below the criteria	Grade 4 – No evidence of the criteria	Comments
Attitude		They conveyed a positive attitude through positive vocal and written tone, facial expressions and body language.			
Motivation		They expressed confidence about the importance of the task and the team's ability to accomplish it.			
Assistance	They always helped their group members when they were having trouble or needed assistance even if they had their own work to be doing.	They provided assistance and encouragement to their team members.			
Category 9 – Response to conflict		They identified and acknowledged conflict, addressing it in constructive ways.			

SOURCE: adapted from Estell et al., 2016, p. 23. Used with permission.

REFLECTION ON LEARNING EVALUATION OF CREATIVITY

We note here that part of any evaluation of the final product of creativity should be the opportunity for students to have some time for reflective practice. Handing students back a mark or even a rubric might have some use, but the experience of learning will be deeper if the students are involved in reflecting on their process, the final product and what attitudes and skills they have learned or consolidated throughout the process. We understand that these things take time, but the benefits are far more substantial. In addition, the comprehensive nature of the rubric gives students stimulus for conversation on how they may improve their own work based on the features of creativity demonstrated in other students work.

As the level of knowledge and skills expected to be manifested by students in their final years of schooling involves even more substantial detail in the assessment process of creativity, we provide a further example. The criteria may be the same in each subject, but how they are manifest, and are recognised, differs. For instance, the criteria for measuring creativity in mathematical problem-solving would be different from the criteria for measuring creativity in poetry writing (Baer & Kaufman, 2017). Creativity in mathematics or poetry is still a matter of effectiveness, novelty and so on, but what constitutes effectiveness is different across the subjects.

CONCLUSION

This chapter has explored in some detail the components and facets of creativity and how they can be assessed using a range of tools, including a variety of adaptable rubrics. In summary, it is possible for teachers to evaluate, formally or informally, formatively or summatively, all the components that make up creativity. We stress that you do this slowly and steadily, building student understanding and skills over time.

CHAPTER 7

THE CREATIVE SCHOOL: HOW CAN WHOLE-SCHOOL CLIMATE BUILD ORGANISATIONAL CREATIVITY?

Teachers do not teach in a vacuum. They are part of an education system that includes policies and practices at multiple levels, government regulations and a range of relationships with key stakeholders such as school leaders, colleagues, students, parents and other community representatives. Similarly, students are negotiating relationships with families, classmates, their social connections both online and in person, and people who work in the education system, such as teachers, administrators and sports coaches. School leaders have the most complex set of relationships, being responsible for not only the internal mechanisms of how the school functions, but also successfully communicating a representation of the school that is both positive and stable. One of the most powerful influences on teachers, students and, ultimately, parents is what is known as school climate.

On a day-to-day basis school climate is determined by four main dimensions: physical and human ecologies (perception of the material environment, including buildings and facilities, administration, decision-making and planning structure), cultural (the system of values, norms, beliefs and assumptions), social (relationships between agents in the school), and individual (the attitude of teachers, students and parents to learning and a sense of belonging to the school (Chirkina, & Khavenson, 2018; Ismail et al., 2020). This chapter will focus primarily on the cultural, social and individual elements of school climate.

SCHOOL CLIMATE, CULTURE AND CREATIVITY

HOW SCHOOL MANAGEMENT INFLUENCES CREATIVITY

Schools are their own ecological systems, with individuals having their own perspective of how the system operates, how it affects them and how they can affect the system (Ryberg et al., 2020). A critical part of school management is negotiating the school culture they desire, with the education department authorities, school board or council, and to implement this throughout the various systems that operate within and outside the school. The implementation is manifest daily through what teachers, parents and students experience as the mood and culture of the school.

Dealing with what is essentially a subjective reality can be challenging for school leaders, hence the need for clarity in purpose and communication to all stakeholders. Given that teacher and student creativity can have a positive impact on the school climate (Moraru, 2019), school leaders need to understand creativity conceptually and how building creative competencies throughout the organisation can build a positive and flourishing organisational climate. To achieve this, school leaders need to look beyond grades and fiscal responsibility, to how creative competencies can complement traditional outcomes. A term used for this style of educational leadership is *edupreneurial* (Brauckmann-Sajkiewicz & Pashiardis, 2020).

We know that creativity consists of the physical and social environments, appropriate attitudes and attributes, understanding and applying the processes that build creative competencies, and having quantifiable outcomes. The following section will look at these elements of the creative ecosystem from the perspective of current and aspiring school leaders. There is ample evidence from the field of organisational creativity that demonstrates leaders can impact the creativity of organisations, but little which relates specifically to the influence of school leaders on the creative culture of their schools (Allen, 2016). We will also endeavour to provide practical advice and ideas that we believe can be implemented incrementally and sustainably, without the need to build a 'twenty-first century school' from scratch.

THE CULTURE OF THE CREATIVE SCHOOL ENVIRONMENT

The school environment goes beyond the confines of the classroom, both physically and socially. We know that a rich physical environment, in terms of buildings and outdoor spaces, aids individuals in feeling psychologically safe and confident to be creative. Encouraging the evolution of indoor and outdoor learning spaces is one way school leaders can support creative learning environments. Relatively simple ideas, such as adding colour to outdoor surfaces, or increasing plantings around school grounds, can be introduced incrementally and cost-effectively, but may not directly impact creativity. (We refer back to Chapter 3, where we showed that the research on things like colour is completely contradictory, with no real findings emerging as consistent. It is the contrast between environments that may stimulate creativity).

Another way to enhance creative physical environments is to offer students, parents and teachers the opportunity to impact the outdoor learning environment of a school. David has been a parent and a teacher at several schools, both primary and secondary, where parents collaborated on the design and implementation of outdoor learning spaces. In some schools, students are asked to contribute their ideas as to how the learning environment could better suit their individual needs. Parents and students often come up with ideas which would never have been considered by school leadership or teachers. In terms of setting up a positive psychological environment of creativity, outlining realistic constraints for time and budget and asking that, in the spirit of creativity, suggestions are new, relevant and useful to the context, will help those involved remain engaged and on-task. Validating their contributions through active listening and implementation can significantly improve the creative culture of a school. We also note here that what is possible is highly dependent on your context. It will be easier to implement such strategies in some schools rather than others.

An example of a successful creative project collaborating with multiple stakeholders is given here from a primary science class in South Africa.

CREATIVE ACTIONS

Science, primary, South Africa

WHAT THE TEACHER FOUND:

"Apparently, there are school principals who have the vision and the skills to bring about changes in the internal and external environments of their school. Creativity, as an additional resource, is made financially and pedagogically usable by those entrepreneurs." (Brauckmann-Sajkiewicz & Pashiardis, 2020, p. 9)

Component of creativity	Facet(s) of creativity	Teaching with or for creativity
Creative environment	Collaboration between school and community	For
Process of creativity	Real-world problem-solving	For
Evaluating creativity	Building of relationships	For

PURPOSE OF LESSON: SUBJECT KNOWLEDGE OR SKILLS

The purpose of this lesson was for students to build their knowledge of healthy nutrition and different types of fruits and vegetables by working in the school garden and cooking with the produce. Each student was allocated a small plot of land for which they were responsible. They sowed, planted and harvested the produce and regularly cooked healthy food for and with younger students (from their own school and neighbouring schools).

The garden also served as a link between students and their home and school. Parents participated in the project with the students, and their produce was contributed to the school and healthy cooking projects. Parents, as well as the students, learned about the educational and teaching importance of the school garden.

PURPOSE OF THE LESSON: TEACHING WITH OR FOR CREATIVITY

In terms of creativity, the purpose of this lesson was for students to develop their collaboration skills by tending the land together. They also learned another layer of collaboration, between the school and their families in sharing the produce. The second purpose was for students to understand real-world problem-solving through the success or failure of the crop.

REFERENCE

Brauckmann-Sajkiewicz, S., & Pashiardis, P. (2020). Entrepreneurial leadership in schools: Linking creativity with accountability. *International Journal of Leadership in Education*. https://doi.org/10.1080/13603124.2020.1804624.

ACCESS

THE ATTITUDES AND ATTRIBUTES OF A CREATIVE SCHOOL

To build an attitudinal culture of creativity, 'school leaders need to demonstrate the attitudes of creativity, both explicitly and implicitly, to all stakeholders' (Patston in Henebery, 2021 para. 7). The attitudes and behaviours of school leaders can certainly influence the attitudes and attributes of their teachers and students (Allen, 2016). To successfully build the attitudes and skills required for a creative school, we recommend a structured three-stage approach to professional learning.

Stage 1 includes the whole staff. It is important to involve the whole staff base to ensure a foundational level of the content and concepts of creativity is understood. By involving the whole school community, the professional learning becomes more cost-effective, sharing a small amount of explicit information with many teachers in one go.

Stage 2 focuses on the individual departments. The learning at this stage should focus on the practices relevant to subjects and how they are applied within the context of that subject. Teachers tend to respect the expertise and opinions of their colleagues and, through a sense of psychological safety, are more willing to receive feedback than from a so-called external expert.

Stage 3 is for small groups and individuals. In this third stage, individual teachers work in small groups or pairs, through either a collaborative or coaching framework. High levels of teacher agency and collaboration in professional development have proven successful in shifting teacher practice in a sustainable way, and in building teachers' creativity and innovation (Imants & Van der Wal, 2020). Research also indicates that teachers are willing to spend more time on professional development done in collaboration with their colleagues (Gore et al., 2017).

Another 'way to do this is to explore with a body of stakeholders how the attitudes and attributes of creativity may be impacted by the context of their particular working environment' (Patston in Henebery, 2021, para. 9). We would suggest that school leaders reflect on the following questions, and others they may generate related to creativity, when developing the strategic plan for moving towards a more creative organisational climate. As you will see, being informed and having open and transparent forms of communication are key. We would even go so far as to suggest that in a meeting with all teaching staff, school leaders may share some of these questions and how they answered them.

- 'How may a school leader demonstrate curiosity?
- How may a classroom teacher demonstrate curiosity?
- Where are teachers encouraged to demonstrate independence in the workplace?
- How does a school leader demonstrate openness to new experiences?
- What are the consequences of demonstrating these creative attitudes or attributes from the perspective of a school leader?
- How are these consequences currently communicated to staff, students and parents?' (Patston in Henebery, 2021, para. 10)
- What are some examples where a school leader needs to demonstrate resilience?
- How might these attitudes and attributes positively contribute to the organisation?
- What are the associated potential risks?

THE PROCESSES OF CREATIVITY IN A CREATIVE SCHOOL

IDENTIFYING AND SOLVING PROBLEMS

It is reasonable to say that the life of a school leader is the life of a creative problem-solver. In terms of strategic planning, it is also essential that a school leader can foresee problems that may need to be solved in the future. While there are many standard problems faced by leaders, new challenges and problems are constantly arising (Visone, 2018). School leaders need to be able to recognise a problem and its constituent variables, prioritise a problem, decide who can provide input to any appropriate methods or solutions, select an appropriate method or methods for solving the problem, and consider the consequences across a range of stakeholders for any proposed solution, before implementing the chosen solution.

Given the real-world, and often complex, nature of problems facing school leaders, having appropriate, efficient, effective, evidence-based techniques for problem-solving is a key competency for them to develop. A study involving 473 secondary school principals in Jordan reported that principals were most confident in solving problems relating to teachers and students, and least confident in dealing with parents and environmental issues (Al-Jaradat & Zaid-Alkilani, 2015). The extensive problem-solving tools detailed in Chapter 5 will provide school leaders with a broad range from which to choose. Having logical, systematic, evidence-based approaches to problem-solving is essential for school leaders. As with teachers working at the department level, school leaders may feel more comfortable developing these competencies with colleagues in similar positions from other organisations.

THE PRODUCTS OF A CREATIVE SCHOOL CULTURE

All school leaders are measured on their performance. When embarking on the journey of building a culture of creativity and creative competencies, it is ideal to have some form of baseline data. This measure can be replicated over time points to assess progress.

The Innovation Phase Assessment Instrument (IPAI; Cropley & Cropley, 2012) is used to assess the extent to which an organisation, such as a school, is aligned to the ideal conditions for fostering creativity and innovation at each stage of the innovation process (the innovation process being the practical application of the elements of creativity; Cropley, 2015). The IPAI models innovation across a series of seven phases – preparation, activation, generation, illumination, verification, communication and validation. In a practical sense, the IPAI enables school leaders to pinpoint weaknesses in the broad culture of the school that are inhibiting creativity. To maximise its capacity for innovation, an organisation must align itself to the favourable conditions in each phase. The IPAI tells an organisation where it is currently well-aligned and where it is currently poorly aligned. This then makes it possible to take targeted actions to address weaknesses and build strengths.

It also recognises that the attitudes and attributes of a person, the creative processes, the product and the organisational culture (the creative environment) differ in each phase. Divergent thinking, for example, may be most favourable to innovation in one phase, but convergent thinking may be most favourable in another. Innovation is no longer modelled as a one-size-fits-all process, and the IPAI allows school leaders to develop a highly differentiated understanding of their capacity for innovation. While this measure is both detailed and comprehensive, it has proved a very useful tool for the schools who have used it.

There are several other means to demonstrate evidence of creativity building across the organisation. Encouraging teachers to build a database of examples of teaching with creativity, and some form of sharing and celebrating examples, is a powerful way to build both teacher creativity and teacher agency and independence. Communicating with students, teachers and parents about the strategies of building creative competencies in independent learning, and building a shared database of effective examples, or sharing examples via school newsletters or online communications, helps build an organisational culture which supports creativity. Highlighting the results of students who have improved their academic outcomes by building their creative competencies is an extremely effective form of communication for all school stakeholders.

PROFESSIONAL DEVELOPMENT FOR THE CREATIVE SCHOOL

SELECTING PROFESSIONAL DEVELOPMENT

> *"To be successful, professional development must be seen as a process, not an event" (p. 388) and it needs to provide teachers with "specific, concrete, and practical ideas that directly relate to the day-to-day operation of their classrooms (p. 382)."* (Guskey, 2002, as cited in Bautista & Ortega-Ruíz, 2015, p. 245)

This section is aimed at both school management and teachers, when choosing the most relevant and useful professional development for their schools. We discuss the current state of play in international professional development, offer suggestions as to the most effective types of professional development and give examples of professional development in practice from a range of countries.

Professional learning, also called professional development, is a significant investment and expense for education systems around the world (Bautista & Ortega-Ruíz, 2015). The shift to a digitally connected global economy has led to significant reforms in education. As a result of these reforms the profession of teaching has evolved considerably. It is beyond the scope of this chapter to cover all the new attitudes, attributes and skills required by teachers in what is an increasingly fluid and complex landscape. However, we acknowledge that the profession of teaching is increasingly demanding in terms of skills, time, constraints and emotional investment.

Professional development is essential in developing teachers' knowledge, beliefs and practices in creativity (Thurm & Barzel, 2020). We believe that the integrated model of continuous professional learning proposed in this chapter is manageable, achievable and indeed essential for teachers in this time of rapid change.

HOW PROFESSIONAL LEARNING IS CURRENTLY EXPERIENCED

While we as authors believe in an asset-based approach to incremental change, it is sometimes easier to put things in context by summarising approaches to professional development, which we know do not work. As Popova and colleagues (2022) assert, 'few PD programs are rigorously evaluated, and among those that are, the evidence of their effectiveness is wildly mixed' (p. 108).

Unfortunately, a large body of research indicates that much professional learning is largely ineffective in building teacher competence and translating to an improvement in student outcomes (Popova et al., 2022). By far the most ineffective form of professional learning is the 'one-hit wonder' approach, where staff are sent to one-off workshops, lectures, seminars or conferences, or academics and private providers are invited to deliver whole-staff presentations or one-off workshops (Borko, 2004). In these environments, teachers are passive receivers of information, and it is extremely difficult under these circumstances to deliver information with any sense of individual targeted relevance, as revealed in this quote from a South African teacher:

> *... It is unfortunate that teachers are summoned for a workshop only to be given materials or should I call them individual study materials ... which are first read to us by the presenters ... then why calling a workshop instead of just sending the materials to schools and spare teachers from wasting valuable teaching time for nothing.* (Chigonga & Mutodi, 2020, p. 5)

Despite knowing for many years that this method of delivery is ineffective in terms of investment in change of practice or student outcomes, this continues to be the most popular form of teacher development around the world (Chen, 2020; Moore & Pharis, 2019).

HOW PROFESSIONAL LEARNING COULD BE EXPERIENCED

Our overall approach toward professional learning for teachers is ongoing professional development through a layered asset-based approach, delivered within an individual school. Asset-based teaching and learning is about focusing on students' and teachers' strengths and building learning around those strengths and their existing knowledge, instead of highlighting any deficits or gaps. School-embedded professional learning incorporates the teaching experience, the school context, teachers' collegiality to collaborate to improve teacher instruction, is cost-effective and leverages off existing effective practice (Kraft et al., 2018).

Where should the strategic and philosophic approach to teaching professional development in creative competencies begin? Every teacher will have had their own experiences with professional development, but this is what we find works best for creativity. We refer to three of the concepts that have been prevalent throughout the book.

1. For something to be creative it must be new, relevant and useful. Professional development should begin with research from providers into where teachers are in terms of their understanding and current application of creativity in the classroom.
2. Teachers reasonably like to feel a sense of understanding but also a sense of psychological safety when building their creative capacities through professional learning. This is essential if they are to engage in the research and risk-taking required when testing and trialling new pedagogies.
3. Building attitudes and skills in creativity will take time. Teachers need to understand the concepts and competencies of creativity in education, and in their personal lives and those of their colleagues and students. They should incrementally build an individual, department-based or school-based database of effective strategies which can be used in building teacher and student creative competencies.

In each stage, teachers need to be aware of the three ways in which creativity can be infused into the classroom: teaching *with* creativity in their pedagogic approaches; teaching *about* creativity in an explicit manner; and teaching *for* creativity, building the creative competencies of their students.

PROFESSIONAL LEARNING FOR TEACHING WITH CREATIVITY

All teachers need to understand what creativity is, why it is needed in schools (by teachers and students), and how it can be taught, learned and assessed. They also need to understand why building creative competencies as an educator is both relevant and useful in their teaching practice. The tangible benefits of having a bigger toolkit of pedagogic approaches must be clearly articulated in any professional development regarding teaching with creativity.

Rather than delivering this information in a lecture or seminar style, whether in person or via webinar, a blended learning approach (known in some countries as hybrid or mixed-method learning) is more effective in deepening and sustaining learning (Şentürk, 2021). The blended learning method integrates face-to-face teaching with computer mediated instruction. It gives teachers the opportunity to reflect and revisit materials that have been delivered. If the first time a teacher sees online content is with their colleagues, they are more likely to engage in pedagogy-based discussion and use the information presented (Philipsen et al., 2019).

PROFESSIONAL LEARNING FOR TEACHING WITH CREATIVITY

When it comes to teaching with creativity in the classroom, it is preferable for teachers to be given examples from their own subjects, topics and, if possible, year level. Throughout the book we have striven to provide examples from a wide range of subjects and year levels. Of course, these are not the only source of information teachers can access. Teachers are often members of professional networks and many of these have publications with examples of classroom practice. A less formal, frequently used and highly cost-effective method of building teacher understanding in a particular area (in this case teaching with creativity), is an online sharing platform such as Facebook. Teachers around the world, from Sweden (Liljekvist et al., 2020), to Indonesia (Sari & Tedjasaputra, 2013a), and Kenya (Bett & Makewa, 2020) use Facebook to share information regarding professional practice and pedagogy as well as subject content.

Professional learning can also happen at the department level. Every teacher is creative in their pedagogy. If a department can gather examples of current best practice from its own members, this can be the beginning of an evolving database of shared experiences.

THE CREATIVE SCHOOL

Mathematics, primary, South Africa

WHAT THE TEACHER FOUND:

"Teacher growth was evident through their professional experimentation and changes in their personal domain. The design features emanating from the study are that teachers be given opportunities to experience reform tasks (e.g. model-eliciting tasks) in the role of learners themselves and teachers should be encouraged to use contextual problems to initiate concept development." (Biccard, 2019, p. 1)

Component of creativity	Facet(s) of creativity	Teaching with or for creativity
Creative environment	Collaboration between teachers from different schools	For
Process of creativity	Real-world problem solving in lesson plans	For
Evaluating creativity	Change in pedagogy	For

PURPOSE OF LESSON: SUBJECT KNOWLEDGE OR SKILLS

The purpose of this lesson was for teachers to build knowledge in subject-based pedagogies from fellow mathematics teachers in other schools by sharing a range of pedagogic practices which they had found effective.

PURPOSE OF THE LESSON: TEACHING WITH OR FOR CREATIVITY

In terms of creativity, the purpose of this project was for teachers to build their collaboration skills with colleagues from other schools, thus developing skills using multiple perspectives to solve the problem of trialling new pedagogies. Creative ideas should be of the correct 'grain size' for teachers to be able to use them in their own lesson planning. Interventions should be able to transfer to everyday classrooms but are only meaningful if they result in changes in the pedagogy of mathematics classrooms. By presenting collaborative professional development sessions, the mobility of the innovation and how it can be supported was the primary focus. Mathematics was also put into context for the students. During observations, teachers used some other contexts as starting points (for example, word problems) while two teachers presented truly problematic situations where no known procedures could simply be applied to the problems (sharing pizzas and constructing 3D objects).

REFERENCE

Biccard, P. (2019). The professional development of primary school mathematics teachers through a design – based research methodology. *Pythagoras, 40*(1), Article a515. https://doi.org/10.4102/pythagoras.v40i1.515.

ACCESS

CREATIVE ACTIONS

PROFESSIONAL LEARNING FOR TEACHING ABOUT CREATIVITY

Throughout the book we have stressed that teachers must understand that creativity is a system, and students also need to understand this conceptually. We have also suggested that, while some explicit teaching about creativity is necessary, this should usually be short and specific, targeted to the skills and subject content that will follow in the lesson or unit of work. Professional learning for teaching about creativity is most effectively delivered in bite-size pieces, modelling the method used for delivery in the classroom.

When teaching about creativity, teachers should use language and concepts appropriate to the age and stage of the students they are working with. When looking at curriculum documentation, it is clear that students are building a developmental sequence of knowledge and skills. As yet, there is no evidence-based developmental trajectory of many of the various elements of creativity. For example, openness to new experiences in Year 7 geography will be different to openness to new experiences in Year 9 science. The capabilities of collaboration also vary between ages, stages and subject levels.

Professional development in teaching about creativity should break down creativity into its individual components, as we have done in this book. It should cover both the social and physical environments needed for creativity, and which environmental elements can potentially crush creativity. The attitudes and attributes students need to develop throughout their school journey also need to be discussed. It is at this point where teacher experience will come to the fore. Over time teachers will have seen students demonstrate elements such as intellectual curiosity or intercultural understanding. They will also have observed students who do not do as well as they could academically in a subject because they lack particular creative attitudes, such as curiosity or tolerance for ambiguity. Teachers can explore what the attitudes and attributes of creativity look like in their particular subject, and how they can teach about these concepts to their students. Once again, building these skills by interleaving them into subject content over time is more effective than just focusing intensively on creativity.

Given that creativity lies both within and between all subject areas, it is also worth heads of department sharing with other heads of department when particular creative competencies, such as the process of problem-solving, or attitudes and attributes, are being integrated into subject and year levels. This coordinated approach shares the load of teaching about creativity between departments, while at the same time ensuring that students are exposed to as many elements of creativity as possible throughout their school journey. This project-based example of real-world problem-solving from Portugal demonstrates how creative competencies can be built over time in both teachers and students.

THE CREATIVE SCHOOL

e7.3
Interdisciplinary real-world problem-solving, secondary, Portugal

WHAT THE TEACHER FOUND:

> *The obtained results also suggest the importance of planning instruction and learning, in order to meet students' curiosity and provide them the opportunity to express their creativity in learning.* (de Fátima Morais et al., 2015, p.293)

Component of creativity	Facet(s) of creativity	Teaching with or for creativity
Creative environment	Collaboration between teachers from different schools	For
Process of creativity	Real-world problem solving in lesson plans	For
Evaluating creativity	Change in pedagogy	For

PURPOSE OF LESSON: SUBJECT KNOWLEDGE OR SKILLS

The purpose of this lesson was for teachers to build their understanding of and skills in problem-solving by examining how these skills can be applied to problems in the community (community problem-solving) and in domains such as education, culture or environmental issues. For this project teachers received previous training and, during the program's implementation, participated in biweekly meetings. Teachers had to analyse and develop creative solutions for a real-world problem, considering the impending problem and future implications.

PURPOSE OF THE LESSON: TEACHING WITH OR FOR CREATIVITY

In terms of creativity, the purpose of this lesson was for teachers to learn creative problem-solving skills, including critical thinking skills, problem-solving strategies, research skills and collaboration skills by working together over an extended period of time. They were then equipped to teach these skills explicitly to their students to solve the real-world problems proposed.

REFERENCE

de Fátima Morais, M., Neves de Jesus, S., Azevedo, I., Araújo, A. M., & Viseu, J. (2015). Intervention Program on adolescent's creativity representations and academic motivation. *Paidéia (Ribeirão Preto)*, 25(62), 289–297. https://doi.org/10.1590/1982-43272562201502.

ACCESS

CREATIVE ACTIONS

PROFESSIONAL DEVELOPMENT OF TEACHING FOR CREATIVITY

It is one thing for education departments, tertiary providers, governments and businesses to demand students leave school with so-called twenty-first century skills. It is quite another for teachers to integrate the development of these skills into their curriculum, when facing what may seem to be conflicting demands in terms of content delivery and standardised testing.

It needs to be made clear 'that building creative competencies in students and teachers has positive and tangible outcomes in many areas, such as motivation, but, perhaps more importantly from a teacher, school or parent perspective, academic outcomes' (Patston in Henebery, 2021, para. 8; Conradty & Bogner, 2020; Kaufman et al., 2021).

This coordinated approach also gives students a better grasp of the overall purpose of education, as they see relevance both within and between subject areas. This coordinated approach of incremental gain in attitudes, skills and competencies over the whole school journey will lead to students being comfortable and capable in creative competencies by the time they leave school. The following example demonstrates this approach with a group of primary and secondary science teachers from Oman.

THE CREATIVE SCHOOL

Science, primary and secondary, Oman

WHAT THE TEACHER FOUND:

> *At one end is a group of teachers who have an interest and belief in teaching for creativity and who possess an aptitude to design and implement instructional activities that foster student creativity; at the other end is a group of teachers who value knowledge most, who teach for the test, and who pay no attention to promoting their students' creativity.* (Al-Abdali & Al-Balushi, 2016, p. 255)

Component of creativity	Facet(s) of creativity	Teaching with or for creativity
Creative environment	Open-ended questions with psychological safety	For
Process of creativity	Critical thinking	For
Process of creativity	Divergent thinking	For

PURPOSE OF LESSON: SUBJECT KNOWLEDGE OR SKILLS

The purpose of this lesson was for teachers to transfer their knowledge and skills to students by asking students to provide applications for the concepts under study, asking them to design graphic organisers or sketches to present their data, and assigning homework to foster creative thinking.

PURPOSE OF THE LESSON: TEACHING WITH OR FOR CREATIVITY

In terms of creativity, the purpose of this lesson was for teachers to explore a range of creative pedagogies to determine their effectiveness within their particular context. This project examined the six strategies observed in teachers who taught for building creativity in their students:
- asking divergent and open-ended questions
- using follow-up questions such as 'Why?', 'What if?' and 'What can you add to this idea?'
- encouraging students to think of all possible answers
- pausing after asking a question to allow students to think
- waiting after receiving a student's response to encourage more participation
- asking higher-order questions that challenge students' thinking to generate novel solutions for real problems.

REFERENCE
Al-Abdali, N. S., Al-Balushi, S. M. (2016). Teaching for creativity by science teachers in grades 5–10. *International Journal of Science and Mathematics Education*, 14, 251–268. https://link.springer.com/article/10.1007/s10763-014-9612-3

ACCESS

CONCLUSION

This chapter has demonstrated that teachers can build their creative competencies through professional learning, and school leaders can build a climate and culture of organisational creativity which benefits all stakeholders. Such evolution of practice and climate takes time, but with incremental change, and the load shared between students, teachers, parents and school leaders, progress can be sustained and embedded over time.

CHAPTER 8

THE CREATIVE INDEPENDENT LEARNER: BEING CREATIVE INSIDE AND OUTSIDE THE CLASSROOM

8

In an ideal world, every teacher would teach a wonderful and useful lesson every time they entered the classroom, and students would be focused and see relevance and need in every piece of information they are offered. Students would take immaculate notes, create beautiful summaries and study efficiently and effectively to achieve full marks in every test and exam. As we know, the reality is quite different. For students the process of independent learning is in fact a series of problems, large and small, that they need to solve to reach their potential at school.

So far, this book has been about the theory and practice of creativity through the lens of teachers and school management. This chapter is viewed through the lens of the student and how teachers can support students' independent learning. Students do not just spend time in the classroom. They spend time doing homework, revision and preparing for tests and exams. Essentially this chapter is about how students can discover which independent learning strategies are best for them. They will need attitudes and attributes, such as openness, curiosity and resilience (see Chapter 4), combined with the skills and tools of problem-solving (see Chapter 5), to find solutions that best meet their individual learning needs within their individual learning context. They will also need to think about the best physical and social learning environments, including when and where they study (see Chapter 3).

A key reason for this chapter comes from Tim's most recent experience at two schools where he was responsible for F–12 learning, initially for a large department and then for a four-campus school. What began as informal discussions with other heads of department led to confirmation that, while there was a clear scope and sequence of subject content and skills, there appeared to be no such scope and sequence for the elements of independent learning. Tim's experience taught him that, even though teachers are incredibly important, if students do not have efficient and appropriate methods to record, consolidate and retrieve their understanding, their learning may be inefficient and ineffective. It is true that some subjects do offer explicit note-taking strategies, but often teachers in one subject are not aware of the note-taking, summarising and study strategies suggested by their colleagues in another. Tim's observations are supported

CREATIVE ACTIONS

by evidence – schools spend little time explicitly building the skills associated with efficient information processing (Dukhan, 2018; Dukhan et al., 2019). Despite education being global, there is a surprising dearth of research as to which are the best information transfer, consolidation and retrieval strategies in schools.

One promising avenue of exploration is the idea of generative learning (Brod, 2021). The principle behind generative learning is that students make sense of the learning as it occurs and use a range of strategies to support their individual learning. In other words, they need to be creative independent learners. As you will see in Table 8.1, different strategies may be required at different age levels.

Table 8.1: Evidence on the effectiveness of generative learning strategies in different age groups

	University students	Secondary school students	Upper primary students	Lower primary students
Concept mapping	Favourable	Favourable	Favourable	Insufficient
Explaining	Favourable	Favourable	Mixed	Mixed
Predicting	Favourable	Favourable	Favourable	Favourable
Questioning	Favourable	Mixed	Mixed	Unfavourable
Testing	Favourable	Favourable	Favourable	Favourable
Drawing	Favourable	Favourable	Unfavourable	Unfavourable

SOURCE: Brod, 2021, p. 1298, https://doi.org/10.1007/s10648-020-09571-9. Used with permission under Creative Commons Attribution License 4.0.

It is a timely reminder that an important part of creativity is doing something new, relevant and useful for an individual within their context. Working explicitly with students on their individual independent learning skills, by coming up with new and creative alternatives, has proven highly effective for Tim in building his students' academic outcomes. Research conducted by the authors of this book in 2021 found that students who used a range of creative independent learning strategies felt less anxious, more engaged with their learning and found their learning more relevant (Patston, Kennedy et al., 2021).

How do you as a teacher expect students to take notes, summarise key facts, concepts and ideas, and retrieve and apply them in assessments? Do you have a specific approach, or do you expect that students know how to do it and you just let them get on with it? It goes without saying that students are in school to learn. How they learn is critically important for the rest of their lives. For younger students, teachers should offer some differing approaches. Older students should research and trial personalised solutions. In this next section we will explore a range of evidence-based methods that students can use at each of these three stages. We stress that some of these solutions might not be creative for one teacher or student, but may be highly innovative and creative for another.

CREATIVE TRANSFER

Students are most frequently exposed to new knowledge and ideas for the first time in the classroom. At some point in the lesson students may need to transfer and record some type of information. The teacher might talk and ask the students to take notes, there might be notes on the board to write down, or notes to be taken from a textbook, a video, or some other form of presentation. What are the most efficient and effective tools that students can use in these tasks? Given the importance of these tools, it was somewhat surprising there is little empirical research in this field from schools, with the majority of studies focusing on university students (Brod, 2021). Taking notes is not just a skill for school; it is a skill for life (Dukhan, 2018).

Taking notes is not easy. Students must listen, comprehend, identify important details, and then record these details as a physical or digital copy (Sun & Li, 2019; White, 2017). So, what are the best ways for students to take notes in the classroom? Once again, we return to our two key words, context and purpose. As with any of the other attitudes and skills discussed in this book, it is best not to run separate sessions on note-taking, consolidation and retrieval strategies but to embed the various strategies within the content of the subject (Hattie & Donoghue, 2016). It is also worth stressing that any note-taking or consolidation strategy must be relevant and useful to the particular subject and topic. We will discuss this in more detail later in the chapter.

Do students take notes because they want to, or need to, or because they are told to? In the latter years of primary and the early years of high school, it is the teacher's responsibility to identify the purpose for students to be taking notes in class, and advise the appropriate methodology. In this developmental phase students need to be given a range of possible tools to use when taking notes, eventually having the freedom to make a decision about what suits their personal needs as a learner. We also believe that context is very important; a method that is successful in a science class may not be suitable in a geography class. Further, a note-taking strategy for one topic in geography may not be suitable for another topic. Students need to build their toolkit of note-taking strategies over time. It is clear that note-taking facilitates learning and is, therefore, an essential skill for students to develop (Aragón-Mendizábal et al., 2016).

Students achieve this by being open to new ideas, being curious about what might be effective for their peers, using critical thinking and trialling different methods to decide which strategy is most effective for them for a particular topic in a particular subject at a particular time. Openness to new experiences and flexibility in learning are attitudes that are key predictors of creativity, as discussed in Chapter 4.

CREATIVE ACTIONS

HANDWRITTEN OR TYPED?

With the ubiquitousness of digital devices, students are increasingly using laptops, tablets, or even smartphones, to take notes. Students see this as efficient, particularly those who have poor handwriting. However, the evidence is clear – even though typed notes may be longer in terms of quantity, they are poorer in terms of quality (Aragón-Mendizábal et al., 2016). Recent evidence has found that students' cognitive processes are more focused on the typing than on the listening (Bouriga & Olive, 2021). This is true in both Asian and European languages (Buriga & Olive, 2021; Siok & Liu, 2018). This means that students are less likely to remember the information that was conveyed in the class if the notes are typed. Because handwriting is a slower process, students tend to listen and think before putting pen to paper. It is not unreasonable to say that just typing notes bypasses the brain altogether. It appears that while taking notes on a laptop does not necessarily inhibit factual recall, handwritten notes are much better for long-term conceptual understanding (Mueller & Oppenheimer, 2014). However, despite this strong body of evidence, many teachers around the world are defaulting to digital note-taking without fully appreciating the consequences in terms of learning (Franco-Mariscal et al., 2021). This does not mean that digital representations of notes have no value (this will be discussed later in the chapter).

Taking notes has two primary functions. Firstly, notes can be taken as a method of building understanding. Secondly, notes can be taken as a means of recording understanding that needs to be accessed at a later time. Trying to take verbatim notes of everything the teacher says in a class is clearly inefficient as a tool for learning. In the most comprehensive studies of their kind, Witherby and Tauber (2019), and Dukhan (2018) reported that, despite rating the quality of their notes as satisfactory, most students wished they had more explicit instructions from their teachers in note-taking methodologies. In fact, there is evidence that explicit note-taking strategies enhance student learning in science in students as young as eleven or twelve years old in Taiwan (Lee et al., 2013) and Nigeria (Segun, 2017). Students also reported that they only noted down what the teachers said were important. This lack of autonomy or agency could have clear ramifications when students are referring to notes. If they do not attempt to clarify something so they can understand, and instead copy down what the teacher told them to, there could be gaps in their understanding.

In another study, students also seemed to take more notes in classes that they perceived as difficult but went for quantity over quality instead of finding an alternative creative strategy to record and summarise difficult information (Rapanta et al., 2020). (The experience of the authors of this book is that students' quality of note-taking is often very poor, lacking structure and organisation.) This study also reported that students took fewer notes in online classes than in-person classes. Given the changes to teaching during the COVID-19 pandemic, and the shift to online instruction or blended learning in many countries, this could be a significant issue in the future.

If you wish to quickly ascertain what note-taking strategies students currently use and generate discussion about the most effective methods, the following example will help.

THE CREATIVE INDEPENDENT LEARNER

e8.1

French language, secondary, France

WHAT THE TEACHER FOUND:

"Very few students are taught even basic 'note taking' skills. This, despite the fact that students are expected to take extensive notes during their courses across the curriculum, and despite the recognized usefulness of note taking for storing, learning and thinking about what is being taught. Primary schools, secondary schools, and universities provide their students with no (or very little) help." (Boch & Piolat, 2005, p. 101–2)

Component of creativity	Facet(s) of creativity	Teaching with or for creativity
Creative environment	Social environment, multiple perspectives of note-taking and collaboration. Peer to peer learning and reflection	For
Process of creativity	Information transfer and retrieval	For
Evaluating creativity	Improved academic results	For

PURPOSE OF LESSON: SUBJECT KNOWLEDGE OR SKILLS

The purpose of this lesson was for students to build their information transfer and information consolidation (summarising) skills by producing a summary that required sorting, selecting and combining information with a standardised language format (respecting spelling, syntax and linearity of the text).

PURPOSE OF THE LESSON: TEACHING WITH OR FOR CREATIVITY

In terms of creativity, the purpose of this lesson was for students to build their creative independent learning strategies by using a written synthesis to explain to one of their newly arrived classmates a point that had been the subject of a class during which the student had taken notes (in this case, the functioning of French spelling). Comparison and reflection work was then done collectively, through questioning about the various aspects of note-taking (peer-to-peer instruction and reflection). The students worked in pairs to rewrite a passage of their notes and compared their text with that of another pair that had been assigned the same passage. This dual task made it possible to better define the difficulties related to this activity and thereby to clarify where the stumbling blocks were.

REFERENCE

Boch, F., & Piolat, A. (2005). Note taking and learning: A summary of research. *The WAC Journal, 16*, 101–113. https://doi.org/10.37514/WAC-J.2005.16.1.08

ACCESS

HANDWRITTEN NOTES IN A LECTURE FORMAT

There is currently a global tension in pedagogy, between a move towards more learner-centred education and international standardised testing (Schweisfurth & Elliott, 2019). Consequently, particularly in the senior years of schooling, the default position in the classroom remains a lecture-style format, frequently supported by some form of technology such as a PowerPoint or video (Dukhan et al., 2019). If the teacher is not delivering the content in creative ways, it is up to the student to find creative ways to transfer and consolidate the information. The challenge for students in this scenario is whether to focus on the teacher's voice or the content of the digital material. Despite evidence that students with high, medium and low ability have clear differences in their note-taking skills, few studies have attempted to assess which note-taking strategy is most effective for each of these distinct cohorts (Boyle & Forchelli, 2014).

Perhaps the second least effective method of taking notes in class, after verbatim transcription, is the linear method. In this method students merely take notes in the chronological sequence of the lesson, with no attempt at making connection between information and ideas. Students finish up with a list of sentences and ideas. Unless students undertake a review of their notes soon after the class and reorganise them in a more structured format, this type of note-taking is ineffective for long-term consolidation of knowledge, skills and recall.

An increasingly popular and more structured approach to note-taking across a range of subjects is the Cornell method (Pauk & Owens, 2010). This method allows students to take notes in sequence, using the right side of the page for formal notes and the left side of the page for cues, headings or topics. This method allows space for students to add summaries using keywords, questions relevant to the notes on the right, and notes for material which needs to be reviewed later. At the bottom or footer of each page, the note taker writes a brief summary of that page of notes to be reviewed. The effectiveness of Cornell note-taking has been demonstrated in a range of high school students, including with middle school students of social studies in an international school in China (Evans & Shively, 2019), and in an English as a foreign language class in Jordan (Alzu'bi, 2019).

Table 8.2: Cornell method of note-taking

Lesson:	Name: Date: Paper:
Cue Column:	**Notes Column:**
Most important information Headings Topics	1. **Record:** During the lecture, use the note taking column to record the lecture using short sentences. 2. **Questions:** After class, formulate questions based on the notes in the note taking column. Writing questions helps to clarify meanings, reveal relationships, establish continuity, and strengthen memory. Also, the writing of questions sets up a perfect stage for exam- studying later. 3. **Recite:** Cover the note-taking column with a sheet of paper. Then, looking at the questions or cue-words in the question and cue column only, say aloud, in your own words, the answers to the questions, facts, or ideas indicated by the cue-words. 4. **Reflect:** Reflect on the material by asking yourself questions, for example: "What's the significance of these facts? What principle are they based on? How can I apply them? How do they fit in with what I already know? What's beyond them? 5. **Review:** Spend at least ten minutes every week reviewing all your previous notes. If you do, you'll retain a great deal for current use, as well as, for the exam.

CREATIVE ACTIONS

The T method of note-taking is similar to Cornell but is used more often in the sciences and mathematics where students are using equations. In these subjects students need to take two types of notes, notes that explain the concepts, ideas and information that are being discussed, and notes that articulate the procedures that need to be followed when completing tasks. In discussion with mathematics teachers when preparing this book, they expressed concern that students are much more likely to write down formulas and step-by-step procedures than to take notes on how these mathematical processes work and are why they are needed. In these subjects, students are also often asked to take notes from their textbooks. This pedagogy requires a creative response from the students in terms of how they transfer the information to deepen their understanding. The T method is also a good consolidation tool.

Table 8.3: Middle school mathematics example of the T method of note-taking

Lesson: Problem 1	Date: Notes column
Terms 'solve' and 'equation'	Definition of 'solve': to find a value of an unknown quantity that makes the equation true Definition of 'equation': a mathematical expression using an = sign Example: Solve $X + 1 = 4$. Solution is $X = 3$ because $3 + 1 = 4$ is true
Term 'formula'	Definition of 'formula': an equation that describes the relationship between several quantities Example – Pythagoras $a^2 = b^2 + c^2$ describes the relationship between the three sides of a right-angled triangle

Non-linear methods of note-taking involve students not merely writing longhand notes but engaging with the content, perhaps creating dot points for keywords and using diagrams or images to demonstrate relationships between concepts and ideas. These non-linear methods can be handwritten or digital. There are many varied non-linear methods, such as concept mapping and mind mapping (see Chapter 5). The following examples shows the use of digital concept mapping in secondary school history in Malaysia and digital mind mapping in secondary school biology in Jordan.

History, secondary, Malaysia

WHAT THE TEACHER FOUND:

> *The respondents were able to develop a structural flow of events that consisted of certain detailed understanding of historical events. Thus, the concept map was considered successful in presenting history facts in a visual form that could easily be applied by respondents in a computer-based application. The tool has evidently outperformed the conventional approach.* (Salleh & Ismail, 2013, p. 692)

Component of creativity	Facet(s) of creativity	Teaching with or for creativity
Creative environment	Explore a broader set of resources than in a textbook	With
Process of creativity	Critical thinking and exploring relationships	For
Evaluating creativity	Improved academic results	For

PURPOSE OF LESSON: SUBJECT KNOWLEDGE OR SKILLS

The purpose of this lesson was for students to build their history knowledge, specifically around relationships between historical events, by engaging with the topic content in different ways and with different strategies. A first-time user would use the course materials in a sequenced manner. After completing the teaching module, users then proceeded with the quizzes, which were represented as concept maps. Users were facilitated with features like 'drag and drop' to choose the correct answer.

PURPOSE OF THE LESSON: TEACHING WITH OR FOR CREATIVITY

In terms of creativity, the purpose of this lesson was for students to improve their creative problem-solving skills by examining how categorising and exploring the relationships between ideas, using the tool of concept maps, are important components of the process. The second purpose of this lesson was for students to build their critical thinking skills by exploring historical ideas through multiple perspectives, using a wide range of digital resources.

REFERENCE

Salleh, S. S., & Ismail, R. (2013). Effectiveness of concept map approach in teaching history subject. In H. B. Zaman, P. Robinson, P. Olivier, T. K. Shih, & S. Velastin (Eds.). Advances in visual informatics (IVIC 2013: Lecture Notes in Computer Science, Vol. 8237). Springer, Cham. https://doi.org/10.1007/978-3-319-02958-0_62.

ACCESS

CREATIVE ACTIONS

Biology, secondary, Jordan

WHAT THE TEACHER FOUND

"E-mind maps ... are more effective than conventional maps especially in the learning process as it employs modern technologies in education enabling the learner to create maps, insert images, colourful drawings, modify, revise, print and share with others. This method helps the learner to form an integrated knowledge structure that qualifies them to deeply explore ideas." (Al-Omari & Al-Dhoon, 2020, p. 6430)

Component of creativity	Facet(s) of creativity	Teaching with or for creativity
Creative environment	Explore a broader set of resources than in a textbook	With
Process of creativity	Critical thinking and exploring relationships	For
Evaluating creativity	Improved academic results	For

PURPOSE OF LESSON: SUBJECT KNOWLEDGE OR SKILLS

The purpose of this lesson was for students to build understanding around taxonomy and Prokaryotes by using a building of knowledge structure technique, rather than a linear form of learning. Each student may have used a different method to acquire knowledge, information and experiences to organise the acquired knowledge through recording, symbolising and assimilating this information in their cognitive repository.

PURPOSE OF THE LESSON: TEACHING WITH OR FOR CREATIVITY

In terms of creativity, the purpose of this lesson was for students to use the tool of e-mind maps to structure information as a means of categorising ideas. Participants of the experimental group learned through a teaching method that focused on scientific concepts and the links between them, while the control group learned by using the conventional method that focuses on memorising and recalling information without exploring the links. The use of mind maps harmonises with the constructivist theory that depicts knowledge as an activity that is constructed and formed by the learner.

REFERENCE

Al-Omari, A. A. H., & Al-Dhoon, B. A. (2020). The impact of e-mind mapping strategy and learning styles on the achievement of the tenth-grade students in biology. *Universal Journal of Educational Research, 8*(12), 6429–6438, 2020. https://doi.org/10.13189/ujer.2020.081208.

ACCESS

DIGITAL NOTES IN A LECTURE FORMAT

Given the rapid uptake of digital technologies around the world, many countries now have digital devices in the classroom. As discussed previously, students typing their notes run the risk of not absorbing and understanding key information and concepts. On the other hand, one advantage of digital note-taking is that students can change colour, font and size while taking notes. They can also use digital highlighters for points which they need to review later. A recent study with university students in Finland found several advantages in taking notes using a digital device: notes were always available in one place, could be supplemented by further information or research, and had easy access to digital applications to annotate and draw (if their device was handwriting enabled or had a digital stylus; Pyörälä et al., 2019). This method of note-taking can be both visually and content rich. However, school-age students would need some explicit instruction in how to take notes effectively using this strategy (Sun & Li, 2019).

NOTE-TAKING IN A NON-LECTURE FORMAT

Not all teaching occurs in a lecture format and not all subjects require the same type of note-taking. Notes need to be content elaborative rather than just content reproductive. Students need to take generative notes in a thoughtful manner that connects instructional information with prior knowledge or with information transmitted earlier. Under these circumstances, students often do not take any notes at all during the process, which impairs their ability to recall information later. A recent study (Jiang et al., 2018) with a sample of middle school science students in the United States reported that students who took generative notes had significantly higher academic outcomes in a unit test. Such findings indicate that it is worth investing time in explaining the purpose of note-taking in your subject area when beginning a particular topic or unit of work.

Students may be offered information in a visual format, such as a video or some form of graphic presentation (Hibbit, 2020). One type of generative note-taking that combines the textual and the visual is sketch noting. At first glance this method, combining sketches with text, can seem quite daunting, as many of the examples online show a high level of artistic skill. It is perhaps easier to think of sketch noting as a form of doodling. Sketches can include writing, symbols or images, or any combination of the three. A study by Treptow (2020) with a Year 11 English class in the United States reported that sketch noting met multiple student reading needs, increased student engagement and motivation, and positively influenced student reading comprehension. This study stressed the importance of student autonomy when it came to the style and structure of the sketches and how they were integrated into the overall note-taking strategy.

CREATIVE ACTIONS

HOW CAN TEACHERS HELP?

GRADUAL RELEASE OF RESPONSIBILITY

Apart from offering students some explicit instruction in note-taking and offering students a variety of methods with which to take notes, teachers can also provide information to students in a more scaffolded way. It is useful to begin by advising students that they are not *taking* notes, they are *making* notes. One method of note-making that has proven effective with students, ranging from Year 6 students studying English in Taiwan (Lin & Cheng, 2010) to undergraduate mathematics students in Thailand (Riyapan et al., 2021), is the gradual release of responsibility model (Fisher & Frey, 2008). In this method the teacher begins with brief direct instructions of which notes to take and how to take them. They then model the note-taking strategy along with the students. They ask students to collaborate to construct notes and finally students are asked to develop their own notes independently. When explaining this method to students a simple way to write it on the board is to use the terminology of Fisher and Frey (2021).

1. Directed instruction: 'I do it'
2. Guided instruction: 'We do it'
3. Collaboration: 'You do it together'
4. Independent practice: 'You do it alone' (Fisher & Frey, 2021, p. 3).

FINDING CREATIVE NOTE-TAKING

Another way to help students is to help them find new ways of creative note-taking. Open-ended prompts such as the following are very useful for senior students to challenge and examine their note-taking strategies. We suggest beginning this process with an opening discussion:

1. Explain the purpose of note-taking. What are its functions?
2. Do you always take notes in the same way in all your lessons? Why?
3. How do you use the notes you take during your lessons? Do you use them as they are? If not, what do you do with them between the lesson and the exam?

Have a five-minute delivery of content, followed by the open-ended questions detailed in Table 8.4, building up over time to a whole lesson. (We stress that these two options need to be done relatively infrequently but should be covered throughout the year to see how the students are developing these skills in your subject area. If students have found more creative ways to do this between discussions, then it is positive reinforcement for them to discuss this in the class).

Table 8.4: Metacognitive questionnaire on note-taking for students

Part 1: Your notes taking during the teacher's presentation
1. Give a detailed description of how you took your notes during this presentation. Give reasons, saying what you did and why. 2. Are you satisfied with your notes? Why? 3. Compare your notes with those of another student. In your opinion, which is better? Why?
Part 2: Possible improvements
1. If you had to start taking these notes again, what would you change? Why? 2. What advice would you give to students whose notes you read, to help improve their note-taking? 3. What could the teacher have done to help you with your note-taking?

SOURCE: adapted from Romainville & Noël, 2003

GUIDED NOTES

Guided notes, also known as skeleton notes, are a useful tool in the guided instruction phase. The concept of guided notes has been around for many years and has proven to be a highly effective way of increasing the efficacy of student notes (Biggers & Luo, 2020; Lazarus, 1996). There are a multitude of ways to provide skeleton notes, but the fundamental premise is the same. Students are provided a skeleton outline of the content, on paper or digitally, by the teacher. How much information is missing from the skeleton resource is at the discretion of the teacher and is dependent on the learning goals. It may be that the students have to fill in key terms or are provided with key terms and need to complete the definitions. This type of guided notes allows students to follow the course of the lesson while having the opportunity to write down their own thoughts, observations and questions.

A comprehensive study in middle school mathematics in the United States (Asselanis, 2017) highlighted the challenges involved in assessing the efficacy of different note-taking strategies. The study reported that although graphic organisers were the most effective note-taking strategy, followed by guided notes and the Cornell method, in terms of student achievement in tests, they were the least favoured note-taking strategy by the students. The students strongly favoured guided note-taking. Such findings clearly demonstrate the need for creative experimentation with various types of note-taking in all levels of schooling.

CREATIVE ACTIONS

COLLABORATIVE NOTE-TAKING

It is also possible to teach students how to take notes in pairs or small groups. There is evidence that notes taken in pairs are more original and comprehensive than notes taken individually (Luo, Kiewra & Samuelson, 2016). However, it is not sufficient merely to put students together and hope that they will make notes of quality. In a study by Yim and colleagues (2017), students without explicit instruction in how to make notes collaboratively demonstrated four key ways of working:

1. In one style, used by 31 per cent of groups, one or two students dominated, writing most of the text, while the other members participated minimally. This method is frequently a cause of frustration for the students who contribute the majority of work.
2. In another method the authors called *divide and conquer*, used by 20 per cent of groups, students are allocated to a particular element, such as definitions, quotes, examples or key concepts. They write their own parts and rarely edit each other's text. They then combine their notes at the end of the collaboration. This method reduces students' cognitive load by allowing them to listen intently for their particular elements of work, while other details are being captured by their classmates.
3. In the third method, called *cooperative revision*, used by 40 per cent of the groups, members divided their sections but freely edited each other's work, mostly at the later stage of writing.
4. In the least popular method, used by 9 per cent of groups, members create sentences together by simultaneously building off each other's text.

In terms of the quality of notes generated by the groups, despite being used by only 20 per cent of groups, the divide and conquer method proved the most effective. These groups participated more actively and equally than the other three groups. The cooperative revision group, despite it being popular between the students, was less effective. It may be that for students comprehending the content from a teacher as well as information from another student may possibly overburden someone taking notes in a group (Costley & Fanguy, 2021).

An extension of the divide and conquer method is known in some schools as the *jigsaw technique*. In this technique students make notes for their section of a concept or topic, and then deepen their learning by teaching this to other groups in the class (Arthurs & Krieger, 2017). They then share their notes with the other groups.

As students experiment over time, using verbal, visual and graphic note-taking strategies, they will develop a personalised approach which suits them individually. However, making notes is not enough. After classes are complete it is essential for students to consolidate their learning and understanding.

CREATIVE CONSOLIDATION

One of the best books we have read in the past few years regarding the consolidation of knowledge to deepen learning is *Make it stick: The science of learning* (Brown et al., 2014). This book addresses some of the key myths of learning. Its findings have been supported empirically through the meta-analyses of Hattie and Donoghue (2016). In this section we will focus on busting the myths to do with the consolidation of knowledge which is later needed for retrieval.

MYTH 1: LEARNING STYLES

Perhaps one of the biggest myths that still pervades education is that people have distinct learning styles and can only learn using their particular style. The reality is that just because a student finds a particular method such as visual or verbal learning more comfortable does not mean that it is more effective. This finding is aligned with the overall philosophy of this book – expose students to a variety of methods and then test them to see which are the most effective. Our experience as educators is that few students take the time to think about how they learn, preferring to replicate methods they have been told will be successful, rather than trialling and comparing methods. Our experience tells us that learning, just like creativity, is context dependent, and developing consolidation techniques for particular subjects, or even topics within subjects, is the most effective way to go.

MYTH 2: REVIEWING, REREADING AND HIGHLIGHTING

The second key myth when it comes to creative consolidation is that reviewing, rereading and highlighting information are effective study strategies. Students believe that by just rereading the notes they have taken during the day they will consolidate their knowledge and understanding. There is now ample scientific evidence that this is not the case. Repetition gives the illusion of knowing but does not demonstrate understanding. In fact, active cognitive strategies, such as elaboration or re-representation (putting ideas into your own words or another format), generation (creating examples, analogies or metaphors to expand and understand a concept), and reflection (thinking about a topic or a class discussion which occurred that day) are significantly more effective study strategies (Wiggins & Sanjekdar, 2019).

MYTH 3: ONE AT A TIME

The third key myth is that students should only focus on one particular subject or topic in a study or consolidation session. Evidence shows that the practice of interleaving – working for a period of time on one subject before moving on to another before returning to the first – does in fact consolidate and deepen learning (Bertilsson et al., 2021).

CREATIVE ACTIONS

STRATEGIES FOR CREATIVE CONSOLIDATION

So, what does this mean for students in practical terms? Research has found that the quality of a student's consolidation materials deepens learning and is a predictor of successful academic outcomes (Friedman, 2014). David has been successfully using some of the following consolidation strategies with students and seen a significant increase in their GPA results. While these habits may take some time, being efficient and effective in the consolidation process will have positive results.

The first stage of knowledge and skill consolidation can in fact take place during the class. One simple method is colour-coding notes that have been taken. At the end of each section students should mark the section with a red tick, an orange tick or a green tick. Red represents an idea or concept that the student does not understand and need to actively research. Orange represents an idea or concept they may be uncertain about and should revise to check understanding after the class. Green is for concepts or ideas students feel comfortable with in terms of understanding. Over time students need to be able to convert their red and orange ticks to green.

With students in the senior years of high school, an ideal time to do such revision is in the breaks such as recess, lunch and immediately after school. It is extremely difficult at the end of the day for students to remember something which they were uncertain about from the first lesson of the day. Taking a few minutes to scan over their notes during the break is much more effective in identifying areas which need to be further explored. This type of revision, essentially a form of interleaving, only adds ten or twenty minutes to a student's day but has very tangible benefits. It can encourage students to ask targeted questions of their teacher and allows them to be better planners of their afternoon or evening study time.

Consolidating notes also has another purpose – that of building a sequence of knowledge and understanding that will build competency within a subject. The best way to achieve this is through a dynamic, not static, process. The student must be involved attitudinally and cognitively in the consolidation process. Building a toolkit of strategies across a number of subjects will also build confidence, self-efficacy and motivation, as students find they have resources to build on. Students will also be able to build existing connections and make new connections between ideas.

The after-school consolidation process should begin with an active and dynamic review of the notes that were taken that day. This is called retrieval practice or self-testing. This will give students a clearer picture about how they learn, consolidating existing knowledge and filling gaps in understanding. It may have been that in a lesson a student was unwilling or unable to ask a particular question, but by self-testing they can check their level of understanding. Another benefit of self-testing is that students build competencies in problem-posing. Over time this will assist students in understanding how teachers construct questions in exams.

If students are using the Cornell or T method of note-taking, they can cover up the content side of the page and use the questions and keywords as prompts for recall. They can even write their responses down and compare them to the notes they took during the class.

Another dynamic method of consolidation is for a student to work with a peer, comparing each other's notes from the day and testing each other. Since every student has a different perspective and experiences a lesson differently, this collaborative approach can be a very successful method of consolidation (Luo et al., 2016).

THE MECHANICS OF CONSOLIDATION

What is the best format to summarise notes? The answer is whatever best facilitates the learning needs of the individual student for the particular purpose and context for which the summary is created. More comprehensive summaries are an excellent way of having an overview of a topic or concepts. They are also useful when preparing an essay or an assignment. These may be presented using the Cornell or T method, serving as both revision and self-testing. It is also possible to include diagrams, images or sketch notes within the Cornell framework. The combination of images and text may aid students with understanding and active recall.

The next layer down from this may be verbal, perhaps using cue cards, or visual, using mind maps or concept maps and posters. It is essential that these forms of summary only include essential information and, if using colours or images, a clear and simple coding system that the student understands. Some students might like making their notes look as attractive as possible. However, if form overwhelms function, the summaries will not be as useful. In addition, students should use their own words to describe the content being summarised. Taking slabs of text from lengthy handwritten notes and putting them onto cue cards does not deepen learning. Rephrasing notes requires cognitive effort and deepens learning and understanding. Students may change the order of the information, the grammar and the sentence structure, but keep the meaning as well as the emphasis on and relationships between main and supporting points.

Students can also develop digital resources as summaries. Simple tools such as PowerPoint or Prezi may be an effective way to summarise notes. Students could also use animation software such as Powtoon or Minecraft Education to make short videos. Class groups can collaborate to make study videos which can be used by a whole class. The same can be true of posters which can be displayed in the classroom.

It requires effort, but it is worthwhile for students to think about and trial a variety of summarising techniques and strategies. Over the course of a school year students might present their strategies to the class and discuss how effective they were or how they might be improved. In the early years of high school, teachers can assess notes and summaries as part of the formative assessment for a subject. This will demonstrate to the students the importance of their skills and their individual strategies which suit their learning. In terms of creativity, the assessment could be based on the student trying something new and rating its relevance and usefulness. By supporting students through the process of identifying and trialling strategies, the teacher is supporting the process of building creative capacity as an independent learner. We know that creative approaches build cognitive flexibility and deepen learning. For students, achieving better outcomes builds the understanding that creative attitudes and skills can benefit much of their learning and encourages further creative exploration.

CREATIVE RETRIEVAL

At some point in time students need to demonstrate their knowledge, understanding and skills. This may be in a class discussion, a class test, an assignment or a summative written exam. What are the most effective ways to construct information so that it can be readily recalled in an assessment situation?

As cognitive science has developed over the past twenty years it has become increasingly clear that students prefer to use study techniques that are less than optimal, choosing the familiar or immediate strategy rather than taking a considered evidence-based approach (Miyatsu et al., 2018). Teachers therefore have two choices: they can either explicitly teach the study strategies which students prefer to use to increase student efficacy, or they can suggest and teach new strategies which are posited by cognitive science. Explicit instruction in how to use each of the strategies and a combination of strategies may in fact be the most effective (Nakayama, 2021; Wong et al., 2021). Retrieval is more successful if the student is actively engaged and uses trial and error when considering which strategy best suits them in a particular retrieval context (Lee, 2020). We strongly suggest that teachers actively review student notes to give feedback and support development of these skills. Table 8.5 shows some of the common errors in application of some of the retrieval strategies preferred by school-age students, and how they can be remedied.

Table 8.5: Common errors in application of retrieval strategies

Retrieval strategy	Student error	Correct approach
Using one type of retrieval strategy	Using only one type of retrieval strategy rather than a combination of strategies best suited to the content	Engage with a variety of retrieval strategies for each subject to determine which works best for the individual and the different content
Photos of teacher notes from the board in the classroom	Not engaging with the content in a meaningful way, allowing the mind to wander during the lesson, assuming the photos will be an effective retrieval prompt	Converting photos to written notes to create thorough engagement and understanding
Rewriting notes before an exam	Copying notes verbatim without review	Review notes and actively edit them, engaging with the content to ensure understanding, changing wording if necessary

Retrieval strategy	Student error	Correct approach
Cue cards	Only using cards for one successful retrieval in the same order	Randomly reorder cards and aim for at least three successful retrievals
Marking up notes	Marking up notes in the first reading and limited use of colours or symbols	Only mark up key points and terms to identify core concepts and information, while also using a variety of colours and symbols to aid retrieval
Organising notes in chronological order of delivery of topic	Assuming the final lessons are the most important in terms of content and skills	Review notes by level of individual understanding of content and skills and review gaps in knowledge
Rereading notes before an exam	Mistaking repeated reading for understanding	Use spaced retrieval reading over time and check for understanding by testing between readings

It is clear from educational and cognitive psychology that generative study is the most effective form for a range of student ages (Brod, 2020; Onanuga, 2020). Students select relevant material, which transfers information from sensory memory to working memory. They then organise incoming material into a personalised coherent internal cognitive structure, improving their working memory. Finally, they integrate connecting cognitive structures with each other and with relevant material activated from long-term memory. This is an iterative process (you can see how it relates to the process of interleaving we discussed earlier). Evidence-based strategies include summarising, mapping, drawing, imagining, self-testing, self-explaining, teaching and enacting (a number of the strategies that also have a positive impact on students' creative capacities). Each of these requires a certain amount of cognitive effort. Evidence indicates that the most effective strategies are peer-to-peer teaching, mapping strategies and imagining drawings of text (Fiorella & Mayer, 2016).

One final strategy is worth exploring. Mnemonics have been used for years as an effective recall strategy (Putnam, 2015). However, there are a variety of mnemonic strategies which can be used, as illustrated in the following table.

CREATIVE ACTIONS

Table 8.6: Descriptions of popular mnemonic techniques and systems

Mnemonic	Description
Link method	Interactive visual imagery connects items in a list, making a chain. Item 1 is joined with item 2; a separate image joins item 2 with item 3 and so on. Thus, retrieving one item in the list cues the next item.
Method of loci	First, a memory palace – a mental map of a building or walk that you know well, such as your house – is memorised. Then, imagery is used to store list items at different locations throughout that palace. Items are retrieved by 'walking' through the palace.
Peg system	A 'peg list', or a list of concrete objects in a specific order (for example, *one* is a bun, *two* is a shoe, *three* is a flea) is learned. Then, visual imagery combines the to-be-remembered items with the peg items. Items can be retrieved by thinking of a number and the corresponding peg, which cues the target item.
Keyword method	First, a keyword is found that sounds like the unfamiliar word (for example, *dentist* sounds like *la dent*). Then imagery joins the keyword with the definition of the unfamiliar word (an image of a dentist holding a large tooth). Seeing la dent activates dentist, which in turn should activate tooth.
Phonetic system	Each number corresponds to a consonant sound (1 = t, 2 = n, 3 = m etc.) Then numbers can be remembered as words, using vowels as necessary. For example, 321 can be remembered as *manatee*. Words can be decoded back into numbers.
Acronyms	The first letter of a list of words are used to create a new word. For example, the colours of the rainbow (red, orange, yellow, green, blue indigo and violet) can be remembered as ROYGBIV. Each letter serves as a retrieval cue for the target items.
Acrostics	The first letters in a list of words serve as the first letters in a new sentence or phrase. For example, the colours of the rainbow can be remembered as Richard Of York Gave Battle In Vain. The first letter in each word of the acrostic serves as a retrieval cue.
Songs, stories and rhymes	Words in a list are joined together by being elements in a story, or by being included in a song or rhyme. Songs and rhymes can also be written to remember specific pieces of information (for example, *i* before *e* except after *c*).

SOURCE: Putnam, 2015, p. 131. Used with permission.

James has been experimenting with a variety of these strategies with students. He found that students need to try two or three different mnemonic methods before finding the one which suited them best individually. One student was struggling to remember the sequence of events that led to the French Revolution. James discovered that they took a bus to and from school each day. The student drew a rough map of their journey and highlighted some key locations on the way. Each location represented a key event which led to the revolution. While the student was travelling to and from school, they would look out the bus window and connect the location with the event by imagining a large sign placed on the building. After a week of bus journeys, the student had embedded the sequence of events in their memory. In the weeks leading up to their final exam, in the spirit of interleaving and retrieval practice, the student would repeat the exercise. This method worked very well for this particular student, and they received an excellent result in their exam.

Visual mnemonics, known as the croque method, is a method of symbolisation or picture writing. When children draw sketch diagrams of objects, animals, people, phenomena or concepts, they store in memory everything that they have sketched. When working on the croque method, several complex thought processes are simultaneously turned on at once.

CONCLUSION

We finish this chapter by tying it to the four elements that make up creativity. For students to be effective independent learners, they need the opportunity to experience and trial the processes of transfer, consolidation and retrieval mentioned throughout the chapter. However, processes do not happen in isolation. They also need the most appropriate physical and social environments for learning to be effective, the right attitudes and attributes, and clear long-term and short-term goals in terms of the outcomes of any period of study. Students should also aim to incorporate the evidence-based strategies mentioned in this chapter, rather than just copying out notes.

You can see in this chapter that many of the attitudes, attributes, processes and environments related to building capacity and competency in creativity are also related to building capacity and competency in student independent learning. Once again, we stress that if each teacher in a school takes a small amount of responsibility for giving students new tools to use and the opportunities to practise them, students will build their creative and independent learning competencies incrementally over the six years of high school. This investment of time and expertise will benefit students, not only in their academic outcomes but also in life after school.

CHAPTER 9

THE CREATIVE PARENT: HOW CAN FAMILIES BUILD CREATIVE COMPETENCIES IN THEIR CHILDREN?

When conducting parent–teacher interviews, Tim asks parents if they solved any problems at work that day, came up with new ideas, used critical thinking, or collaborated with colleagues. They usually answer in the affirmative, at which point he asks how they developed those skills. The answer is usually something like 'The school of life, but I wish I knew more about these things before I started working.' Often the examples parents give from their work or family life are new to the students. These conversations give both students and parents a clear understanding of why creative competencies must be integrated into school education. It also opens a new doorway of conversation in the family.

Just as students learn things at school, they also learn things at home. We know that the home learning environment has a significant impact on student learning outcomes and social development (Lehrl et al., 2020). Research shows that if parents are aware of the science of creativity and given examples of how it might be applied in their home, their children's creative attitudes and skills develop more quickly (Jankowska & Karwowski, 2019). Schools and teachers can help parents become aware of the science of creativity.

Throughout this book we have tried to take an asset-based rather than a deficit-based approach towards building creativity in students, focusing on strengths rather than weaknesses. We understand that life is becoming increasingly complex as the ubiquitous use of digital devices enters education, and with COVID-19 having disrupted parenting and education models that have developed over the last fifty years. This is not a chapter about how to parent; it is rather about the elements of life in the home and family relationships that can have a positive impact on a child developing their creativity.

We will now look at the four key elements that make up creativity – environment, attitudes, processes and outcomes – and how they can be influenced and supported by parents.

PARENTING AND THE CREATIVE ENVIRONMENT

The home environment is multi-faceted, combining both the physical and social environments of family life. Family dynamics are very important and vary significantly depending on context. Parents may act as instructors, demonstrators, facilitators or collaborators with their children. These roles are often quite fluid, changing depending on time and circumstance. It is in the home environment that children first experience creativity; for the majority of children, the home environment is far more creative than the school environment (Zielińska, 2020). When discussing creativity with students it is often useful to start with their own experiences of creativity outside school and in the home.

For all of us, our first exposure to creativity is mini-c creativity: personal creativity in everyday activities (Kaufman & Beghetto, 2009). Children build an understanding of the world through play, imagination, exploration, and experimentation. This ongoing journey of discovery means children experience new insights or thoughts that they feel are creative. As we have stressed throughout the book, creativity can happen in any element of life at any time. Having a resource-rich home environment is a good way to stimulate creativity in children; they can explore, manipulate, imagine and construct. For instance, if giving a child a new toy, you do not need to show them how it works. If they use the toy in an unexpected and imaginative way (but also appropriate – we do not mean swallowing it or using it inappropriately as a projectile), allow them to enjoy the process of exploration. Openness to new experience is a key personal characteristic of creativity and needs to be encouraged throughout one's life. Children should also be exposed to a broad variety of physical and social environments during their upbringing, from walks in nature, to experiencing foods, music, sport, and pastimes as well as art and literature from a variety of cultures.

Another key element to developing creativity as an individual is having a sense of psychological safety in their environment (Pugsley & Acar, 2020). Psychological safety means that children are free to express their ideas without purely negative external evaluation or judgement, and that parents have a sense of empathy for their child exploring their creativity (Fearon et al., 2013). This does not mean, of course, that parents should feel as though they can never give feedback on their children's creative activities. Teachers can discuss with parents how children can build their creative capacities at home and approaches parents might like to take to facilitate this. For example, a teacher might discuss problem-solving activities occurring in the classroom or explain the use of open-ended questions to stimulate imagination and curiosity. Parents can also be encouraged to explore nature with their children, loose-parts play (objects that can be combined without being permanently joined) or joining as a participant in their child's play rather than leading or instructing, and allowing their child to determine the direction and materials of the play.

THE DIGITAL HOME ENVIRONMENT AND CREATIVITY

Digital devices are becoming ubiquitous around the globe, with young children having access to various types of screens from an increasingly early age. There is much gloom and doom, particularly in popular media, about how screens are dumbing down our youth, but it would be foolish for us to suggest that children be prohibited from using any type of screen. Our view is that digital devices are like any other tool or object – the purpose and function need to be understood by the user and they must be used appropriately within context.

A recent study of over 4000 Australian children explored the contexts in which children use screens over a four-year period (Sanders et al., 2019). They identified four different types of screen use: social screen time such as social media; passive screen time such as television or YouTube; interactive screen time such as video games; and educational screen time such as using a computer for homework. They reported that the type of screen time had a greater impact on children's academic performance than the amount of screen time. Educational screen time had positive effects on children's persistence and educational outcomes, and no significant negative effects on psychological or health outcomes. Interactive screen time showed unfavourable temperament outcomes and worse socioemotional outcomes. Social screen time was associated with poorer health-related quality of life, heightened reaction to stress and worse socioemotional outcomes. These findings have significant implications for creativity, which requires persistence, a healthy psychology and temperament suited to positive collaboration with others. It is certainly worth parents discussing with their children the ways in which different types of screen functionality can be used and the impact that it may have on their children's lives. Such information could be conveyed by teachers in a school newsletter or mentioned during parent teacher interviews. Even something as simple as encouraging parents to engage in educational screen time at home with their children could have positive benefits.

For primary school students, digital devices such as tablets can enhance students' reading and writing development, as information can be delivered in a variety of colours and formats, giving students greater variety as they receive information (Flewitt et al., 2015). Digital game-based learning devised by educators has been shown to enhance the problem-solving abilities of three- to six-year-olds (Behnamnia et al., 2020). Studies of older children and adults have shown that video games, particularly but not exclusively educational ones, can have positive effects on creativity (Green & Kaufman, 2015).

Parents can also demonstrate digital creativity by showing their children new and useful ways to use digital tools (Pérez-Fuentes et al., 2019). One of the unexpected benefits of lockdowns and remote learning was that children got to see how their parents work, in particular their opportunities for creativity. Teachers can encourage students to ask their parents how they solve problems in the digital world and the creative ways in which they use digital tools.

In terms of the other ways that schools can influence parents, most schools have some form of communication forum, physical or online. Most parents like to know that the school understands current research trends in education and are willing to help their children succeed in any way possible. A simple paragraph outlining how both the time and type of digital interaction affect children's learning would be appropriate in such communication. It can also be tailored to the digital tools students are using at each year level.

PARENTING AND THE ATTITUDES AND ATTRIBUTES OF CREATIVITY

Parental attitudes demonstrated during early childhood can have an impact up to and including adolescence (Fang & Shen, 2021). Parental attitudes toward creativity are no exception. There is ample evidence from the literature that an authoritarian parenting style increases the chance of children developing maladaptive perfectionism and lower levels of creativity (Miller et al., 2012). Demonstrating attitudes such as enthusiasm, curiosity (and intellectual curiosity), openness to new experience, sensible risk-taking and perseverance encourage children to also adopt these attributes. By supporting and praising these attitudes when demonstrated by children, parents can help build and maintain their child's creativity.

Encouraging parents to read to their children, and eventually have the children read to them, is an excellent way to stimulate imagination, curiosity and creativity. Children can also create their own stories and act them out through drama and role-play, which has been shown to enhance creative thinking skills in school-age children (Celume et al., 2019).

Another relatively simple method of building a child's curiosity is to ask open-ended questions. Questioning is a prelude to creative thinking. Asking questions such as 'Why?', 'What if …?', 'How do you think …?', or 'Can you describe …', give children confidence in both their thinking and communication skills. As children get older they can be asked more abstract questions and begin to develop qualities such as tolerance for ambiguity. It is also important to admit to children that sometimes you don't know something and that perhaps you could work together to find it out.

Children also need to develop a sense of creative self-efficacy – the belief that they are capable of being creative. Parents who support child autonomy from an early age produce children with a higher sense of creative self-efficacy and higher academic outcomes (Liang & Yuan, 2020; Vansteenkiste et al., 2010). Children with more supportive parents are also likely to be able to be more comfortable and confident in social situations, thus improving their collaboration and problem-solving skills in group creativity (Zhang et al., 2018).

MOTIVATION AND ENGAGEMENT

Children can also be creative in their recreational life, whether that be in sports, hobbies or the arts. At some point in time most children find something they are interested in and then captivated by. This desire to explore an interest further is part of the transition from mini-c to little-c creativity. Rather than just enjoying something as an experience, children desire to learn more and to build their knowledge and skills. In some cases, this may be a passing phase and for others it could be a passion for the rest of their life. In terms of creativity, it is preferable that parents are supportive of their children's choices. This type of creativity is often under recognised and undervalued (Zielińska, 2020), yet it is where children and adolescents (and adults) initially feel most comfortable as creative individuals. It is also where they have their first experience of intrinsic rather than extrinsic motivation.

In Zielińska's 2020 study involving over a thousand students in Poland, children and adolescents revealed a rich diversity across approximately seventy activities that they considered to be creative. The majority of participants took part in at least one activity they considered to be creative, with three out of four of these activities taking place outside of school. This paper supported the findings of Agnoli and colleagues (2018), with students reporting intrinsic motivation in their activities outside of school and extrinsic motivation of most of their activities within school. If children show higher levels of intrinsic motivation, they are more open to receiving feedback. In discussions between parents and their adolescent children, it is important that their intrinsic motivation and their creativity are acknowledged and supported. Parallels can then be drawn between the differences in their attitudes and behaviours in recreational versus academic activities, since adolescents have different perceptions about evaluation and feedback between subject areas. It is also important that parents show enthusiasm for the subjects which their children do at school. Parental enthusiasm has been shown to improve both motivation and academic outcomes in STEM subjects (Jungert et al., 2020). There will certainly be many school subjects which parents are not enthusiastic about, but sometimes a personal view needs to be set aside and students encouraged to explore the potential value that any subject may offer them. And most parents are, at least, enthusiastic about their child's happiness.

Tim wondered why there appeared to be a link between students who play a musical instrument and academic achievement (Guhn et al., 2020). Initially it was suggested that this was because learning an instrument took so much time that the students needed to be very efficient with the rest of their time, and therefore better at studying and getting better results. It now appears that the reason may be the concept of motivational spill-over, where a high level of intrinsic motivation in one area of life spills over into others (Pierce et al., 2016). Learning an instrument also requires persistence and enables children to build a sense of mastery. Practising an instrument also develops a sense of autonomy as well as a sense of wellbeing (Guhn et al., 2020; Patston & Waters, 2015). Adolescents who are highly motivated are also more likely to have higher levels of intellectual risk-taking, which in turn improves both creativity and academic outcomes (Beghetto, 2009). When speaking to parents about why children should learn a musical instrument, schools often talk about the social benefits. By demonstrating that learning a musical instrument has other tangible benefits in terms of motivation, autonomy and mastery, and has a positive impact on academic outcomes, teachers can present a more compelling argument.

The creative identity and creative self-efficacy of parents may also have an impact on their child's creativity (Lebuda et al., 2020). Parents with a strong creative identity and sense of creative self-efficacy are more likely to have a positive home environment, and encourage novelty, fantasy and perseverance in their children. It is worth parents explaining to their children why they have particular interests and hobbies or passions, and how they express their creativity through these activities. They could also discuss how solving a problem in a recreational pursuit or showing perseverance in a hobby was useful in their working lives or in the family environment. As the school helps parents build their understanding of creativity, they can personalise their creative experiences to their children. Over time, as students build their creative capacities, they may in fact be able to help their parents build better attitudes towards creativity and become more effective and efficient problem-solvers.

HOW PARENTS CAN SUPPORT CREATIVITY

The following table, adapted from Cropley (2014), demonstrates what parents can do to encourage their children's creative capacity and also how to do it. The following questions are phrased for the middle primary level but could be adapted for older students. Using the language of pedagogy and the terminology used in the book with both students and parents can help the learning to transfer at home.

In the following example, students were asked to try and work out what a particular object is without touching it. Teachers could use this investigation to create a brief video for parents to help students with their problem-solving activities at home. This investigation includes a number of features of the social environment, the attitudes and attributes, the processes and the outcomes of creativity. By putting them in a logical sequence and applying them to one particular task, it gives parents an idea of how many elements and aspects of creativity there are. It also demonstrates to them how they can help to build these elements and aspects in their children.

Table 9.1: Developing children's creative capacity

Keys to develop children's creativity	Practical responses and strategies
WHAT?	HOW?
Redefine or break down the problem	What has to be done to solve this problem? At this stage, any success criteria should be open-ended and stated in general terms only. For example, what are some of the first things you might need to think about when trying to solve this problem?

Keys to develop children's creativity	Practical responses and strategies
WHAT?	**HOW?**
Question and analyse any assumptions you might make	You might give some constraints here but encourage the students to ask questions. For example, you might ask a student not to touch the object with their body. The student might ask 'Can I touch it with a tool such as a pencil?' These types of questions represent the beginning of intellectual curiosity in students.
Justify your creative thinking	After generating an idea students need to justify what they have done. For example, you could ask 'Why did you put foil around the pencil before you touched the object?'
Encourage idea generation	Children need to get used to asking more than one question when trying to solve a problem. For example, if the student is stuck you might ask them 'What else could you touch the object with to find out something more about it?'
The role of knowledge	Pre-existing knowledge is essential when people are trying to be creative. Often students struggle with what we call functional fixedness, the idea that an object can only be used for one purpose. You might ask the student 'What else have you seen that looks or feels like this?' to stimulate new ideas.
Overcoming obstacles	Problem-solving consists of several steps and students might struggle with certain parts of the process. If open-ended questioning doesn't work, perhaps go back a step. Sometimes just restating the problem will help students overcome a block. Any new attempts to overcome the obstacle should be praised and encouraged.

continued ...

CREATIVE ACTIONS

Keys to develop children's creativity **WHAT?**	Practical responses and strategies **HOW?**
Encourage sensible risk-taking	Students should be encouraged to explore when problem-solving. Using the object example, depending on what the object is, you may ask the students find out how much it weighs without using a scale. If they suggest putting it in water to see how much water is displaced, you might first suggest they put a drop of water on the object to see if it causes a reaction.
Encourage tolerance for ambiguity	In chemistry objects can be solid, liquid or gas, or sometimes a combination, such as quicksand. When faced with uncertainty, students can either immediately exclude an option or include an option. Encourage them to explore a range of options no matter how ambiguous they may seem.
Build creative self-efficacy	Sometimes the processes of creativity can appear quite daunting and students may begin to doubt themselves. By showing them that you are open to a large range of ideas, they are building their skills in idea generation and their confidence. Compliment a student if they have come up with an idea that no one else thought of.
Find out what excites them	Many students like the process of being a detective when trying to solve a problem. In this example, students were given an object and needed to use their deductive reasoning skills to find out what it was. Students were much more engaged in this process than being given a lecture on the different states of matter. Encourage parents to ask their children what excites them and what they are curious about. They could even say something like 'I am curious about fish and have learnt a lot of interesting things. What are you curious about?'

Keys to develop children's creativity	Practical responses and strategies
WHAT?	**HOW?**
The importance of delayed gratification	Students need to understand that resilience is an important tool when being creative. Offering extrinsic rewards, such as 'If you solve this problem in five minutes you can watch television', encourage hasty thinking and do not build students capacity for cognitive load. The satisfaction from solving a difficult problem is sufficient reward.
Provide a favourable environment	Many parents speak too often and make too many suggestions when their students are solving problems. That could be because they want to help or because they get impatient with how their children are solving a particular problem. Try and put students under minimal time pressure. Offer positive, constructive and encouraging feedback. Focus on what has been achieved rather than what hasn't and use the problem-solving process to demonstrate the importance of resilience in all aspects of life.

SOURCE: Adapted from Cropley, 2014, pp. 16–19. Used with permission.

CONCLUSION

Young children are curious, inquisitive, resilient and playful – all positive personal characteristics of creativity. By striving to maintain these qualities through exploration, modelling, consistency and humour, parents can build their children's creative competencies for life. It is also possible for schools and individual teachers to communicate with parents and support them in understanding and developing their own creativity and that of their children.

CHAPTER 10

WHERE TO FROM HERE?

> *The current economic environment is characterized by a high speed of development, where the need to generate and implement novel and useful ideas is not considered a competitive advantage but rather a necessity for survival.* (Liu et al., 2021, p. 129)

> *Teachers are intelligent professionals who desire to improve their pedagogy of many years, adapting to change – in fact, leading change by trialling new ideas – and improving the education and engagement of students.* (Patston, 2015, p. 10)

These ideas summarise both the future of work and the future of education, and touch on two important reasons we wrote this book. We know the future is about change, and we know that teachers are willing to change; they just need the skills, tools, opportunities and support to make change happen.

In writing this book, we have been heartened by how many examples of creativity in education there are around the world. In fact, during the COVID-19 pandemic individual creativity flourished as the changing domestic environment and isolation led to new attitudes and ways of problem-solving. People found new and useful ways to manage learning and working from home. The collaborative approach to finding vaccines showed human creativity and innovation at their very best. In education, the rapid transition to online learning once again showed that teachers are leading change by trialling new ideas. They actively explored and then demonstrated new creative pedagogies (not all of them digital). Students found creative solutions to learning in different physical and social environments. We must continue to support them to do so.

THE FUTURE OF WORK

We know that success in the workplace is not the only goal of education or the only setting where people must be creative. However, many people will spend a large portion of their time in the workplace, and the workplace is where many challenges humans face will be addressed.

When people talk about the future of work, it is often with a sense of fear and trepidation. Will their job be replaced by a robot or even exist at all? Given the rapid rise of technology and the fact that we now live in a truly global economy, these fears may seem reasonable. We would argue that while technological change is indeed rapid, and brings with it many challenges, there will always be a need for human input in most elements of work. But two questions do need to be asked: What jobs will people perform in the future? and What skills will be needed to perform these jobs? We discussed this in Chapter 1 as a reason that creativity is now *essential*.

Humans are both creative and adaptive. Historically, while technological change may destroy jobs, it does generate new ones. The OECD (2019a) and the World Economic Forum (2020), while acknowledging the disruptive qualities of technology, believe that the future of work is in human qualities and attitudes (such as the creative attitudes and attributes discussed in this book). Humans will need to learn, unlearn and relearn (Ra et al., 2019). In other words, they will need education.

This broader impact also extends to the kind of activities within industries. In the past, automation has mostly impacted predictable physical work – a robot arm could replace a human within a simple production line. However, automation, thanks to the addition of artificial intelligence, is now also able to perform a wide range of activities including cognitive tasks. The reason many jobs are automatable is because they are routine, algorithmic, predictable or analytical in nature. Tasks that are now within the capability of artificial intelligence.

This means that the unpredictable, more cognitive and less routine tasks become the focus of human work. Humans do the things that artificial intelligence and automation cannot, including complex problem-solving, negotiation, decision-making under uncertainty, communication, empathy, and … creativity. The reason we focus on creativity as the key is that it is integral to many of the other elements on this list. Creativity is, at its core, about developing novel and useful solutions to problems. The ability to do this depends on a complex combination of who we are, where we work or study and how we think.

Once we put creativity into a professional or educational context, we can expand the view of creativity mentioned throughout this book. In addition to the person (attitudes and dispositions), cognitive skills (process) and the social and physical environment, creativity also depends on domain knowledge – for example, knowledge of mathematics or physics – and on other domain-specific skills (perhaps the ability to code). The important thing about this expanded view is that this defines a competency. We strongly favour looking at creativity in this way (as a competency and not merely a skill). Skills are specific, narrow and often not transferable, whereas competencies are broader, general and transferable. Competencies represent the application of skills in a practical setting. Whether cognitive (involving ideas), technical (involving, for example, manual activities) or interpersonal (involving people), competencies represent a combination of skills, abilities, dispositions and knowledge. The ability to find new and effective solutions to problems is exactly that. It is a vital, broad, transferable twenty-first century competency.

However, we see challenges with this future. At the same time as the need for creativity is growing, global workplaces are hampered by not only a shortage of workers but also a shortage of the right kind of workers with diversity central to creative problem-solving. If, as a society, we are going to solve the challenging problems that arise from continuous and rapid change, we need to tap into all of the available creative problem-solving resources at our disposal. Otherwise, we fear another risk to the future of work could be an ideas recession.

The good news, in our opinion, is that it is entirely within our capacity to solve this. Of course, the issue of preparing the next generation of learners, who will become workers, is a complex problem, and there are already many initiatives seeking to address this. The challenge is doing these things within the constraints of the curriculum and the expectations of authorities, parents and administrators. This is the main reason why the examples in this book are structured through the lens of subjects. Despite ongoing calls across the world to blow up the traditional model of education, the reality is that change at the system-level is glacial. All the suggestions in the book can be implemented within current curriculum and subject structures.

As the world continues to change, there will always be problems that require new and creative solutions. The growth of artificial intelligence and automation will drive us further towards a focus on science, technology, engineering and mathematics (STEM) occupations, with many jobs of the future focused on creative problem-solving in these areas. Virtually all workers, from cleaners to cardiologists, will have to understand their relationship with digital technology. If we are to avoid an ideas recession, we need to ensure that students are well versed in the attitudes and processes of creativity.

This discussion hammers home the importance of treating creativity not as a skill but as a competency. The first step in achieving this, we think, may be a fundamental rebranding of education. We know that's easier said than done, but the rationale behind this is that as long as the essential twenty-first century competencies are secondary, we won't be able to fix the problem. In the case of young learners, we think this rebranding is also an essential element of retaining them and keeping them engaged.

THE FUTURE OF EDUCATION

> *Education policy makers must support the laborious task of improving teachers' competences and classroom environment while simultaneously providing teachers with due respect and trust in relation to their crucial roles in society.* (Sotiriou et al., 2020, para. 24)

> *Students who used their phones in class took fewer notes and had poorer overall academic performance, compared to those who did not.* (Tanil & Yong, 2020, para. 2)

These quotes summarise two key challenges relating to the future of education. Calls for breaking the model of education have echoed since the beginning of national education systems.

However, as we have constantly stressed throughout this book, change at the government or systems level in education is incredibly slow. Governments and education departments know that their citizens need educating and that current methods of schooling can provide literacy, numeracy and a sense of citizenship. These methods culminate in some kind of standardised test or assessment at the end of around twelve years schooling (or less in some countries), after which students begin work or further study. We believe that this model is not under threat; rather, the model and modes of delivery and assessment are under threat. This is where teachers need support.

We know, that around the globe, employers are concerned with the lack of practical human skills university graduates develop during their courses, and universities are disappointed with the level of these skills students bring from their schooling. So, how can this situation be fixed?

While there may be a perception that online delivery of education is a panacea, international pedagogic practice has not kept up with the pace of technological change (Dhawan, 2020). We also believe that this is not the fault of the teachers, rather of an inflexible, slow-moving system, where international league tables appear to have become drivers of education.

Hopefully, some of the answers lie in this book. In an ideal world, teachers would be offered professional development to build both their digital literacy and their creative competencies in pedagogy. Education systems would find a way to document the developmental progression of creative competencies and to value these in their final documentation, which students would then use for employment or further study. Tim is currently trialling such documentation in schools in Australia.

There are certainly hotspots of activity in these areas throughout the world. Many universities and some schools are moving towards a micro-credential or portfolio model in 'soft skills', although there is increasing confusion as to what this term actually means (Touloumakos, 2020). Unfortunately, these micro-credentials tend to be generic rather than specific to a particular subject or discipline. As we have stressed throughout the book, creativity is a system that varies according to the context or subject and needs to be taught and learned as such. A student who has demonstrated problem-solving and critical thinking in science will still need to experience problem-solving in English.

Another proposed future of education lies in changing the subjects that are taught in schools. The movement towards so called inquiry or real-world learning, which gained popularity in many countries, is now coming under question. The original open inquiry model, which relied on students having the attitudes, skills and knowledge to be independent learners, is gradually being replaced by a scaffolded inquiry model (Cairns, 2019). The reason is that students need literacies, knowledge and skills to conduct research-based inquiry. In other words, they need competencies.

We clearly favour a competency-based approach toward teaching and learning, as evidenced by the many examples in the book. There are times in the classroom when students need explicit instruction, whether in how to read, how to write, how to count or how to learn the various methods of problem-solving. The systems-based approach toward creativity covers the skills, abilities, dispositions and knowledge needed to be creative. These can be taught concurrently with the skills, abilities, dispositions and knowledge in the context of any subject.

THE FUTURE OF CREATIVITY IN EDUCATION

> "*Artificial systems do not need to mimic the attitudes, behaviours, or actions of the creative human. They must replicate only the cognitive process and the result.*" (Cropley et al., 2021, p. 4–5)

The science of creativity is booming. Never before have so many papers been published in the field. Countries around the globe have included creativity in their curriculum statements. The authors of this book are developing and trialling measures and assessment of creative competencies in individual subject areas.

The future for creativity in education is a question of application. Thanks to the catalysing effect of digital transformation, creativity theory is now driving the development of the tools that teachers need. Faced with the task of ensuring that children leave school equipped not only with the traditional hard skills (for example, the three Rs) but also with the vital cross-functional competencies such as creativity, teachers need to know *what* creativity is as well as *how to develop i*t. As the digital transformation continues to grow, teachers need to be able to recognise, foster and measure creativity across every part of the curriculum.

A key to this process may be that researchers have to leave behind certain debates for the sake of facilitating this application. For example, does it matter to teachers whether creativity is a general competency spanning all subjects, or unique to each subject, or some complex combination of the two? Or do teachers simply need tools that allow them to assess, quickly and accurately, whether or not a child shows some sort of psychological preference for new ideas; is able to think in ways that lead to the generation of many possible solutions to a problem; and can actually produce something that is creative? Furthermore, teachers need to know if anything they are doing, or anything in the school environment, is impeding creativity.

Fortunately, as the focus on creativity in education grows, the demands of end-users are leading to the development of the kinds of tools needed. Measuring instruments that answer statistical research questions are being transformed into tools, in the language of the end-users, that are more streamlined and practical. Not only that, but the same technologies that are driving digital transformation are themselves driving changes to how creativity is assessed in school settings. For example, the growing field of learning analytics is seeing the development of approaches that integrate measurement, evaluation and feedback into the normal, everyday classroom activities of teachers and students. Instead of interrupting the flow of learning, learning analytics is making it possible to monitor and foster creativity as a seamless part of the learning process.

Simultaneously, the same digital technologies are also transforming creativity assessment of a more general kind. Even with the best will in the world, there are times when more intrusive assessments are needed. These present two challenges. First, they interrupt the learning process which, for many teachers, is already crowded. Second, they are frequently slow to administer, costly to analyse and the results are often only available after a long delay, meaning that any opportunity to make use of the results in a formative manner is lost. In the past, this has been a significant barrier to the application described in this section. If the assessment is intrusive, costly and unhelpful, the easiest decision for schools and teachers is to not use it. However, emerging research is giving new impetus to this issue. New creativity assessment processes are turning previously cumbersome creativity tests into fast, accurate, and therefore much more useful, formative assessments.

Two examples show what is now possible, both in how the tests can be used and in the kinds of information they can deliver. Firstly, one of the long-standing forms of general creativity test uses a drawing activity to assess elements such as divergent thinking, openness, risk-taking and novelty. Students draw a picture based on a pre-existing set of shapes. Such tests can now be scored by a neural network (a form of artificial intelligence) and can do so as accurately as a human (Cropley and Marrone, 2022). Critically, the artificial intelligence can score this type of test instantaneously, where a human might take fifteen to twenty minutes. The advantages are self-evident. Artificial intelligence is now also helping to produce creativity tests that are more specific in nature. For example, computational methods can now assess written responses (such as lists of words or captions for a picture) with high speed and accuracy. Our research continues to apply similar innovations to the assessment of creativity in responses to mathematics, science, verbal and divergent thinking questions, and no doubt other subject areas will follow.

We are now seeing the application of creativity research in the form of more streamlined, user-friendly, fast and seamless assessment tools for teachers. We are witnessing the development of learning analytics systems as a way to integrate creativity, and other cross functional skills, into a busy curriculum. Coupled with the pressure to respond that is coming out of digital transformation, we can see, in fact, a bright future for creativity in education.

So how does this all fit together in the classroom for teachers? We believe that teachers have the attitude and motivation to build their own creative competencies and those of their students. We believe that as employers and tertiary providers increasingly insist for evidence of these creative competencies, they will become an essential and integral part of school education.

While the global pandemic has shone a light on human resilience, adaptability and perseverance, it has also shone a light on some of the systemic problems facing education.

WHERE TO FROM HERE?

We believe that the key to successfully moving to a more creative future in education begins with the teachers. In this book we have demonstrated that the system of creativity is already building creative competencies in students and teachers around the world. As teachers grow in confidence and skills, feeling psychologically safe enough to explore new pedagogies into the classroom, students will become critical and creative thinkers, collaborative problem-solvers, and take openness and curiosity into the world. Nothing we have suggested in this book could not be implemented in a classroom tomorrow. Nothing we have suggested in this book would do anything other than improve academic results of students and prepare them more thoroughly for their future after school, whether that be in education or work.

The history of the human race is the history of creativity. It will also be its future.

REFERENCES

Agnoli, S., Runco, M. A., Kirsch, C., & Corazza, G. E. (2018). The role of motivation in the prediction of creative achievement inside and outside of school environment. *Thinking Skills and Creativity*, *28*, 167–176. https://doi.org/10.1016/j.tsc.2018.05.005

Aguilar, D., & Pifarre Turmo, M. (2019). Promoting social creativity in science education with digital technology to overcome inequalities: A scoping review. *Frontiers in Psychology*, *10*, 1474. https://doi.org/10.3389/fpsyg.2019.01474

Aiamy, M., & Haghani, F. (2012). The effect of synectics & brainstorming on 3rd grade students' development of creative thinking on science. *Procedia – Social and Behavioral Sciences*, *47*, 610–613. https://doi.org/10.1016/j.sbspro.2012.06.704

Al-Abdali, N. S., Al-Balushi, S. M. (2016). Teaching for creativity by science teachers in grades 5–10. *International Journal of Science and Mathematics Education*, *14*, 251–268. https://doi.org/10.1007/s10763-014-9612-3

Alawad, A. (2012). How to influence students' risk-taking behaviour in order to enhance their creative and critical thinking processes. *Life Science Journal*, *9*, 4483–4443. http://www.lifesciencesite.com/lsj/life0904/669_12384life0904_4438_4443.pdf

Al-Jaradat, M. K. M., & Zaid-Alkilani, K. K. (2015). Successful leadership practices in school problem-solving by the principals of the secondary schools in Irbid Educational Area. *Review of European Studies*, *7*(3), 20–32. http://dx.doi.org/10.5539/res.v7n3p20

Allen, K.-A., & van der Zwan, R. (2019). The myth of left- vs right-brain learning. *International Journal of Innovation, Creativity and Change*, *5*(1), 189–200. https://www.ijicc.net/index.php/volume-5-2019/51-vol-5-iss-1

Allen, R. F. (2016). Fostering a school culture and climate where creativity can thrive: A case study of an international school principal. *Theses and Dissertations – Education Science*, *19*. https://doi.org/10.13023/ETD.2016.456

Allsopp, D. H. (1997). Using classwide peer tutoring to teach beginning algebra problem-solving skills in heterogeneous classrooms. *Remedial and Special Education*, *18*(6), 367–379. https://doi.org/10.1177/074193259701800606

Almahameed, Y. S. (2020). Resolving lexical and structural ambiguity by Jordanian learners of English. *Journal of Critical Reviews*, *7*(8), 2565–2573. http://www.jcreview.com/admin/Uploads/Files/61c9bc66423a74.09059604.pdf

Al-Omari, A. A. H., & Al-Dhoon, B. A. (2020). The impact of e-mind mapping strategy and learning styles on the achievement of the tenth-grade students in biology. *Universal Journal of Educational Research*, *8*(12), 6429–6438, 2020. https://doi.org/10.13189/ujer.2020.081208

Alzu'bi, M. A. (2019). The influence of suggested Cornell note-taking method on improving writing composition skills of Jordanian EFL learners. *Journal of Language Teaching and Research*, *10*(4), 863–871. https://doi.org/10.17507/jltr.1004.26

Amabile, T. M. (1979). Effects of external evaluation on artistic creativity. *Journal of personality and social psychology*, *37*(2), 221–233. https://doi.org/10.1037/0022-3514.37.2.221

Amabile, T. M. (1982). Social psychology of creativity: A consensual assessment technique. *Journal of Personality and Social Psychology*, *43*(5), 997–1013. https://doi.org/10.1037/0022-3514.43.5.997

Amabile, T. M. (1996). *Creativity in context: Update to "The Social Psychology of Creativity."* Westview Press.

Amabile, T. M. (1998). *How to kill creativity*. Harvard Business Review. https://hbr.org/1998/09/how-to-kill-creativity

Amabile, T. M. (2013). Componential theory of creativity. In E. H. Kessler (Ed.), *Encyclopedia of management theory* (pp. 134–139). Sage Publications. http://dx.doi.org/10.4135/9781452276090.n42

REFERENCES

Amabile, T. M., & Pratt, M. G. (2016). *The dynamic componential model of creativity and innovation in organizations: Making progress, making meaning. Research in Organizational Behavior, 36*, 157–183. https://doi.org/10.1016/j.riob.2016.10.001

Andrade, H. L. (2019). A critical review of research on student self-assessment. *Frontiers in Education, 4*, Article 87. https://doi.org/10.3389/feduc.2019.00087

Apriliani, L. R., Suyitno, H., & Rochmad, R. (2016). Analyze of mathematical creative thinking ability based on math anxiety in creative problem solving model with SCAMPER technique. *Proceeding of ICMSE, 3*(1), 131–141.

Aragón-Mendizábal, E., Delgado-Casas, C., Navarro-Guzmán, J.-I., Menacho-Jiménez, I., & Romero-Oliva, M.-F. (2016). A comparative study of handwriting and computer typing in note-taking by university students. *Comunicar, 24*(48), 101–107. https://doi.org/10.3916/C48-2016-10

Arthurs, L. A., & Bailey B. Z. (2017). An integrative review of in-class activities that enable active learning in college science classroom settings, *International Journal of Science Education, 39*(15), 2073–2091. https://doi.org/10.1080/09500693.2017.1363925

Asselanis, S. M. (2017). Effective note taking strategies in the secondary mathematics classroom [Master's Thesis, University of Mary Washington]. *Eagle Scholar.* https://scholar.umw.edu/student_research/206

Astutik, S., & Mahardika, I. K. (2020). HOTS student worksheet to identification of scientific creativity skill, critical thinking skill and creative thinking skill in physics learning. *Journal of Physics: Conference Series, 1465*, Article 012075. https://doi.org/10.1088/1742-6596/1465/1/012075

Auger, P., & Woodman, R. W. (2016). Creativity and intrinsic motivation: Exploring a complex relationship. *The Journal of Applied Behavioral Science, 52*(3), 342–366. https://doi.org/10.1177/0021886316656973

Azer S. A. (2005). The qualities of a good teacher: how can they be acquired and sustained? *Journal of the Royal Society of Medicine, 98*(2), 67–69. https://doi.org/10.1258/jrsm.98.2.67

Baas, M., Koch, S., Nijstad, B. A., & De Dreu, C. K. W. (2015). Conceiving creativity: The nature and consequences of laypeople's beliefs about the realization of creativity. *Psychology of Aesthetics, Creativity, and the Arts, 9*(3), 340–354. https://doi.org/10.1037/a0039420

Baek, Y., & Touati, A. (2020). Comparing collaborative and cooperative gameplay for academic and gaming achievements. *Journal of Educational Computing Research, 57*(8), 2110–2140. https://doi.org/10.1177/0735633118825385

Baer, J. (2019). Theory in creativity research: The pernicious impact of domain generality. In C. Mullen (Ed.), *Creativity under duress in education? Creativity Theory and action in education* (Vol. 3; pp. 119–135). Springer, Cham. https://doi.org/10.1007/978-3-319-90272-2_7

Baer, J., & Kaufman, J. C. (2017). The amusement park theoretical model of creativity: An attempt to bridge the domain-specificity/generality gap. In J. C. Kaufman, V. P. Glăveanu, & J. Baer (Eds.), *The Cambridge handbook of creativity across domains.* Cambridge University Press.

Baer, M., & Oldham, G. R. (2006). The curvilinear relation between experienced creative time pressure and creativity: Moderating effects of openness to experience and support for creativity. *Journal of Applied Psychology, 91*(4), 963–970. https://doi.org/10.1037/0021-9010.91.4.963

Baer, R. A. (2014). Introduction to the core practices and exercises. In R. A. Baer (Ed.), *Mindfulness-based treatment approaches: Clinician's guide to evidence base and applications* (pp. 3–25). Elsevier Academic Press. https://doi.org/10.1016/B978-0-12-416031-6.00001-3

Banaji, S., Cranmer, S., & Perrotta, C. (2013). What's stopping us? Barriers to creativity and innovation in schooling across Europe. In K. Thomas & J. Chan (Eds.), *Handbook of research on creativity* (pp. 450–463). Edward Elgar Publishing. https://doi.org/10.4337/9780857939814.00044

Banister, C. (2020). Exploring peer feedback processes and peer feedback meta-dialogues with learners of academic and business English. *Language Teaching Research*, 1–19. https://doi.org/10.1177/1362168820952222

Barnett, L. A. (1990). Playfulness: Definition, design, and measurement. *Play & Culture, 3*(4), 319–336.

Barrett, P., Davies, F., Zhang, Y., & Barrett, L. (2015). The impact of classroom design on pupils' learning: Final results of a holistic, multi-level analysis. *Building and Environment, 89*, 118–133. https://doi.org/10.1016/j.buildenv.2015.02.013

Barrett, P., Davies, F., Zhang, Y., & Barrett, L. (2017). The holistic impact of classroom spaces on learning in specific subjects. *Environment and Behavior, 49*(4), 425–451. https://doi.org/10.1177/0013916516648735

Barron, B. (2003). When smart groups fail. *The Journal of Learning Sciences, 12*, 307–359. http://dx.doi.org/10.1207/S15327809JLS1203_1

Barth, P., & Stadtmann, G. (2021). Creativity assessment over time: Examining the reliability of CAT ratings. *Journal of Creative Behavior, 55*(2), 396–409. https://doi.org/10.1002/jocb.462

Baruah, J., & Paulus, P. B. (2019). Collaborative creativity and innovation in education. In *Creativity Under Duress in Education?* (pp. 155–177). Springer, Cham.

Bautista, A., & Ortega-Ruíz, R. (2015). Teacher professional development: International perspectives and approaches. *Psychology, Society and Education, 7*(3), 240–251. https://doi.org/10.25115/psye.v7i3.1020

Beghetto, R. A. (2009). Correlates of intellectual risk taking in elementary school science. *Journal of Research in Science Teaching, 46*(2), 210–223. https://doi.org/10.1002/tea.20270

Beghetto, R. A. (2014). Creative mortification: An initial exploration. *Psychology of Aesthetics, Creativity, and the Arts, 8*(3), 266–276. https://doi.org/10.1037/a0036618

Beghetto, R. A. (2016). Creativity and conformity: A paradoxical relationship. In J. A. Plucker (Ed.), *Creativity and innovation: Theory, research and practice*. Prufrock.

Beghetto, R. A., Karwowski, M., & Reiter-Palmon, R. (2021). Intellectual risk taking: A moderating link between creative confidence and creative behavior? *Psychology of Aesthetics, Creativity, and the Arts, 15*(4), 637–644. https://doi.org/10.1037/aca0000323

Beghetto, R. A., & Kaufman, J. C. (2014). Classroom contexts for creativity. *High Ability Studies, 25*(1), 53–69. https://doi.org/10.1080/13598139.2014.905247

Beghetto, R. A., Baer, J., Kaufman, J. C., & Patston, T. (2017). *Teaching for creativity in the Australian curriculum classroom*. Hawker Brownlow Education.

Beghetto, R. A., Kaufman, J. C., & Baxter, J. (2011). Answering the unexpected questions: Exploring the relationship between students' creative self-efficacy and teacher ratings of creativity. *Psychology of Aesthetics, Creativity, and the Arts, 5*(4), 342–349. https://doi.org/10.1037/a0022834

Behnamnia, N., Kamsin, A., & Ismail, M. A. B. (2020). The landscape of research on the use of digital game-based learning apps to nurture creativity among young children: A review. *Thinking Skills and Creativity, 37*, 100666. https://doi.org/10.1016/j.tsc.2020.100666

Benedek, M., Karstendiek, M., Ceh, S. M., Grabner, R. H., Krammer, G., Lebuda, I., Silvia, P. J., Cotter, K. N., Li, Y., Hu, W., Martskvishvili, K., & Kaufman, J. C. (2021). Creativity myths: Prevalence and correlates of misconceptions on creativity. *Personality and Individual Differences, 182*, 111068. https://doi.org/10.1016/j.paid.2021.111068

Benavides, F., Dumont, H., & Istance, D. (2008). *The search for innovative learning environments*. In *Innovating to learn, learning to innovate*. OECD Publishing. https://doi.org/10.1787/9789264047983-en

Bergmann, J., & Sams, A. (2014). *Flipped learning: Gateway to student engagement*. International Society for Technology in Education.

Bertilsson, F., Stenlund, T., Wiklund-Hörnqvist, C., & Jonsson, B. (2021). Retrieval practice: Beneficial for all students or moderated by individual differences? *Psychology Learning & Teaching, 20*(1), 21–39. https://doi.org/10.1177/1475725720973494

Besemer, S. P., & Treffinger, D. J. (1981). Analysis of creative products: Review and synthesis. *The Journal of Creative Behavior, 15*(3), 158–178. https://doi.org/10.1002/j.2162-6057.1981.tb00287.x

REFERENCES

Besemer, S. P., & O'Quin, K. (1987). Creative product analysis: Testing a model by developing a judging instrument. In S. G. Isaksen (Ed.), *Frontiers of creativity research: Beyond the basics* (pp. 367–389). Brady.

Bett, H., & Makewa, L. (2020). Can Facebook groups enhance continuing professional development of teachers? Lessons from Kenya. *Asia-Pacific Journal of Teacher Education, 48*(2), 132–146. https://doi.org/10.1080/1359866X.2018.1542662

Biccard, P. (2019). The professional development of primary school mathematics teachers through a design – based research methodology. *Pythagoras, 40*(1), Article a515. https://doi.org/10.4102/pythagoras.v40i1.515

Bicer, A., Lee, Y., Perihan, C., Capraro, M. M., & Capraro, R. M. (2020). Considering mathematical creative self-efficacy with problem posing as a measure of mathematical creativity. *Educational Studies in Mathematics, 105*(3), 457–485. https://doi.org/10.1007/s10649-020-09995-8

Biggers, B., & Luo, T. (2020). Guiding students to success: A systematic review of research on guided notes as an instructional strategy from 2009–2019. *Journal of University Teaching & Learning Practice, 17*(3). http://dx.doi.org/10.14453/jutlp.v17i3.12

Black, P., & Wiliam, D. (1998). Assessment and classroom learning. *Assessment in Education: Principles, Policy & Practice, 5*(1), 7–74. https://doi.org/10.1080/0969595980050102

Blackmore, J., Bateman, D., Loughlin, J., O'Mara, J., & Aranda, G. (2011). Research into the connection between built learning spaces and student outcomes (Paper No. 22). *Department of Education and Early Childhood Development*. https://www.education.vic.gov.au/Documents/about/programs/infrastructure/blackmorelearningspaces.pdf

Bledow, R., Rosing, K., & Frese, M. (2013). A dynamic perspective on affect and creativity. *Academy of Management Journal, 56*(2), 432–450. https://doi.org/10.5465/amj.2010.0894

Bluth, K., & Mullarkey, M., & Lathren, C. (2018). Self-compassion: A potential path to adolescent resilience and positive exploration. *Journal of Child and Family Studies, 27*, 3037–3047. https://doi.org/10.1007/s10826-018-1125-1

Boch, F., & Piolat, A. (2005). Note taking and learning: A summary of research. *The WAC Journal, 16*, 101–113. https://doi.org/10.37514/WAC-J.2005.16.1.08

Bolden, B., DeLuca, C., Kukkonen, T., Roy, S., & Wearing, J. (2020). Assessment of creativity in K–12 education: A scoping review. *Review of education, 8*(2), 343–376. https://doi.org/10.1002/rev3.3188

Boud, D., Cohen, R., & Sampson, J. (2001). Peer learning and assessment. *Assessment and Evaluation in Higher Education, 24*(4), 413–426.

Bouriga, S., & Olive, T. (2021). Is typewriting more resources-demanding than handwriting in undergraduate students? *Reading and Writing, 34*, 2227–2255. https://doi.org/10.1007/s11145-021-10137-6

Borko, H. (2004). Professional development and teacher learning: Mapping the terrain. *Educational Researcher, 33*(8), 3–15. https://doi.org/10.3102/0013189X033008003

Boyle, J. R., & Forchelli, G. A. (2014). Differences in the note-taking skills of students with high achievement, average achievement, and learning disabilities. *Learning and Individual Differences, 35*, 9–14. https://doi.org/10.1016/j.lindif.2014.06.002

Brauckmann-Sajkiewicz, S., & Pashiardis, P. (2020). Entrepreneurial leadership in schools: Linking creativity with accountability. *International Journal of Leadership in Education*. https://doi.org/10.1080/13603124.2020.1804624

Britton, B. K., & Tesser, A. (1991). Effects of time-management practices on college grades. *Journal of Educational Psychology, 83*(3), 405–410. https://doi.org/10.1037/0022-0663.83.3.405

Brod, G. (2021). Generative learning: Which strategies for what age? *Educational Psychology Review, 33*, 1295–1318. https://doi.org/10.1007/s10648-020-09571-9

Brookhart, S. (2010). *How to assess higher-order thinking skills in your classroom*. ASCD.

Brown, P. C., Roediger, H. L., & McDaniel, M. A. (2014). *Make it stick: The science of successful learning*. The Belknap Press of Harvard University Press.

Bunprom, S., Boontemsuk, C., Tupsai, J., & Yuenyong, C. (2021). Examining grade 11 students' existing ideas of engineering design process of fluid and Bernoulli's principle through predict-observe-explain (POE). *Journal of Physics: Conference Series*, 1835(1), Article 012026. http://dx.doi.org/10.1088/1742-6596/1835/1/012026

Burnard, P., Craft, A., Cremin, T., Duffy, B., Hanson, R., Keene, J., Haynes, L., & Burns, D. (2006). Documenting 'possibility thinking': A journey of collaborative enquiry. *International Journal of Early Years Education*, 14(3) 243–262. https://doi.org/10.1080/09669760600880001

Buzan, T., & Buzan, B. (1995). *The mind map book*. BBC Books.

Cairns, D. (2019). Investigating the relationship between instructional practices and science achievement in an inquiry-based learning environment. *International Journal of science education*, 41(15), 2113–2135. https://doi.org/10.1080/09500693.2019.1660927

Carmeli, A., Gelbard, R., & Reiter-Palmon, R. (2013). Leadership, creative problem-solving capacity, and creative performance: The importance of knowledge sharing. *Human Resource Management*, 52(1), 95–121. https://doi.org/10.1002/hrm.21514

Carmeli, A., Reiter-Palmon, R., & Ziv, E. (2010). Inclusive leadership and employee involvement in creative tasks in the workplace: The mediating role of psychological safety. *Creativity Research Journal*, 22(3), 250–260. https://doi.org/10.1080/10400419.2010.504654

Carmeli, A., Sheaffer, Z., Binyamin, G., Reiter-Palmon, R., & Shimoni, T. (2013). Transformational leadership and creative problem-solving: The mediating role of psychological safety and reflexivity. *Journal of Creative Behavior*, 48(2), 115–135. https://doi.org/10.1002/jocb.43

Castañer, X., & Oliveira, N. (2020). Collaboration, coordination, and cooperation among organizations: Establishing the distinctive meanings of these terms through a systematic literature review. *Journal of Management*, 46(6), 965–1001. https://doi.org/10.1177/0149206320901565

Catterall, K., Mickenberg, J., & Reddick, R. (2019). Design thinking, collaborative innovation, and neoliberal disappointment: Cruel optimism in the history and future of higher education. *Radical Teacher*, 114, 34–47. https://doi.org/10.5195/rt.2019.548

Celume, M.-P., Besançon, M., & Zenasni F. (2019). Fostering children and adolescents' creative thinking in education. *Theoretical model of drama pedagogy training. Frontiers in Psychology*, 9, Article 2611. https://doi.org/10.3389/fpsyg.2018.02611

Central Advisory Council for Education (CACE). (1967). *Children and their primary schools* (The Plowden Report). HMSO. http://www.educationengland.org.uk/documents/plowden/plowden1967-1.html

Cents-Boonstra, M., Lichtwarck-Aschoff, A., Denessen, E., Aelterman, N., & Haerens, L. (2021). Fostering student engagement with motivating teaching: An observation study of teacher and student behaviours. *Research Papers in Education*, 36(6), 754–779. https://doi.org/10.1080/02671522.2020.1767184

Chan, D. W., & Chan, L.-K. (1999). Implicit theories of creativity: Teachers' perception of student characteristics in Hong Kong. *Creativity Research Journal*, 12(3), 185–195. https://doi.org/10.1207/s15326934crj1203_3

Chan, J. C. Y., & Lam, S.-F. (2010). Effects of different evaluative feedback on students' self-efficacy in learning. *Instructional Science*, 38, 37–58. https://doi.org/10.1007/s11251-008-9077-2

Chandra Sekhar, S., & Lidiya, K. (2012). *Brainstorming. Management*, 2(4), 113–117. https://doi.org/10.5923/j.mm.20120204.05

Chang, C.-P. (2013). Relationships between playfulness and creativity among students gifted in mathematics and science. *Creative Education*, 4(2), 101–109. https://doi.org/10.4236/ce.2013.42015

REFERENCES

Chang, J. H., Hsu, C.-C., Shih, N.-H., & Chen, H.-C. (2014). Multicultural families and creative children. *Journal of Cross-Cultural Psychology*, *45*(8), 1288–1296. https://doi.org/10.1177/0022022114537556

Chen, L. (2020). A historical review of professional learning communities in China (1949–2019): Some implications for collaborative teacher professional development. *Asia Pacific Journal of Education*, *40*(3), 373–385. https://doi.org/10.1080/02188791.2020.1717439

Chen, X., He, J., & Fan, X. (2022). Relationships between openness to experience, cognitive flexibility, self-esteem, and creativity among bilingual college students in the US. *International Journal of Bilingual Education and Bilingualism*, *25*(1), 342–354. https://doi.org/10.1080/13670050.2019.1688247

Chen, L., Inoue, K., Goda, Y., Okubo, F., Taniguchi, Y., Oi, M., Konomi, S., Ogata, H., & Yamada, M. (2020). Exploring factors that influence collaborative problem solving awareness in science education. *Technology, Knowledge and Learning*, *25*, 337–366. https://doi.org/10.1007/s10758-020-09436-8

Cheng, C.-Y., & Leung, A. K.-Y. (2013). Revisiting the multicultural experience-creativity link: The effects of cultural distance and comparison mindset. *Social Psychological and Personality Science*, *4*(4), 475–482. https://doi.org/10.1177/1948550612462413

Chigonga, B., & Mutodi, P. (2019). The cascade model of mathematics teachers' professional development in South Africa: How well did it suit them? *EURASIA Journal of Mathematics, Sciences and Technology Education*, *15*(10), Article em1761. https://doi.org/10.29333/ejmste/109261

Chirkina, T. A., & Khavenson, T. E. (2018). School climate: A history of the concept and approaches to defining and measuring it on PISA questionnaires. *Russian Education & Society*, *60*(2), 133–160. https://doi.org/10.1080/10609393.2018.1451189

Chou, C.-L., Hung, M.-L., Tsai, C.-W., & Chang, Y.-C. (2020). Developing and validating a scale for measuring teachers' readiness for flipped classrooms in junior high schools. *British Journal of Educational Technology*, *51*(4), 1420–1435. https://doi.org/10.1111/bjet.12895

Christensen, B. T., Halskov, K., & Klokmose, C. N. (Eds.). (2019). *Sticky creativity: Post-it® note cognition, computers, and design*. Academic Press.

Christensen, B. T., & Abildgaard, S. J. J. (2021). Kinds of 'moving' in designing with sticky notes. *Design Studies*, *76*, Article 101036. https://doi.org/10.1016/j.destud.2021.101036

Christensen, C. M., Horn, M. B., & Staker, H. (2013). Is K–12 blended learning disruptive? An introduction to the theory of hybrids. *Clayton Christensen Institute for Disruptive Innovation*. https://files.eric.ed.gov/fulltext/ED566878.pdf

Chua, R. Y. J. (2018). Innovating at cultural crossroads: How multicultural social networks promote idea flow and creativity. *Journal of Management*, *44*(3), 1119–1146. https://doi.org/10.1177/0149206315601183

Chylińska, M., & Gut, A. (2020). Pretend play as a creative action: On the exploratory and evaluative features of children's pretense. *Theory & Psychology*, *30*(4), 548–566. https://doi.org/10.1177/0959354320931594

Cizek, G., Andrade, H., Furtak, E., Middlestead, A., & Wiliam, D. (2019, June 24). Formative assessment in the disciplines: Advances in theory and practice [Conference presentation]. *National Conference on Student Assessment*, Orlando, Florida, June 24–26, 2019.

Collard, P., & Looney, J. (2014). Nurturing creativity in education. *European Journal of Education*, *49*(3), 348–364. https://doi.org/10.1111/ejed.12090

Conradty, C., & Bogner, F. X. (2020). STEAM teaching professional development works: Effects on students' creativity and motivation. *Smart Learning Environments*, *7*, Article 26. https://doi.org/10.1186/s40561-020-00132-9

Costa, P. T., & McCrae, R. R. (1992). Revised NEO Personality Inventory (NEO-PI-R) and NEO Five-Factor Inventory (NEO-FFI) professional manual. *Psychological Assessment Resources*.

Costley, J., & Fanguy, M. (2021). Collaborative note-taking affects cognitive load: The interplay of completeness and interaction. *Educational Technology Research and Development*, *69*, 655–671. https://doi.org/10.1007/s11423-021-09979-2

Cropley, A. J. (1967). Creativity, intelligence, and achievement. *Alberta Journal of Educational Research*.

Cropley, A. J. (1997). *More ways than one: Fostering creativity in the classroom (4th ed.)*. Ablex Publishing.

Cropley, A. J. (2001). *Creativity in education and learning: A guide for teachers and educators*. Routledge.

Cropley, A. J. (2006). In praise of convergent thinking. *Creativity Research Journal*, 18(3), 391–404. https://doi.org/10.1207/s15326934crj1803_13

Cropley, A. J. (2020). Ancient world conceptualizations of creativity. In M. A. Runco & S. R. Pritzker (Eds.), *Encyclopedia of creativity* (pp. 42–46). Academic Press.

Cropley, D. H. (2022). Why are we creative? Novel and effective products. In J. Plucker (Ed.), *Creativity and Innovation: Theory, Research, and Practice (Second Ed.)* Chapter 10 (pp. 249 – 264), New York, NY: Routledge.

Cropley, A. J., & Cropley, D. H. (2007). Using assessment to foster creativity. In A.-G. Tan (Ed.), *Creativity: A handbook for teachers* (pp. 209–230). World Scientific.

Cropley, D. H. (In press). Product creativity assessment. In M. Runco & S. Acar (Eds.), *Handbook of Creativity Assessment*. Edward Elgar Publishing.

Cropley, D. H. (2014). Fighting the slump: A multi-faceted exercise for fostering creativity in children. *International Journal of Creativity and Problem Solving*, 24(2), 7–22.

Cropley, D. H. (2015). *Creativity in engineering: Novel solutions to complex problems*. Academic Press. https://doi.org/10.1016/C2013-0-18511-X

Cropley, D. H. (2020). *Femina problematis solvendis – problem solving woman: A history of the creativity of women*. Springer.

Cropley, D. H., & Cropley, A. J. (2000). *Fostering creativity in engineering undergraduates*. High ability studies, 11(2), 207–219. https://doi.org/10.1080/13598130020001223

Cropley, D. H., & Cropley, A. J. (2005). Engineering creativity: A systems concept of functional creativity. In J. C. Kaufman & J. Baer (Eds.), *Faces of the muse: How people think, work and act creatively in diverse domains* (pp. 169–185). Lawrence Erlbaum.

Cropley, D. H., & Cropley, A. J. (2012). A psychological taxonomy of organizational innovation: Resolving the paradoxes. *Creativity Research Journal*, 24(1), 29–40. https://doi.org/10.1080/10400419.2012.649234

Cropley, D. H., Kaufman, J. C., & Cropley, A. J. (2011). Measuring creativity for innovation management. *Journal of Technology Management & Innovation*, 6(3), 13–30. https://doi.org/10.4067/S0718-27242011000300002

Cropley, D. H., & Marrone, R. L. (2021, October 7). *Automated Scoring of Figural Creativity using a Convolutional Neural Network*. https://doi.org/10.31234/osf.io/8qe7y

Cropley, D. H., Medeiros, K. E., & Damadzic, A. (2021, August 25). *The intersection of human and artificial creativity*. https://doi.org/10.31234/osf.io/t7nv2

Cropley, D. H., & Patston, T. (2019). Supporting creative teaching and learning in the classroom: Myths, models, and measures, In C. Mullen (Ed.), *Creativity under duress in education? Resistive theories, practices, and actions*. Springer.

Cropley, D. H., Patston, T., Marrone, R. L., & Kaufman, J. C. (2019). Essential, unexceptional and universal: Teacher implicit beliefs of creativity. *Thinking Skills and Creativity*, 34, Article 100604. https://doi.org/10.1016/j.tsc.2019.100604

Csikszentmihalyi, M., & Wolfe, R. (2014). New conceptions and research approaches to creativity: Implications of a systems perspective for creativity in education. In M. Csikszentmihalyi (Ed.), *The systems model of creativity* (pp. 161-184). Springer. https://doi.org/10.1007/978-94-017-9085-7_10

Dann, R. (2013). *Be curious: Understanding 'curiosity' in contemporary curriculum policy and practice*. Education 3–13, 41(6), 557–561. https://doi.org/10.1080/03004279.2013.850256

Davies, D., Jindal-Snape, D., Collier, C., Digby, R., Hay, P., & Howe, A. (2013). Creative learning environments in education: A systematic literature review. *Thinking Skills and Creativity*, *8*, 80–91. https://doi.org/10.1016/j.tsc.2012.07.004

Davis, S. (2018). Flexibility, constraints and creativity: Cultivating creativity in teacher education. In K. Snepvangers, P. Thomson & A. Harris (Eds.), *Creativity policy, partnerships and practice in education* (pp. 331–352). Palgrave Macmillan. https://doi.org/10.1007/978-3-319-96725-7_15

De Bono, E. (1985). *Six thinking hats*. Penguin.

de Buisonjé, D. R., Ritter, S. M., de Bruin, S., ter Horst, J. M.-L., & Meeldijk, A. (2017). Facilitating creative idea selection: The combined effects of self-affirmation, promotion focus and positive affect. *Creativity Research Journal*, *29*(2), 174–181. https://doi.org/10.1080/10400419.2017.1303308

de Fátima Morais, M., Neves de Jesus, S., Azevedo, I., Araújo, A. M., & Viseu, J. (2015). Intervention Program on adolescent's creativity representations and academic motivation. *Paidéia (Ribeirão Preto)*, *25*(62), 289–297. https://doi.org/10.1590/1982-43272562201502

Dean, D. L., Hender, J., Rodgers, T., & Santanen, E. (2006). Identifying good ideas: constructs and scales for idea evaluation. *Journal of Association for Information Systems*, *7*(10), 646–699.

Demarin, V., & Derke, F. (2020). Creativity – The story continues: An overview of thoughts on creativity. In V. Demarin (Ed.), *Mind and brain: Bridging neurology and psychiatry* (pp. 1–20). Springer.

Deng, L., Wang, L., & Zhao, Y. (2016). How creativity was affected by environmental factors and individual characteristics: A cross-cultural comparison perspective. *Creativity Research Journal*, *28*(3), 357–366. https://doi.org/10.1080/10400419.2016.1195615

Department for Education. (2014). *The national curriculum in England: Complete framework for key stages 1 to 4*. https://www.gov.uk/government/publications/national-curriculum-in-england-framework-for-key-stages-1-to-4

DeYoung, C. G. (2014). Openness/intellect: A dimension of personality reflecting cognitive exploration. In M. L. Cooper & R. J. Larsen (Eds.), *APA handbook of personality and social psychology: Personality processes and individual differences* (Vol. 4, pp. 369–399). American Psychological Association.

DeYoung, C. G. (2015). Cybernetic big five theory. *Journal of Research in Personality*, *56*, 33–58. https://doi.org/10.1016/j.jrp.2014.07.004

DeYoung, C. G., Quilty, L. C., & Peterson, J. B. (2007). Between facets and domains: 10 aspects of the Big Five. *Journal of Personality and Social Psychology*, *93*(5), 880–896. https://doi.org/10.1037/0022-3514.93.5.880

Dhawan S. (2020). Online learning: A panacea in the time of COVID-19 crisis. *Journal of Educational Technology Systems*, *49*(1), 5–22. https://doi.org/10.1177/0047239520934018

Dollinger, S. J. (2011). "Standardized minds" or individuality? Admissions tests and creativity revisited. *Psychology of Aesthetics, Creativity, and the Arts*, *5*(4), 329–341. https://doi.org/10.1037/a0023659

Double, K. S., McGrane, J. A., & Hopfenbeck, T. N. (2020). The impact of peer assessment on academic performance: A meta-analysis of control group studies. *Educational Psychology Review*, *32*, 481–509. https://doi.org/10.1007/s10648-019-09510-3

Dukhan, S. (2018). Note-making in biology: How the school experience influences note-making practice and approach at university. *African Journal of Research in Mathematics, Science and Technology Education*, *22*(3), 265–275, https://doi.org/10.1080/18117295.2018.1476050

Dukhan, S., Brenner, E., & Cameron, A. (2019). The influence of lecturers' expectations of students' role in meaning making on the nature of their PowerPoint slides and the quality of students' note-making: A first-year biology class context. *African Journal of Research in Mathematics, Science and Technology Education*, *23*(1), 100–110. https://doi.org/10.1080/18117295.2019.1598625

Dul, J. (2019). The physical environment and creativity: A theoretical framework. In J. C. Kaufman & R. Sternberg (Eds.), *The Cambridge handbook of creativity* (Cambridge Handbooks in Psychology; pp. 481–510). Cambridge University Press. https://doi.org/10.1017/9781316979839.025

Eberle, B. F. (1997). *Scamper*. DOK Publishers.

Estell, J. K., Sapp, H. M., & Reeping, D. (2016, June). *Work in progress: Developing single point rubrics for formative assessment* [Paper presentation]. ASEE Annual Conference & Exposition, New Orleans, Louisiana. https://doi.org/10.18260/p.27221

Evans, B., & Shively, C. T. (2019). Using the Cornell note-taking system can help eighth grade students alleviate the impact of interruptions while reading at home. *Journal of Inquiry and Action in Education*, *10*(1), 1–35. https://eric.ed.gov/?id=EJ1205170

Fairweather, E. C., & Cramond, B. (2010). Infusing creative and critical thinking into the curriculum together. In R. A. Beghetto & J. C. Kaufman (Eds.), *Nurturing creativity in the classroom* (pp. 113–141). Cambridge University Press.

Fan, M., & Cai, W. (2020). How does a creative learning environment foster student creativity? An examination on multiple explanatory mechanisms. *Current Psychology*, *41*, 4667–4676. https://doi.org/10.1007/s12144-020-00974-z

Fang, Y., & Shen, Y. (2021). The relationship between undergraduate students' parenting style and creativity. *Psychology*, *12*(4), 498–510. https://doi.org/10.4236/psych.2021.124031

Faturrochman, R. G., Darmawan, A. A., & Hadi, F. (2021). Teacher talk in scientific approach in EFL classroom: A speech acts perspective. *SAGA: Journal of English Language Teaching and Applied Linguistics*, *2*(1), 35–46. https://doi.org/10.21460/saga.2020.21.66

Fearon, D., Copeland, D., & Saxon, T., (2013) The relationship between parenting styles and creativity in a sample of Jamaican children. *Creativity Research Journal*, *25*(1), 119–128. https://doi.org/10.1080/10400419.2013.752287

Feist, G. J. (1998). A meta-analysis of personality in scientific and artistic creativity. *Personality and Social Psychology Review*, *2*(4), 290–309. https://doi.org/10.1207/s15327957pspr0204_5

Fernández-Castillo, A., Chacón-López, H., & Fernández-Prados, M. J. (2022). Self-esteem and resilience in students of teaching: Evolution associated with academic progress. *Education Research International*, 2022, Article 4854332. https://doi.org/10.1155/2022/4854332

Ferrero, M., Konstantinidis, E., & Vadillo, M. A. (2020). An attempt to correct erroneous ideas among teacher education students: The effectiveness of refutation texts. *Frontiers in Psychology*, *11*, Article 577738. https://doi.org/10.3389/fpsyg.2020.577738

Fiorella, L., & Mayer, R. E. (2016). Eight ways to promote generative learning. *Educational Psychology Review*, *28*(4), 717–741. https://doi.org/10.1007/s10648-015-9348-9

Fischer, J. F. & Davis, J. F (2005). *Algorithms: Through the ages and around the world*. Texas University Press.

Fisher, D., & Frey, N. (2008). Homework and the gradual release of responsibility: Making "responsibility" possible. *English Journal*, *98*(2), 40–45.

Fisher, D., & Frey, N. (2021). *Better learning through structured teaching: A framework for the gradual release of responsibility* (3rd ed.). ASCD.

Fleer, M. (2019). Scientific playworlds: A model of teaching science in play-based settings. *Research in Science Education*, *49*(5), 1257–1278. https://doi.org/10.1007/s11165-017-9653-z

Flensner, K. K., & Von der Lippe, M. (2019). Being safe from what and safe for whom? A critical discussion of the conceptual metaphor of 'safe space'. *Intercultural Education*, *30*(3), 275–288. https://doi.org/10.1080/14675986.2019.1540102

Flewitt, R., Messer, D., & Kucirkova, N. (2015). *New directions for early literacy in a digital age: The iPad. Journal of Early Childhood Literacy*, *15*(3), 289–310. https://doi.org/10.1177/1468798414533560

Florida, R. (2012). *The Rise of the creative class revisited*. Basic Books.

Fluckiger, J. (2010). Single point rubric: A tool for responsible student self-assessment. *Delta Kappa Gamma Bulletin*, *76*(4), 18–25.

REFERENCES

Ford, C., & Sullivan, D. M. (2004). A time for everything: How timing of novel contributions influences project team outcomes. *Journal of Organizational Behavior, 25*(2), 279–292. https://doi.org/10.1002/job.241

Franco-Mariscal, A.-J., Hierrezuelo-Osorio, J. M., Cruz-Lorite, I. M., & Cebrián-Robles, D. (2021). The dilemma of replacing traditional calligraphic skills with technology in the teaching of writing. *International Journal for 21st Century Education, 8*(1), 18–36. https://doi.org/10.21071/ij21ce.v8i1.13342

Frazier, M. L., Fainshmidt, S., Klinger, R. L., Pezeshkan, A., & Vracheva, V. (2017). Psychological safety: A metaanalytic review and extension. *Personnel Psychology, 70*(1), 113–165. https://doi.org/10.1111/peps.12183

Freeman, S., Eddy, S. L., McDonough, M., Smith, M. K., Okoroafor, N., Jordt, H., & Wenderoth, M. P. (2014). Active learning increases student performance in science, engineering, and mathematics. *Proceedings of the National Academy of Sciences of the USA, 111*(23), 8410–8415. https://doi.org/10.1073/pnas.1319030111

Friedman, M. C. (2014). *Notes on note-taking: Review of research and insights for students and instructors. Harvard Initiative for Learning and Teaching*, Harvard University. https://hwpi.harvard.edu/files/hilt/files/notetaking_0.pdf

Gajda, A., Karwowski, M., & Beghetto, R. A. (2017). Creativity and academic achievement: A meta-analysis. *Journal of Educational Psychology, 109*(2), 269–299. https://psycnet.apa.org/doi/10.1037/edu0000133

Galatti, L. R., Machado, J. C., Motta, M. D. C., Misuta, M. S., & Belli, T. (2019). Nonlinear Pedagogy and the implications for teaching and training in table tennis. *Motriz: Revista de Educação Física, 25*(1), Article e101999. https://doi.org/10.1590/s1980-6574201900010015

Gazizov, E. R., Gazizova, S. E., Kiseleva, N. G., & Zinnatullina, A. N. (2018). Heuristic methods for solving the creative problems. *Вісник Національної академії керівних кадрів культури і мистецтв, 3*, 1024–1026. https://doi.org/10.32461/2226-3209.3.2018.171920

Gerlach, S., & Brem, A. (2017). Idea management revisited: A review of the literature and guide for implementation. *International Journal of Innovation Studies, 1*(2), 144–161. https://doi.org/10.1016/j.ijis.2017.10.004

Gibson, C., & Mumford, M. D. (2013). Evaluation, criticism, and creativity: Criticism content and effects on creative problem solving. *Psychology of Aesthetics, Creativity, and the Arts, 7*(4), 314–331. https://doi.org/10.1037/a0032616

Glăveanu, V. P. (2013). Rewriting the language of creativity: The five A's framework. *Review of General Psychology, 17*(1), 69–81. https://doi.org/10.1037/a0029528

Glăveanu, V. P. (2019). Revisiting the foundations of creativity studies. In V. P. Glăveanu (Ed.), *The creativity reader* (pp. 1–12). Oxford University Press.

Glăveanu, V. P., & Kaufman, J. C. (2019). Creativity: A historical perspective. In J. C. Kaufman & R. J. Sternberg (Eds.), *Cambridge handbook of creativity* (2nd ed., pp. 11–26). Cambridge University Press.

Gobron, S., Barman, C., Sadiku, A., Lince, X., & Capron-Puozzo, I. (2021). *Towards an E-class stimulating social interactivity based on digitized and gamified brainstorming. Gamevironments, 15*, 19–55. https://doi.org/10.48783/gameviron.v15i15.145

Goldberg, L. R. (1992). The development of markers for the Big-Five factor structure. *Psychological Assessment, 4*(1), 26–42. https://doi.org/10.1037/1040-3590.4.1.26

Gonczi, A. L., Bergman, B. G., Huntoon, J., Allen, R., McIntyre, B., Turner, S., Davis, J., & Handler, R. (2017). Decision matrices: Tools to enhance middle school engineering instruction. *Science Activities, 54*(1), 8–17. https://doi.org/10.1080/00368121.2016.1264922

Gong, Y., Cheung, S.-Y., Wang, M., & Huang, J.-C. (2012). Unfolding the proactive process for creativity: Integration of the employee proactivity, information exchange, and psychological safety perspectives. *Journal of management, 38*(5), 1611–1633. https://doi.org/10.1177/0149206310380250

Gonzalez, J. (May 1, 2014). Know your terms: Holistic, analytic, and single-point rubrics. *Cult of pedagogy*. https://www.cultofpedagogy.com/holistic-analytic-single-point-rubrics/

Gordon, William J. J. (1961). *Synectics: The Development of Creative Capacity*. Harper and row.

Gore, J., Lloyd, A., Smith, M., Bowe, J., Ellis, H., & Lubans, D. (2017). Effects of professional development on the quality of teaching: Results from a randomised controlled trial of Quality Teaching Rounds. *Teaching and Teacher Education, 68*, 99–113. https://doi.org/10.1016/j.tate.2017.08.007

Gralewski, J., & Karwowski, M. (2016). Are teachers' implicit theories of creativity related to the recognition of their students' creativity? *The Journal of Creative Behavior, 52*(2), 156–167. https://doi.org/10.1002/jocb.140

Green, G., & Kaufman, J. C. (Eds.). (2015). *Video games and creativity*. Academic Press.

Grigorenko, E. L., Jarvin, L., Diffley, R., Goodyear, J., Shanahan, E., & Sternberg, R. J. (2009). Are SATS and GPA enough? A theory-based approach to predicting academic success in secondary school. *Journal of Educational Psychology, 101*, 964–981.

Guhn, M., Emerson, S. D., & Gouzouasis, P. (2020). A population-level analysis of associations between school music participation and academic achievement. *Journal of Educational Psychology, 112*(2), 308–328. http://dx.doi.org/10.1037/edu0000376

Guilford, J. P. (1950). Creativity. *American Psychologist, 5*(9), 444–454. https://doi.org/10.1037/h0063487

Guilford J. P. (1967). *The Nature of Human Intelligence*. McGraw-Hill.

Guo, Y. (2018). The influence of academic autonomous motivation on learning engagement and life satisfaction in adolescents: The mediating role of basic psychological needs satisfaction. *Journal of Education and Learning, 7*(4), 254–261.

Han, J., Park, D., Hua, M., & Childs, P. R. N. (2021). Is group work beneficial for producing creative designs in STEM design education? *International Journal of Technology and Design Education*. https://doi.org/10.1007/s10798-021-09709-y

Han, K. (2021). Fostering students' autonomy and engagement in EFL classroom through proximal classroom factors: Autonomy-supportive behaviors and student-teacher relationships. *Frontiers in Psychology, 12*, Article 767079. https://doi.org/10.3389/fpsyg.2021.767079

Han, Q., Hu, W., Liu, J., Jia, X., & Adey, P. (2013). The influence of peer interaction on students' creative problem-finding ability. *Creativity Research Journal, 25*(3), 248–258.

Harris, A., & De Bruin, L. R. (2018). Secondary school creativity, teacher practice and STEAM education: An international study. *Journal of Educational Change, 19*(2), 153–179. https://doi.org/10.1007/s10833-017-9311-2

Hattie, J. (2012). *Visible learning for teachers: Maximizing impact on learning*. Routledge.

Hattie, J. A. C., & Donoghue, G. M. (2016). Learning strategies: A synthesis and conceptual model. *NPJ Science of Learning, 1*, Article 16013. https://doi.org/10.1038/npjscilearn.2016.13

Hecht, S. J. (2011). *Transposing Broadway: Jews, assimilation, and the American musical*. Palgrave Macmillan.

Heilmann, G., & Korte, W. B. (2010). *The role of creativity and innovation in school curricula in the EU27: A content analysis of curricula documents*. European Commission Joint Research Centre. www.pim.com.mt/pubs/JRC_curricula.pdf

Henebery, B. (October 22, 2021). 5 tips to help students prepare for their Year 12 exams. *The Educator*. https://www.theeducatoronline.com/k12/news/5-tips-to-help-students-prepare-for-their-year-12-exams/279003

Hennessey, B. A. (2019). Motivation and creativity. In J. C. Kaufman & R. J. Sternberg (Eds.), *Cambridge handbook of creativity* (2nd ed.) (pp. 374–395). Cambridge University Press.

Henriksen, D., Cain, W., & Mishra, P. (2018). Everyone designs: Learner autonomy through creative, reflective, and iterative practice mindsets. *Journal of Formative Design in Learning, 2*(2), 69–81. https://doi.org/10.1007/s41686-018-0024-6

REFERENCES

Hernandez-de-Menendez, M., Escobar Díaz, C. A., & Morales-Menendez, R. (2020). Educational experiences with Generation Z. *International Journal on Interactive Design and Manufacturing (IJIDeM)*, *14*(3), 847–859. https://doi.org/10.1007/s12008-020-00674-9

Herold, J. (1974). Sputnik in American education: A history and reappraisal. *McGill Journal of Education/ Revue des sciences de l'éducation de McGill*, *9*(2), 143–164. https://mje.mcgill.ca/article/view/6971

Herro, D., Quigley, C., Andrews, J., & Delacruz, G. (2017). Co-measure: Developing an assessment for student collaboration in STEAM activities. *International journal of STEM education*, *4*(1), Article 26. https://doi.org/10.1186/s40594-017-0094-z

Hibbitt, C. (2020). Using skeleton typograms to explore comparative anatomy. *The American Biology Teacher*, *82*(2), 120–122. https://doi.org/10.1525/abt.2020.82.2.120

Hickey, M., Healy, D., & Schmidt, C. (2022). A quantitative analysis of two improvisation assessment instruments. *Psychology of Music*, *50*(1), 175–186. https://doi.org/10.1177/0305735620988788

Hill, K. E. (1954). Creativity in the Curriculum. *Childhood Education*, *31*(4), 169-172.

Hirst, G., Van Knippenberg, D., & Zhou, J. (2009). A cross-level perspective on employee creativity: Goal orientation, team learning behavior, and individual creativity. *Academy of Management Journal*, *52*(2), 280–293. https://doi.org/10.5465/AMJ.2009.37308035

Holinger, M., & Kaufman, J. C. (2018). The relationship between creativity and feedback. In A. A. Lipnevich & J. K. Smith (Eds.), *The Cambridge handbook of instructional feedback* (pp. 575–587). Cambridge University Press. https://doi.org/10.1017/9781316832134.028

Hopfenbeck, T. N. (2019). The use and abuse of assessment. *Assessment in Education: Principles, Policy & Practice*, *26*(6), 637–642. https://doi.org/10.1080/0969594x.2019.1689323

Hopson, M. H., Simms, R. L., & Knezek, G. A. (2014). Using a technology-enriched environment to improve higher-order thinking skills. *Journal of Research on Technology in Education*, *34*(2), 109–119. https://doi.org/10.1080/15391523.2001.10782338

Horn, D., & Salvendy, G. (2006). Product creativity: Conceptual model, measurement and characteristics. *Theoretical Issues in Ergonomics Science*, *7*(4), 395–412. https://doi.org/10.1080/14639220500078195

Huang, N.-T., Chang, Y.-S., & Chou, C.-H. (2020). Effects of creative thinking, psychomotor skills, and creative self-efficacy on engineering design creativity. *Thinking Skills and Creativity*, *37*, Article 100695. https://doi.org/10.1016/j.tsc.2020.100695

Hubbard, R. S. (1996). *A workshop of the possible: Nurturing children's creative development*. Stenhouse Publishers.

Iannello, P., Mottini, A., Tirelli, S., Riva, S., & Antonietti, A. (2017). Ambiguity and uncertainty tolerance, need for cognition, and their association with stress. A study among Italian practicing physicians. *Medical Education Online*, *22*(1), Article 1270009. https://doi.org/10.1080/10872981.2016.1270009

Imants, J., & Van der Wal, M. M. (2020). A model of teacher agency in professional development and school reform. *Journal of Curriculum Studies*, *52*(1), 1–14. https://doi.org/10.1080/00220272.2019.1604809

Isaksen S. G., & Gaulin, J. P. (2005). A reexamination of brainstorming research: Implications for research and practice. *Gifted Child Quarterly*, *49*(4), 315–329. https://doi.org/10.1177/001698620504900405

Ishikawa, K. (1990). *Introduction to quality control*. 3A Corporation.

Ismail, S., Rahman, F., & Yaacob, A. (2020). *School climate and academic performance*. Oxford Research Encyclopedia of Education. https://doi.org/10.1093/acrefore/9780190264093.013.662

Ivcevic, Z., & Brackett, M. A. (2015). Predicting creativity: Interactive effects of openness to experience and emotion regulation ability. *Psychology of Aesthetics, Creativity, and the Arts*, *9*(4), 480–487. https://doi.org/10.1037/a0039826

Ivcevic, Z., & Mayer, J. D. (2006). Creative types and personality. *Imagination, Cognition and Personality*, *26*(1), 65–86. https://doi.org/10.2190/0615-6262-G582-853U

Jankowska, D. M., & Karwowski, M. (2019). Family factors and development of creative thinking. *Personality and Individual Differences*, *142*, 202–206. https://doi.org/10.1016/j.paid.2018.07.030

Jeffrey, B., & Woods, P. (1997). The relevance of creative teaching: Pupils' views. In A. Pollard, D. Thiessen & A. Filer (Eds.), *Children and their curriculum: The perspectives of primary and elementary children* (pp. 15–33). Falmer.

Jensen, M. M., Thiel, S.-K., Hoggan, E., & Bødker, S. (2018). Physical versus digital sticky notes in collaborative ideation. *Computer Supported Cooperative Work (CSCW)*, *27*, 609–645. http://dx.doi.org/10.1007/s10606-018-9325-1

Jiang, Y., Clarke-Midura, J., Keller, B., Baker, R., Paquette, L., & Ocumpaugh, J. (2018). Note-taking and science inquiry in an open-ended learning environment. *Contemporary Educational Psychology*, *55*, 12–29. http://dx.doi.org/10.1016/j.cedpsych.2018.08.004

Jirout J., Vitiello V., & Zumbrunn, S. (2018). Curiosity in schools. In G. Gordon (Ed.), *The new science of curiosity*. Nova.

Johnson, D. W., Johnson, R. T., & Holubec, E. J. (1994). *The new circles of learning: Cooperation in the classroom and school*. ASCD.

Johnson, T. M., & King-Sears, M. E. (2020). Eliciting students' perspectives about their co-teaching experiences. *Intervention in School and Clinic*, *56*(1), 51–55. https://doi.org/10.1177/1053451220910732

Johnson, S. R., Pas, E. T., Loh, D., Debnam, K. J., & Bradshaw, C. P. (2017). High school teachers' openness to adopting new practices: The role of personal resources and organizational climate. *School mental health*, *9*(1), 16–27. https://doi.org/10.1007/s12310-016-9201-4

Jong, M. S.-Y. (2020). Promoting elementary pupils' learning motivation in environmental education with mobile inquiry-oriented ambience-aware fieldwork. *International Journal of Environmental Research and Public Health*, *17*(7), Article 2504. https://doi.org/10.3390/ijerph17072504

Jouda, A. A. (2019). *The impact of SCAMPER strategy on developing English vocabulary learning, accomplishment motivation and retention for tenth graders in Gaza Governorate* [Doctoral dissertation, The Islamic University of Gaza]. https://library.iugaza.edu.ps/thesis/126912.pdf

Jovanović, V., & Brdaric, D. (2012). Did curiosity kill the cat? Evidence from subjective well-being in adolescents. *Personality and Individual Differences*, *52*(3), 380–384. https://doi.org/10.1016/j.paid.2011.10.043

Jungert, T., Levine, S., & Koestner, R. (2020). Examining how parent and teacher enthusiasm influences motivation and achievement in STEM. *The Journal of Educational Research*, *113*(4), 275–282. https://doi.org/10.1080/00220671.2020.1806015

Käckenmester, W., Bott, A., & Wacker, J. (2019). Openness to experience predicts dopamine effects on divergent thinking. *Personality Neuroscience*, *2*, Article e3. https://doi.org/10.1017/pen.2019.3

Kapoor, H., & Kaufman, J. C. (2020). Meaning-making through creativity during COVID-19. *Frontiers in Psychology*, *11*, Article 595990. https://doi.org/10.3389/fpsyg.2020.595990

Kariippanon, K. E., Cliff, D. P., Lancaster, S. J., Okely, A. D., & Parrish, A. M. (2019). Flexible learning spaces facilitate interaction, collaboration and behavioural engagement in secondary school. *PloS one*, *14*(10), Article e0223607. https://doi.org/10.1371/journal.pone.0223607

Karwowski, M. (2015). Peer effect on students' creative self-concept. T*he Journal of Creative Behavior*, *49*(3), 211-225. https://psycnet.apa.org/doi/10.1002/jocb.102

Karwowski, M., Gralewski, J., Patston, T., Cropley, D. H., & Kaufman, J. C. (2020). The creative student in the eyes of a teacher: A cross-cultural study. *Thinking Skills and Creativity*, *35*, Article 100636. https://doi.org/10.1016/j.tsc.2020.100636

Kashdan, T. B., Sherman, R. A., Yarbro, J., & Funder, D. C. (2013). How are curious people viewed and how do they behave in social situations? From the perspectives of self, friends, parents, and unacquainted observers. *Journal of Personality*, *81*(2), 142–154. https://doi.org/10.1111/j.1467-6494.2012.00796.xDann, 2013

REFERENCES

Kashdan, T. B., & Silvia, P. J. (2009). Curiosity and interest: The benefits of thriving on novelty and challenge. In S. J. Lopez & C. R. Snyder (Eds.), *Oxford handbook of positive psychology* (pp. 367–374). Oxford University Press.

Kashdan, T. B., & Yuen, M. (2007). Whether highly curious students thrive academically depends on perceptions about the school learning environment: A study of Hong Kong adolescents. *Motivation and Emotion*, *31*, 260–270. https://doi.org/10.1007/s11031-007-9074-9.

Kaufman, J. C. (2001). The Sylvia Plath effect: Mental illness in eminent creative writers. *The Journal of Creative Behavior*, *35*(1), 37–50. https://doi.org/10.1002/j.2162-6057.2001.tb01220.x

Kaufman, J. C. (Ed.). (2014). *Creativity and mental illness*. Cambridge University Press.

Kaufman, J. C. (2016). *Creativity 101*. Springer.

Kaufman, J. C. (2018). Creativity's need for relevance in research and real life: Let's set a new agenda for positive outcomes. *Creativity. Theories–Research–Applications*, *5*(2), 124–137. https://doi.org/10.1515/ctra-2018-0008

Kaufman, J. C., & Baer, J. (2004). Sure, I'm creative – but not in mathematics! Self-reported creativity in diverse domains. *Empirical Studies of the Arts*, *22*(2), 143–155. https://doi.org/10.2190/26HQ-VHE8-GTLN-BJJM

Kaufman, J. C., & Baer, J. (2012). Beyond new and appropriate: Who decides what is creative? *Creativity Research Journal*, *24*(1), 83–91. https://doi.org/10.1080/10400419.2012.649237

Kaufman, J. C., & Beghetto, R. A. (2009). Beyond big and little: The four C model of creativity. *Review of General Psychology*, *13*(1), 1–12. https://doi.org/10.1037/a0013688

Kaufman, J. C., & Beghetto, R. A. (2013a). Fundamentals of creativity. *Educational Leadership*, *70*, 10–15.

Kaufman, J. C., & Beghetto, R. A. (2013b). In praise of Clark Kent: Creative metacognition and the importance of teaching kids when (not) to be creative. *Roeper Review*, *35*, 155–165. http://dx.doi.org/10.1080/02783193.2013.799413

Kaufman, J. C., Kapoor, H., Patston, T., & Cropley, D. H. (2021). Explaining standardized educational test scores: The role of creativity above and beyond GPA and personality. *Psychology of Aesthetics, Creativity, and the Arts*. https://doi.org/10.1037/aca0000433

Kaya, N. G. (2021). Fostering creativity of gifted students. In O. Zahal & Ö. Yahşi (Eds.), *Research and Reviews in Educational Sciences* (pp. 37–54). Gece Publishing.

Keinänen, M., Sheridan, K., & Gardner, H. (2006). Opening up creativity: The lenses of axis and focus. In J. C. Kaufman & J. Baer (Eds.), *Creativity and reason in cognitive development* (pp. 202–220). Cambridge University Press. https://doi.org/10.1017/CBO9780511606915.013

Keller, M. M., Becker, E. S., Frenzel, A. C., & Taxer, J. L. (2018). When teacher enthusiasm is authentic or inauthentic: Lesson profiles of teacher enthusiasm and relations to students' emotions. *Aera Open*, *4*, 1–16. https://doi.org/10.1177/2332858418782967

Kettler, T., Lamb, K. N., & Mullet, D. R. (2021). *Developing creativity in the classroom: Learning and innovation for 21st-century schools*. Routledge.

Khairunnisa, K., Abdullah, A., Khairil, K., & Rahmatan, H. (2022). The influence of problem based learning models combined with flashcard media on creative thinking skills of students. *Jurnal Penelitian Pendidikan IPA*, *8*(1), 247–251. https://doi.org/10.29303/jppipa.v8i1.1154

Khan, A. A., & Mahmood, N. (2018). Effect of synectics model of teaching in enhancing students' understanding of abstract concepts of mathematics. *Pakistan Journal of Distance and Online Learning*, *4*(1), 185–198. https://files.eric.ed.gov/fulltext/EJ1267261.pdf

Kim, K. H., & Pierce, R. A. (2013). Convergent versus divergent thinking. In E. G. Carayannis (Eds.), *Encyclopedia of creativity, invention, innovation and entrepreneurship* (pp. 245–250). Springer. https://doi.org/10.1007/978-1-4614-3858-8_22

Kirjavainen, S., & Hölttä-Otto, K. (2019, August 18–21). To classify or combine: The effects of idea generation mechanisms on the novelty and quantity of ideas. In *Proceedings of the ASME 2019 International Design Engineering Technical Conferences and Computers and Information in Engineering Conference*, Volume 7: 31st International Conference on Design Theory and Methodology, Article DETC2019-97141, V007T06A004. American Society of Mechanical Engineers. https://doi.org/10.1115/DETC2019-97141

Klapwijk R.M. (2017) Formative assessment of creativity. In M. de Vries (Ed.), *Handbook of technology education* (Springer international handbooks of education; pp. 1–20). Springer, Cham. https://doi.org/10.1007/978-3-319-38889-2_55-1

Kong, S.-C., Chiu, M. M., & Lai, M. (2018). A study of primary school students' interest, collaboration attitude, and programming empowerment in computational thinking education. *Computers & Education*, *127*(1), 178–189. http://dx.doi.org/10.1016/j.compedu.2018.08.026

Kraft, M., Blazar, D., & Hogan, D. (2018). The effect of teacher coaching on instruction and achievement: A meta-analysis of the causal evidence. *Review of Educational Research*, *88*(4), 547–588. https://doi.org/10.3102/0034654318759268

Krammer, G., Vogel, S. E., & Grabner, R. (2020). Believing in neuromyths makes neither a bad nor good student-teacher: The relationship between neuromyths and academic achievement in teacher education. *Mind, Brain, and Education*, *15*(1), 54–60. https://doi.org/10.1111/mbe.12266

Lackney, J. A. (2008). Teacher environmental competence in elementary school environments. *Children Youth and Environments*, *18*(2), 133–159.

Lamnina M., & Chase C. C. (2019). Developing a thirst for knowledge: How uncertainty in the classroom influences curiosity, affect, learning, and transfer. *Contemporary Educational Psychology, 59*, Article 101785. https://doi.org/10.1016/j.cedpsych.2019.101785

Lazarides, R., Gaspard, H., & Dicke, A.-L. (2019). Dynamics of classroom motivation: Teacher enthusiasm and the development of math interest and teacher support. *Learning and Instruction, 60*, 126–137. https://doi.org/10.1016/j.learninstruc.2018.01.012

Lazarus, B. D. (1996). Flexible skeletons: Guided notes for adolescents. *Teaching Exceptional Children*, *28*(3), 36–40. https://doi.org/10.1177/004005999602800307

Le, H., Janssen, J., & Wubbels, T. (2018). Collaborative learning practices: Teacher and student perceived obstacles to effective student collaboration. *Cambridge Journal of Education*, *48*(1), 103–122. https://doi.org/10.1080/0305764X.2016.1259389

Lebuda, I., Jankowska, D. M., & Karwowski, M. (2020). Parents' creative self-concept and creative activity as predictors of family lifestyle. *International Journal of Environmental Research and Public Health*, *17*(24), 9558. https://doi.org/10.3390/ijerph17249558

Lee, W. S. (2020). An experimental investigation into the application of a learning-from-mistakes approach among freshmen students. *SAGE Open*, *10*(2). https://doi.org/10.1177/2158244020931938

Lee, C.-C., Hao, Y., Lee, K. S., Sim, S. C., & Huang, C.-C. (2019). Investigation of the effects of an online instant response system on students in a middle school of a rural area. *Computers in Human Behavior, 95*, 217–223. https://doi.org/10.1016/j.chb.2018.11.034

Lee, C. S., Therriault, D. J., & Linderholm, T. (2012). On the cognitive benefits of cultural experience: Exploring the relationship between studying abroad and creative thinking. *Applied Cognitive Psychology*, *26*(5), 768–778. https://doi.org/10.1002/acp.2857

Lee, P.-L., Wang, C.-L., Hamman, D., Hsiao, C.-H., & Huang, C.-H. (2013). Notetaking instruction enhances students' science learning. *Child Development Research*, Article 831591. https://doi.org/10.1155/2013/831591

Lehrl, S., Evangelou, M., & Sammons, P. (2020). The home learning environment and its role in shaping children's educational development. *School Effectiveness and School Improvement*, *31*(1), 1–6. https://doi.org/10.1080/09243453.2020.1693487VV

Lempinen, E. (2020, May 27). *The pandemic could open a door to new technology – and dramatic innovation – in education*. Berkley News. https://news.berkeley.edu/2020/05/27/the-pandemic-could-open-a-door-to-new-technology-and-dramatic-innovation-in-education/

Leopoldino, K. D. M., González, M. O. A., de Oliveira Ferreira, P., Pereira, J. R., & Costa Souto, M. E. (2016). Creativity techniques: A systematic review. *Product: Management and Development, 14*(2), 95–100. https://doi.org/10.4322/pmd.2016.015

Leung, A. K.-Y., & Chiu, C.-Y. (2008). Interactive effects of multicultural experiences and openness to experience on creative potential. *Creativity Research Journal, 20*, 376–382. https://doi.org/10.1080/10400410802391371

Leung, A. K.-y., Maddux, W. W., Galinsky, A. D., & Chiu, C.-y. (2008). Multicultural experience enhances creativity: The when and how. *American Psychologist, 63*(3), 169–181. https://doi.org/10.1037/0003-066X.63.3.169

Li, C.-H., & Liu, Z.-Y. (2017). Collaborative problem-solving behavior of 15-year-old Taiwanese students in science education. *Eurasia Journal of Mathematics, Science and Technology Education, 13*, 6577–6595. https://doi.org/10.12973/ejmste/78189.

Liang, C. C., & Yuan, Y. H. (2020). Exploring children's creative self-efficacy affected by after-school program and parent-child relationships. *Frontiers in Psychology, 11*, Article 2237. https://doi.org/10.3389/fpsyg.2020.02237

Lidåker, T. (2018). *The potential of argument mapping as a tool for teaching critical thinking in secondary school* [Master's thesis, Linköping University]. DiVA. http://liu.diva-portal.org/smash/get/diva2:1229406/FULLTEXT01.pdf

Lieberman, J. N. (1977). *Playfulness: Its relationship to imagination and creativity*. Academic Press.

Liljekvist, Y. E., Randahl, A.-C., van Bommel, J., & Olin-Scheller, C. (2020). Facebook for professional development: Pedagogical content knowledge in the centre of teachers' online communities. *Scandinavian Journal of Educational Research, 65*(5), 723–735. https://doi.org/10.1080/00313831.2020.1754900

Lin, N. C., & Cheng, H. F. (2010). Effects of gradual release of responsibility model on language learning. *Procedia – Social and Behavioral Sciences, 2*(2), 1866–1870. https://doi.org/10.1016/j.sbspro.2010.03.1000

Lin, S.-F. (2019). Students' attitudes towards learning English vocabulary through collaborative group work versus individual work. *Journal of Education and Learning, 8*(4), 93–111. https://doi.org/10.5539/jel.v8n4p93

Litcanu, M., Proştean, O., Oros, C., & Mnerie, A.V. (2015). Brain-Writing Vs. Brainstorming Case Study For Power Engineering Education. *Procedia - Social and Behavioral Sciences, 191*, 387-390. https://doi.org/10.1016/j.sbspro.2015.04.452

Liu, C. C., Lu, K. H., Wu, L. Y., & Tsai, C. C. (2016). The impact of peer review on creative self-efficacy and learning performance in Web 2.0 learning activities. *Journal of Educational Technology & Society, 19*(2), 286–297. http://www.jstor.org/stable/jeductechsoci.19.2.286

Liu, Y., & Huang, X. (2021). Effects of basic psychological needs on resilience: A human agency model. *Frontiers in Psychology, 12*, Article 700035. https://doi.org/10.3389/fpsyg.2021.700035

Lombardi, L., Mednick, F. J., De Backer, F., & Lombaerts, K. (2021). Fostering critical thinking across the primary school's curriculum in the European schools system. *Education Sciences, 11*(9), 505. MDPI AG. http://dx.doi.org/10.3390/educsci11090505

Loscalzo, J. (2014). A celebration of failure. *Circulation, 129*(9), 953–955. https://doi.org/10.1161/CIRCULATIONAHA.114.009220

Lu, J. G., Akinola, M., Mason, M. F. (2017). "Switching on" creativity: Task switching can increase creativity by reducing cognitive fixation. *Organizational Behavior and Human Decision Processes, 139*, 63–75. https://doi.org/10.1016/j.obhdp.2017.01.005

Lucas, B., Claxton, G., & Spencer, E. (2013). *Progression in student creativity in school: first steps towards new forms of formative assessments* (OECD Education Working Papers, No. 86). OECD Publishing. http://dx.doi.org/10.1787/5k4dp59msdwk-en

Lucas, B. J., & Nordgren, L. F. (2015). People underestimate the value of persistence for creative performance. *Journal of Personality and Social Psychology, 109*(2), 232–243. https://doi.org/10.1037/pspa0000030

Luo, L., Kiewra, K. A., & Samuelson, L. (2016). *Revising lecture notes: How revision, pauses, and partners affect note taking and achievement. Instructional Science, 44,* 45–67. https://doi.org/10.1007/s11251-016-9370-4

Ma, X., Bie, Z., Li, C., Gu, C., Li, Q., Tan, Y., Tian, M.-Y., & Fan, C. (2021). The effect of intrinsic motivation and environmental cues on social creativity. *Interactive Learning Environments.* https://doi.org/10.1080/10494820.2021.1874423

Maddux, W. W., & Galinsky, A. D. (2009). Cultural borders and mental barriers: the relationship between living abroad and creativity. *Journal of personality and social psychology, 96*(5), 1047. https://psycnet.apa.org/doi/10.1037/a0014861

Mammadov, S. (2021). A comparison of creativity-relevant personal characteristics in adolescents across personality profiles. *The Journal of Creative Behavior, 55*(2), 294-305. https://doi.org/10.1002/jocb.451

Mannion, J. M. (2019). *The effectiveness of the question formulation technique on open-ended, written response questions in mathematics* [Master's Thesis, Rowan University]. Rowan Digital Works. https://rdw.rowan.edu/etd/2673

Mansour, H., & Al-yahyai, F., & Heiba, E. (2018). The recycling concept in art education at Sultan Qaboos University. *Journal of Education and Social Development, 2*(2), 82–87. https://doi.org/10.5281/zenodo.2526431

Marks, J., & Chase, C. C. (2019). Impact of a prototyping intervention on middle school students' iterative practices and reactions to failure. *Journal of Engineering Education, 108*(4), 547–573. https://doi.org/10.1002/jee.20294

Marshall, B. (2017). The politics of testing. *English in Education, 51*(1), 27–43. https://doi.org/10.1111/eie.12110

Marttunen, M., & Laurinen, L. (2007). Collaborative learning through chat discussions and argument diagrams in secondary school. *Journal of Research on Technology in Education, 40*(1), 109–126. https://doi.org/10.1080/15391523.2007.10782500

May, B. N. (2020). Exploring and Engaging in Music Innovation Through the Engineering Design Process. *General Music Today, 34*(1), 43–48. https://doi.org/10.1177/1048371320942282

McLain, D. L., Kefallonitis, E., & Armani, K. (2015). Ambiguity tolerance in organizations: Definitional clarification and perspectives on future research. *Frontiers in Psychology, 6,* Article 344. https://doi.org/10.3389/fpsyg.2015.00344

Meer, B., & Stein, M. I. (1955). Measures of intelligence and creativity. *the Journal of Psychology, 39*(1), 117-126. https://doi.org/10.1080/00223980.1955.9916164

Mehta, S., & Kulshrestha, A. K. (2014). Implementation of cooperative learning in science: A developmental-cum-experimental study. *Education Research International,* 2014, Article 431542. https://doi.org/10.1155/2014/431542

Miller, A. L., Lambert, A. D., & Speirs Neumeister, K. L. (2012). Parenting style, perfectionism, and creativity in high-ability and high-achieving young adults. *Journal for the Education of the Gifted, 35*(4), 344–365. https://doi.org/10.1177/0162353212459257

Minigan, A. P., & Beer, J. (2017). Inquiring minds: Using the question formulation technique to activate student curiosity. *The New England Journal of History, 74*(1), 114–136.

Miyatsu, T., Nguyen, K., & McDaniel, M. A. (2018). Five popular study strategies: Their pitfalls and optimal implementations. *Perspectives on Psychological Science*, *13*(3), 390–407. https://doi.org/10.1177/1745691617710510

Mo, J. (2017). C*ollaborative problem solving* (PISA in Focus, No. 78). OECD Publishing. https://doi.org/10.1787/cdae6d2e-en

Moliner, L., & Alegre, F. (2020). Effects of peer tutoring on middle school students' mathematics self-concepts. *PloS One*, *15*(4), e0231410. https://doi.org/10.1371/journal.pone.0231410

Molnár, G., & Csapó, B. (2018). The efficacy and development of students' problem-solving strategies during compulsory schooling: Logfile analyses. *Frontiers in psychology*, *9*, Article 302. https://doi.org/10.3389/fpsyg.2018.00302

Moore, L. S., & Pharis, T. (2019). Improving teacher quality: Professional development implications from teacher professional growth and effectiveness system implementation in rural Kentucky high schools. *Educational Research Quarterly 42*(3), 29–48. https://eric.ed.gov/?id=EJ1205241

Moraru, M. (2019). Improving school climate through the teachers' and students' creativity. *Journal of Pedagogy – Revista de Pedagogie*, *2019*(2), 139–149. https://doi.org/10.26755/RevPed/2019.2/139

Mousena, E., & Raptis, N. (2020). Beyond teaching: School climate and communication in the educational context. In S. Waller, L. Waller, V. Mpofu & M. Kureba (Eds.), *Education at the intersection of globalisation and technology*. IntechOpen. https://doi.org/10.5772/intechopen.93575

Mueller, A., & Fleming, T. (2001). Cooperative learning: Listening to how children work at school. *The Journal of Educational Research*, *94*(5), 259–265. http://www.jstor.org/stable/27542333?origin=JSTOR-pdf

Mueller, P. A., & Oppenheimer, D. M. (2014). The pen is mightier than the keyboard: Advantages of longhand over laptop note taking. *Psychological Science*, *25*(6), 1159–1168. https://doi.org/10.1177/0956797614524581

Muir, T. (2020). Self-determination theory and the flipped classroom: A case study of a senior secondary mathematics class. *Mathematics Education Research Journal*, *33*, 569–587 https://doi.org/10.1007/s13394-020-00320-3

Mukhtoraliyevna, Z. S., & Madaminkhonqizi, S. M. (2022). Methods of mnemonics in pedagogical work with elementary school students. *International Journal of Culture and Modernity*, *13*, 44–52. https://ijcm.academicjournal.io/index.php/ijcm/article/view/192

Mullet, D. R., Willerson, A., Lamb, K. N., & Kettler, T. (2016). Examining teacher perceptions of creativity: A systematic review of the literature. *Thinking Skills and Creativity*, *21*, 9–30. https://doi.org/10.1016/j.tsc.2016.05.001

Nakayama, M. (Ed.). (2021). *Note taking activities in e-learning environments*. Springer Singapore.

Naputa, G., Patston, T., & Patston, G. (2019). *Aboriginal sky figures: Your guide to finding the sky figures in the stars, based on Aboriginal dreamtime stories*. ABC.

National Advisory Committee on Creative and Cultural Education. (1999). *All our futures: Creativity, Culture and Education*. https://sirkenrobinson.com/pdf/allourfutures.pdf

Newman, A., Tse, H. H. M., Schwarz, G., & Nielsen, I. (2018). The effects of employees' creative self-efficacy on innovative behavior: The role of entrepreneurial leadership. *Journal of Business Research*, *89*, 1–9, https://doi.org/10.1016/j.jbusres.2018.04.001

Ng, Y. F., Chan, K. K., Lei, H., Mok, P., & Leung, S. (2019). Pedagogy and innovation in science education: A case study of an experiential learning science undergraduate course. *The European Journal of Social & Behavioural Sciences*, *25*(2), 2910–2926. https://doi.org/10.15405/ejsbs.254

Nielsen, J. A., Zielinski, B. A., Ferguson, M. A., Lainhart, J. E., & Anderson, J. S. (2013). An evaluation of the left-brain vs. right-brain hypothesis with resting state functional connectivity magnetic resonance imaging. *PLoS ONE*, *8*(8), Article e71275. https://doi.org/10.1371/journal.pone.0071275

Nijstad, B. A., De Dreu, C. K. W., Rietzschel, E. F., & Baas, M. (2010). The dual pathway to creativity model: Creative ideation as a function of flexibility and persistence. *European Review of Social Psychology, 21*(1), 34–77. https://doi.org/10.1080/10463281003765323

Nordin, A., & Sundberg, D. (2016). Travelling concepts in national curriculum policy-making: The example of competencies. *European Education Research Journal, 15*(3), 314–328. https://doi.org/10.1177/1474904116641697

Mokhtar Noriega, F., Heppell, S., Segovia Bonet, N., & Heppell, J. (2013). Building better learning and learning better building, with learners rather than for learners. *On the Horizon, 21*(2), 138-148. https://doi.org/10.1108/10748121311323030

Nouri, J., Akerfeldt, A., Fors, U., & Selander, S. (2017). Assessing collaborative problem solving skills in technology-enhanced learning environments – the PISA framework and modes of communication. *International Journal of Emerging Technologies in Learning (iJET), 12*(4), 163–174. https://doi.org/10.3991/ijet.v12i04.6737

Novak, J. D. (1990). Concept mapping: A useful tool for science education. *Journal of Research in Science Teaching, 27*(10), 937–949. https://doi.org/10.1002/tea.3660271003

Nüdel Kart. (2021). *Teacher creativity manual*. Nüdel Kart. https://www.nudelkart.com/uploads/1/2/4/9/124932713/nu%CC%88k_creativity_chapter-v1-1.pdf

Nusbaum, E. C., & Silvia, P. J. (2011). Are intelligence and creativity really so different? Fluid intelligence, executive processes, and strategy use in divergent thinking. *Intelligence, 39*(1), 36–45. https://doi.org/10.1016/j.intell.2010.11.002

O'Donovan, R., & McAuliffe, E. (2020). A systematic review exploring the content and outcomes of interventions to improve psychological safety, speaking up and voice behaviour. *BMC Health Services Research, 20*, Article 101. https://doi.org/10.1186/s12913-020-4931-2

Offner, A. K., Kramer, T. J., & Winter, J. P. (1996). The effects of facilitation, recording, and pauses on group brainstorming. *Small Group Research, 27*(2), 283–298. https://doi.org/10.1177/1046496496272005

Oleynick, V. C., DeYoung, C. G., Hyde, E., Kaufman, S. B., Beaty, R. E., & Silvia, P. J. (2017). Openness/intellect: The core of the creative personality. In G. J. Feist, R. Reiter-Palmon, & J. C. Kaufman (Eds.), *The Cambridge handbook of creativity and personality research* (pp. 9–27). Cambridge University Press. https://doi.org/10.1017/9781316228036.002

Onanuga, P. (2020). Relative effectiveness of generative learning strategy on students' academic achievement in senior secondary school biology: Sustainable development perspective. *Annual Journal of Technical University of Varna, Bulgaria, 4*(1), 12–22. https://doi.org/10.29114/ajtuv.vol4.iss1.134

Ong, C. S. L., & Nie, Y. (2016). Promoting students' creative self-efficacy: A field experimental study in Singapore secondary classrooms. In R. B. King & A. B. I. Bernardo (Eds.), *The Psychology of Asian Learners* (pp. 559–575). Springer.

Organisation for Economic Co-operation and Development. (2008, 15-16 May). *Twenty-first century learning: Research, innovation and policy directions from recent OECD analyses* [Conference session]. OECD/CERI International conference on Learning in the 21st century: Research, innovation and policy, Paris, France. https://www.oecd.org/site/educeri21st/40820895.pdf

Organisation for Economic Co-operation and Development. (2013). *PISA 2015 draft collaborative problem solving framework*. https://www.oecd.org/callsfortenders/Annex%20ID_PISA%202015%20Collaborative%20Problem%20Solving%20Framework%20.pdf

Organisation for Economic Co-operation and Development. (2019). *PISA 2021 Creative thinking framework: Third draft*. OECD.

Osborn, A., (1948). *Your Creative Power: how to Use Imagination*. C. Scribner & Sons

Osborn, A. F. (1953). *Applied imagination: Principles and procedures of creative problem-solving*. Charles Scribner's Sons.

REFERENCES

Ozyaprak, M. (2016). The effectiveness of SCAMPER technique on creative thinking skills. *Journal for the Education of Gifted Young Scientists, 4*(1), 31–40. http://dx.doi.org/10.17478/JEGYS.2016116348

Painter, D. (2018). *Using design thinking in mathematics for middle school students: A multiple case study of teacher perspectives* [Doctoral Thesis, Concordia University, St. Paul]. DigitalCommons@CSP. https://digitalcommons.csp.edu/cup_commons_grad_edd/192

Pantaleo, S. (2019). Creativity and elementary students' multimodal narrative representations. *Australian Journal of Language and Literacy, 42*(1), 17–27.

Patston, T. (2015). Why are we waiting? Education research and the lethargy of change (Occasional Paper 143). *Centre for Strategic Education*. http://www.cse.edu.au/zfiles/OccPaper143Sample.pdf

Patston, T. (2019). *What is creativity in education?* The Education Hub. https://theeducationhub.org.nz/wp-content/uploads/2021/03/What-is-creativity-in-education.pdf

Patston, T. (March 17, 2021b). *Creativity at secondary school*. The Education Hub. https://theeducationhub.org.nz/creativity-at-secondary-school/

Patston, T. J., Cropley, D. H., Marrone, R. L., & Kaufman, J. C. (2018). Teacher implicit beliefs of creativity: Is there an arts bias? *Teaching and Teacher Education, 75*, 366–374. https://doi.org/10.1016/j.tate.2018.08.001

Patston, T. J., Kaufman, J. C., Cropley, A. J., & Marrone, R. (2021). What is creativity in education? A qualitative study of international curricula. *Journal of Advanced Academics, 32*(2), 207–230. https://doi.org/10.1177/1932202X20978356

Patston, T. J., Kennedy, J., Jaeschke, W., Kapoor, H., Leonard, S. N., Cropley, D. H., & Kaufman, J. C. (2021). Secondary education in COVID lockdown: More anxious and less creative – maybe not? *Frontiers in Psychology, 12*, Article 613055. https://doi.org/10.3389/fpsyg.2021.613055

Patston, T., & Waters, L. (2015). Positive instruction in music studios: Introducing a new model for teaching studio music in schools based upon positive psychology. *Psychology of Well-Being, 5*, Article 10. https://doi.org/10.1186/s13612-015-0036-9

Pauk, W., & Owens, R. J. Q. (2010). *How to study in college* (10th ed.). Wadsworth.

Peng, C. (2021). A conceptual review of teacher enthusiasm and students' success and engagement in Chinese EFL classes. *Frontiers in Psychology, 12*, Article 742970. https://doi.org/10.3389/fpsyg.2021.742970

Pérez-Fuentes, M. D. C., Molero Jurado, M. D. M., Oropesa Ruiz, N. F., Simón Márquez, M. D. M., & Gázquez Linares, J. J. (2019). Relationship between digital creativity, parenting style, and adolescent performance. *Frontiers in Psychology, 2487*. https://doi.org/10.3389/fpsyg.2019.02487

Pernaa, J., & Wiedmer, S. (2020). A systematic review of 3D printing in chemistry education – analysis of earlier research and educational use through technological pedagogical content knowledge framework. *Chemistry Teacher International, 2*(2), Article 20190005. https://doi.org/10.1515/cti-2019-0005

Pfeiffer, J. W. (1998). *The Pfeiffer Library, Volume 26* (2nd ed). Jossey-Bass and Pfeiffer.

Philipsen, B., Tondeur, J., Pareja Roblin, N., Vanslambrouck, S., & Zhu, C. (2019). Improving teacher professional development for online and blended learning: a systematic meta-aggregative review. *Educational Technology Research and Development, 67*, 1145–1174. https://doi.org/10.1007/s11423-019-09645-8

Pichierri, M., & Guido, G. (2016). When the row predicts the grade: Differences in marketing students' performance as a function of seating location. *Learning and Individual Differences, 49*, 437–441. https://doi.org/10.1016/j.lindif.2016.04.007

Pichugova, I. L., Stepura, S. N., & Pravosudov, M. M. (2016). Issues of promoting learner autonomy in EFL context. *SHS Web of Conferences, 28*, Article 01081. https://doi.org/10.1051/shsconf/20162801081

Pierce, J. L., Gardner, D. G., & Crowley, C. (2016). Organization-based self-esteem and well-being: Empirical examination of a spillover effect. E*uropean Journal of Work and Organizational Psychology, 25*(2), 181–199. https://doi.org/10.1080/1359432X.2015.1028377

Pirola-Merlo, A., & Mann, L. (2004). The relationship between individual creativity and team creativity: Aggregating across people and time. *Journal of Organizational Behavior, 25*(2), 235–257. https://doi.org/10.1002/job.240

Plucker, J. A., & Alanazi, R. (2019). Is creativity compatible with educational accountability? Promise and pitfalls of using assessment to monitor and enhance a complex construct. In I. Lebuda & V. P. Glaveanu (Eds.), *The Palgrave handbook of social creativity research* (pp. 501–514). Palgrave Macmillan.

Plucker, J. A., Beghetto, R. A., & Dow, G. T. (2004). Why isn't creativity more important to educational psychologists? Potentials, pitfalls, and future directions in creativity research. *Educational Psychologist, 39*(2), 83–96. https://doi.org/10.1207/s15326985ep3902_1

Plucker, J. A., Makel, M. C., & Qian, M. (2021). Assessment of creativity. In J. C. Kaufman, & R. J. Sternberg (Eds.), *Creativity: An Introduction* (pp. 41–66). Cambridge University Press. https://doi.org/10.1017/9781108776721

Pluut, H., & Curşeu, P. L. (2013). The role of diversity of life experiences in fostering collaborative creativity in demographically diverse student groups. *Thinking Skills and Creativity, 9*, 16–23. https://doi.org/10.1016/j.tsc.2013.01.002

Poirier, M., Law, J. M., & Veispak, A. (2019). A spotlight on lack of evidence supporting the integration of blended learning in K–12 education: A systematic review. *International Journal of Mobile and Blended Learning, 11*(4), 1-14. https://doi.org/10.4018/IJMBL.2019100101

Polat, Ö., & Aydın, E. (2020). The effect of mind mapping on young children's critical thinking skills. *Thinking Skills and Creativity, 38*, Article 100743. https://doi.org/10.1016/j.tsc.2020.100743

Popova, A., Evans, D. K., Breeding, M. E., & Arancibia,, V. (2022). Teacher professional development around the world: The gap between evidence and practice. *The World Bank Research Observer, 37*(1), 107–136. https://doi.org/10.1093/wbro/lkab006

Post, T., & van der Molen, J. H. W. (2018). Do children express curiosity at school? Exploring children's experiences of curiosity inside and outside the school context. *Learning, Culture, and Social Interaction, 18*, 60–71. https://doi.org/10.1016/j.lcsi.2018.03.005

Power, R. A., & Pluess, M. (2015). Heritability estimates of the Big Five personality traits based on common genetic variants. *Translational Psychiatry, 5*(7), Article e604. https://doi.org/10.1038/tp.2015.96

Powers, D. E., & Kaufman, J. C. (2004). Do standardized tests penalize deep-thinking, creative, or conscientious students? Some personality correlates of Graduate Record Examinations test scores. *Intelligence, 32*(2), 145–153. https://doi.org/10.1016/j.intell.2003.08.003

Priyadi, A. A., & Suyanto, S. (2019, July 12–13). The effectiveness of problem based learning in biology with fishbone diagram on critical thinking skill of senior high school students. *Journal of Physics: Conference Series, 1397*, Article 012047. https://iopscience.iop.org/issue/1742-6596/1397/1

Puente-Díaz, R., Cavazos-Arroyo, J., Puerta-Sierra, L., & Vargas-Barrera, F. (2022). The contribution openness to experience and its two aspects to the explanation of idea generation, evaluation and selection: A metacognitive perspective. *Personality and Individual Differences, 185*, Article 111240. https://doi.org/10.1016/j.paid.2021.111240

Pugsley, L., & Acar, S. (2020). Supporting creativity or conformity? Influence of home environment and parental factors on the value of children's creativity characteristics. *Journal of Creative Behavior, 54*(3), 598–609. https://doi.org/10.1002/jocb.393

Putnam, A. L. (2015). Mnemonics in education: Current research and applications. *Translational Issues in Psychological Science, 1*(2), 130–139. https://doi.org/10.1037/tps0000023

Pyörälä, E., Mäenpää, S., Heinonen, L., Folger, D., Masalin, T., & Hervonen, H. (2019). The art of note taking with mobile devices in medical education. *BMC Medical Education, 19*, Article 96. https://doi.org/10.1186/s12909-019-1529-7

Ra, S., Shrestha, U., Khatiwada, S., Yoon, S. W., & Kwon, K. (2019). The rise of technology and impact on skills. *International Journal of Training Research*, 17(sup1), 26–40. https://doi.org/10.1080/14480220.2019.1629727

Ragupathi K., & Lee A. (2020). Beyond fairness and consistency in grading: The role of rubrics in higher education. In C. Sanger & N. Gleason (Eds.), *Diversity and inclusion in global higher education* (pp. 73–95). Palgrave Macmillan. https://doi.org/10.1007/978-981-15-1628-3_3

Rannastu M., Siiman L. A., Mäeots M., Pedaste M., & Leijen Ä. (2019). Does group size affect students' inquiry and collaboration in using computer-based asymmetric collaborative simulations? [Conference paper]. In M. Herzog, Z. Kubincová, P. Han, & M. Temperini (Eds.), *Advances in web-based learning – ICWL 2019. Lecture Notes in computer science* (Vol. 11841, pp. 143–154). Springer, Cham. https://doi.org/10.1007/978-3-030-35758-0_14

Rapanta, C., Botturi, L., Goodyear, P., Guàrdia, L., & Koole, M. (2020). Online university teaching during and after the Covid-19 crisis: Refocusing teacher presence and learning activity. *Postdigital Science and Education*, 2, 923–945. https://doi.org/10.1007/s42438-020-00155-y

Reinig, B. A., & Briggs, R. O. (2008). On the relationship between idea-quantity and idea-quality during ideation. *Group Decision and Negotiation*, 17, Article 403. https://doi.org/10.1007/s10726-008-9105-2

Reis, S. M., & Renzulli, J. S. (1991). The assessment of creative products in programs for gifted and talented students. *Gifted Child Quarterly*, 35(3), 128–134. https://doi.org/10.1177/001698629103500304

Reiter-Palmon, R., & Robinson, E. J. (2009). Problem identification and construction: What do we know, what is the future? *Psychology of Aesthetics, Creativity, and the Arts*, 3(1), 43–47. https://doi.org/10.1037/a0014629

Reynders, G., Lantz, J., Ruder, S. M., Stanford, C. L., & Cole, R. S. (2020). Rubrics to assess critical thinking and information processing in undergraduate STEM courses. *International Journal of STEM Education*, 7, Article 9. https://doi.org/10.1186/s40594-020-00208-5

Rhodes, M. (1961). An analysis of creativity. *The Phi Delta Kappan*, 42(7), 305–310. https://www.jstor.org/stable/20342603

Rhodes, T. (2010). *Assessing outcomes and improving achievement: Tips and tools for using rubrics*. Association of American Colleges and Universities.

Ribeiro, M. P., & Fleith, D. D. S. (2018). Creativity and multiculturalism: Literature review. *Trends in Psychology*, 26(2), 943–956. https://doi.org/1010.9788/TP2018.2-15Pt

Ricardo-Barreto, C., Llinas-Solano, H., Medina-Rivilla, A., Cacheiro-Gonzalez, M. L., Villegas-Mendoza, A., Lafaurie, A., & Navarro Angarita, V. (2022). Teachers' perceptions of culturally appropriate pedagogical strategies in virtual learning environments: A study in Colombia. *Turkish Online Journal of Distance Education*, 23(1), 113–130. https://doi.org/10.17718/tojde.1050372

Richardson, C., & Mishra, P. (2018). Learning environments that support student creativity: Developing the SCALE. *Thinking Skills and Creativity*, 27, 45–54. https://doi.org/10.1016/j.tsc.2017.11.004

Rickards, T., & De Cock, C. (2012). Understanding organizational creativity: Toward a multiparadigmatic approach. In M. Runco (Ed.), *The creativity research handbook* (pp. 1-31). Hampton Press.

Rietzschel, E. F., Nijstad, B. A., & Stroebe, W. (2006). Productivity is not enough: A comparison of interactive and nominal brainstorming groups on idea generation and selection. *Journal of Experimental Social Psychology*, 42(2), 244–251. https://doi.org/10.1016/j.jesp.2005.04.005

Rietzschel, E. F., Nijstad, B. A., & Stroebe, W. (2010). The selection of creative ideas after individual idea generation: Choosing between creativity and impact. *British Journal of Psychology*, 101(1), 47–68. https://doi.org/10.1348/000712609X414204

Rissanen, I., Kuusisto, E., Tuominen, M., & Tirri, K. (2018). In search of a growth mindset pedagogy: A case study of one teacher's classroom practices in a Finnish elementary school. *Teaching and Teacher Education*, 77, 204–213. https://doi.org/10.1016/j.tate.2018.10.002

Ritchhart, R., Church, M., & Morrison, K. (2011). *Making thinking visible: How to promote engagement, understanding and independence for all learners*. Jossey-Bass.

Ritter, S. M., & Mostert, N. M. (2017). Enhancement of creative thinking skills using a cognitive-based creativity training. *Journal of Cognitive Enhancement, 1*, 243–253. https://doi.org/10.1007/s41465-016-0002-3

Riyapan, P., & Hazanee, A., & Pansombut, T., & Muangprathub, J., & Intarasit, A. (2021). The development of blended learning through learning by teaching for mathematical literacy in general education program on higher education. *Universal Journal of Educational Research, 9*, 556–563. https://doi.org/10.13189/ujer.2021.090315.

Romainville, M., & Noël, B. (2003). Métacognition et apprentissage de la prise de notes à l'université [Metacognition and note-taking learning at the university]. *Arob@se, 1–2*, 87–96. http://www.arobase.to

Rosenstock, L., & Riordan, R. (2017). Changing the subject. In R. A. Beghetto, & J. C. Kaufman (Eds.), *Nurturing creativity in the classroom* (pp. 3-5). Cambridge University Press.

Rott, B. (2021). *Epistemological beliefs and critical thinking in mathematics: Qualitative and quantitative studies with pre-service teachers*. Springer. https://doi.org/10.1007/978-3-658-33539-7_3

Runco, M. A., & Jaeger, G. J. (2012). The standard definition of creativity. *Creativity Research Journal, 24*(1), 92–96. https://doi.org/10.1080/10400419.2012.650092

Russ, S. W., & Lee, A. W. (2021). Pretend play and creativity. In J. A. Plucker (Ed.), *Creativity and innovation: Theory, research and practice* (pp. 133–149). Routledge.

Russ, S. W., & Wallace, C. E. (2013). Pretend play and creative processes. *American Journal of Play, 6*(1), 136–148.

Ryan, R. M., & Deci, E. L. (2020). Intrinsic and extrinsic motivation from a self-determination theory perspective: Definitions, theory, practices, and future directions. *Contemporary Educational Psychology, 61*, Article 101860. https://psycnet.apa.org/doi/10.1016/j.cedpsych.2020.101860

Ryberg, R., Her, S., Temkin, D., Madill, R., Kelley, C., Thompson, J., & Gabriel, A. (2020). Measuring school climate: Validating the education department school climate survey in a sample of urban middle and high school students. *AERA Open, 6*(3). https://doi.org/10.1177/2332858420948024

Sadler-Smith, E. (2015). Wallas' four-stage model of the creative process: More than meets the eye? *Creativity Research Journal, 27*(4), 342–352. https://doi.org/10.1080/10400419.2015.1087277

Şahin, F. (2021). The effects of personality traits of teachers on the development of student creativity. *Education and Science, 46*(205), 191–205. https://doi.org/10.15390/EB.2020.9154

Salazar-Torres, J., Rincón Leal, O., & Vergel Ortega, M. (2021). The rubric as an assessment tool for solving problem situations in the physics and mathematics teaching context. *Journal of Physics: Conference Series, 1981*, Article 012018. https://doi.org/10.1088/1742-6596/1981/1/012018

Salleh, S. S., & Ismail, R. (2013). Effectiveness of concept map approach in teaching history subject. In H. B. Zaman, P. Robinson, P. Olivier, T. K. Shih, & S. Velastin (Eds.). *Advances in visual informatics* (IVIC 2013: Lecture Notes in Computer Science, Vol. 8237). Springer, Cham. https://doi.org/10.1007/978-3-319-02958-0_62

Samsibar, S., & Naro, W. (2018). The effectiveness of role play method toward students' motivation in English conversation. *English, Teaching, Learning and Research Journal, 4*(1), 107–116. https://doi.org/10.24252/Eternal.V41.2018.A8

Sanders, S. (2016). Critical and creative thinkers in mathematics classrooms. *Journal of Student Engagement: Education Matters, 6*(1), 19–27. https://ro.uow.edu.au/jseem/vol6/iss1/4

Sanders, T., Parker, P. D., del Pozo-Cruz, B., Noetel, M., & Lonsdale, C. (2019). Type of screen time moderates effects on outcomes in 4013 children: Evidence from the Longitudinal Study of Australian Children. *International Journal of Behavioral Nutrition and Physical Activity, 16*, Article 117. https://doi.org/10.1186/s12966-019-0881-7

Saqr, M., Nouri, J., & Jormanainen, I. (2019). A learning analytics study of the effect of group size on social dynamics and performance in online collaborative learning. In M. Scheffel, J. Broisin, V. Pammer-Schindler, A. Ioannou, & J. Schneider (Eds.), *Lecture notes in computer science (including subseries Lecture notes in artificial intelligence and Lecture notes in bioinformatics) 11722 LNCS* (pp. 466–479). Springer International Publishing.

Sari, E. K., & Fitrawati, F. (2018). Using 6-3-5 Brainwriting in helping senior high school students doing brainstorming in writing process. *Journal of English Language Teaching, 7*(3). 531–537. https://doi.org/10.24036/jelt.v7i3.101115

Sari, E., & Tedjasaputra, A. (2013a). Engaging stakeholders through Facebook for teacher professional development in Indonesia [Conference paper]. In *Proceedings of the 25th Australian Computer-Human Interaction Conference: Augmentation, Application, Innovation, Collaboration, Adelaide, Austalia*, November 25–29, 2013 (pp. 201–204). https://doi.org/10.1145/2541016.2541056

Sari, E., & Tedjasaputra, A. (2013b). Online learning community for teacher professional development in Indonesia. In *Proceedings of the 21st International Conference on Computers in Education* (pp. 896–905). Asia-Pacific Society for Computers in Education.

Scales, P. C., Pekel, K., Sethi, J., Chamberlain, R., & Van Boekel, M. (2020). Academic year changes in student-teacher developmental relationships and their linkage to middle and high school students' motivation: A mixed methods study. *The Journal of Early Adolescence, 40*(4), 499–536. https://doi.org/10.1177/0272431619858414

Schifferle, T. M., & Kollegger, N. (2021, June 2–3). Enabling agile rapid product development in K12 classrooms by enhancing an educational exoskeleton. In *FabLearn Europe/MakeEd 2021 – An International Conference on Computing, Design and Making in Education* (Article 24). Association for Computing Machinery. https://doi.org/10.1145/3466725.3466768

Schweisfurth, M., & Elliott, J. (2019). When "best practice" meets the pedagogical nexus: Recontextualisation, reframing and resilience. *Comparative Education, 55*(1), 1–8. https://doi.org/10.1080/03050068.2018.1544801

Scott, G., Leritz, L. E., & Mumford, M. D. (2004). The effectiveness of creativity training: A quantitative review. *Creativity Research Journal, 16*(4), 361–388. https://doi.org/10.1207/s15326934crj1604_1

Scoular, C., Duckworth, D., Heard, J., & Ramalingam, D. (2020). Collaboration: Skill development framework. *Australian Council for Educational Research*. https://research/acer/edu.au/ar_misc/42

Seeber, I. (2019). How do facilitation interventions foster learning? The role of evaluation and coordination as causal mediators in idea convergence. *Computers in Human Behavior, 94*, 176–189. https://doi.org/10.1016/j.chb.2018.11.033

Segun, O. (2017). Effects of cognitive restructuring and problem solving strategies on reading and note taking of secondary school students in Ondo State, Nigeria. *Advances in Social Sciences Research Journal, 4*(16), 77–97. https://doi.org/10.14738/assrj.416.3545

Şentürk, C. (2021). Effects of the blended learning model on preservice teachers' academic achievements and twenty-first century skills. *Education and Information Technologies, 26*, 35–48. https://doi.org/10.1007/s10639-020-10340-y

Serrano-Espinoza, J. J., & Argudo-Serrano, J. C. (2022). A strategy based on music activities to promote motivation in a public school. *CIENCIAMATRIA, 8*(1), 490–512. https://doi.org/10.35381/cm.v8i1.687

Serrat, O. (2017). *Knowledge solutions: Tools, methods, and approaches to drive organizational performance*. Springer. https://doi.org/10.1007/978-981-10-0983-9

Shah, P. E., Weeks, H. M., Richards, B., & Kaciroti, N. (2018). Early childhood curiosity and kindergarten reading and math academic achievement. *Pediatric Research, 84*(3), 380–386. https://doi.org/10.1038/s41390-018-0039-3.

Shi, B., Dai, D. Y., & Lu, Y. (2016). Openness to experience as a moderator of the relationship between intelligence and creative thinking: A study of Chinese children in urban and rural areas. *Frontiers in Psychology, 7*, Article 641. https://doi.org/10.3389/fpsyg.2016.00641

Shiever, S., & Maker, C. J. (1991). Enrichment and acceleration: An overview and new direction. In N. Colangelo & G. A. Davis (Eds.), *Handbook of gifted education* (pp. 99–110). Allyn & Bacon.

Shively, K., Stith, K. M., & Rubenstein, L. D. (2018). Measuring what matters: Assessing creativity, critical thinking, and the design process. *Gifted Child Today, 41*(3), 149–158. https://doi.org/10.1177/1076217518768361

Shirvani, M., & Porkar, R. (2021). How do EFL students perceive brainstorming in L2 writing classes? *Theory and Practice in Language Studies, 11*(12), 1602–1609. https://doi.org/10.17507/tpls.1112.12

Sibbaluca, L. M. (2009). Clarification of ambiguous problems: Effects on problem solving ability and attitude towards mathematics. *Alipato: A Journal of Basic Education, 3*(3), 76–87. https://journals.upd.edu.ph/index.php/ali/article/view/1758

Silver, E. A., & Cai, J. (1993). *Mathematical problem posing and problem solving by middle school students* [Paper presentation]. Annual meeting of the American Educational Research Association, Atlanta, Georgia.

Silvia, P. J., & O'Brien, M. E. (2004). Self-awareness and constructive functioning: Revisiting "the human dilemma". *Journal of Social and Clinical Psychology, 23*(4), 475–489. https://doi.org/10.1521/jscp.23.4.475.40307

Silvia, P. J., Nusbaum, E. C., Berg, C., Martin, C., & O'Connor, A. (2009). Openness to experience, plasticity, and creativity: Exploring lower-order, high-order, and interactive effects. *Journal of Research in Personality, 43*(6), 1087–1090. https://doi.org/10.1016/j.jrp.2009.04.015

Silwa, S., Nihiser, A., Lee, S., McCaughtry, N., Culp, B., & Michael, S. (2017). Engaging students in physical education: key challenges and opportunities for physical educators in urban settings. *Journal of Physical Education, Recreation and Dance, 88*(8), 43–48. https://doi.org/10.1080/07303084.2017.1271266

Simonton, D. H. (2012). Creativity, problem solving, and solution set sightedness: Radically reformulating BVSR. *Journal of Creative Behavior, 46*(1), 48–65. https://doi.org/10.1002/jocb.004

Siok, W. T., & Liu, C. Y. (2018). Differential impacts of different keyboard inputting methods on reading and writing skills. *Scientific Reports, 8*(1), 1–13. https://doi.org/10.1038/s41598-018-35268-9

Sotiriou, S. A., Lazoudis, A., & Bogner, F. X. (2020). Inquiry-based learning and e-learning: How to serve high and low achievers. *Smart Learning Environments, 7*, Article 29. https://doi.org/10.1186/s40561-020-00130-x

Steeves, K. A., Bernhardt, P. E., Burns, J. P., & Lombard, M. K. (2009). Transforming American educational identity after Sputnik. *American Educational History Journal, 36*(1), 71–87. https://eric.ed.gov/?id=EJ863681

Stevanovic, M., Marjanović, D., & Štorga, M. (2015, July 27–30). A model of idea evaluation and selection for product innovation. In C. Weber, S. Husung, G. Cascini, M. Cantamessa, D. Marjanovic & F. Montagna (Eds.), *Proceedings of the 20th International Conference on Engineering Design (ICED15; Vol. 8)*, Milan, Italy (pp. 193–202). The Design Society.

Sternberg, R. J. (1987). Questions and answers about the nature and teaching of thinking skills. In J. B. Baron & R. J. Sternberg (Eds.), *Teaching thinking skills: Theory and practice* (pp. 251–259). W. H. Freeman and Co.

Sternberg, R. J. (1998). Styles of thinking and learning. *Canadian Journal of School Psychology, 13*(2), 15–40. https://doi.org/10.1177/082957359801300204

Sternberg, R. J., & Karami, S. (2021). An 8P theoretical framework for understanding creativity and theories of creativity. *The Journal of Creative Behavior, 56*(1), 55–78. https://doi.org/10.1002/jocb.516

Stokhof, H., de Vries, B., Bastiaens, T., & Martens, R. (2020). Using mind maps to make student questioning effective: Learning outcomes of a principle-based scenario for teacher guidance. *Research in Science Education, 50*, 203–225. https://doi.org/10.1007/s11165-017-9686-3

REFERENCES

Stover, D. (2014, January 1). Unleashing the creative mind. *Scientific American*. https://www.scientificamerican.com/article/unleashing-the-creative-mind-creativity-special/

Straker, D. (1997). *Rapid problem solving with Post-it® notes*. Da Capo Press.

Strelan, P., Osborn, A., & Palmer, E. (2020). The flipped classroom: A meta-analysis of effects on student performance across disciplines and education levels. *Educational Research Review, 30*, Article 100314. https://doi.org/10.1016/j.edurev.2020.100314

Sun, D., & Li, Y. (2019). Effectiveness of digital note-taking on students' performance in declarative, procedural and conditional knowledge learning. *International Journal of Emerging Technologies In Learning, 14*(18), 108–119. http://dx.doi.org/10.3991/ijet.v14i18.10825

Svensson, N. (2015). Subjective experiences of creative work after negative feedback. *Thinking Skills and Creativity, 15*, 26–36. https://doi.org/10.1016/j.tsc.2014.11.002

Swennen, A. (2017). We are not stuck! Professional development across generations. *Professional development in education, 43*(2), 157–162. https://doi.org/10.1080/19415257.2017.1282717

Symonds, J., & Schoon, I., Eccles, J., & Salmela-Aro, K. (2019). The development of motivation and amotivation to study and work across age-graded transitions in adolescence and young adulthood. *Journal of Youth and Adolescence, 48*, 1131–1145. https://doi.org/10.1007/s10964-019-01003-4

Tan, J. P-L., Caleon, I., Ng, H. L., Poon, C. L., & Koh, E. (2018). Collective creativity competencies and collaborative problem-solving outcomes: Insights from the dialogic interactions of Singapore student teams. In E. Care, P. Griffin & M. Wilson (Eds.), *Assessment and teaching of 21st century skills: Research and applications* (pp. 95–118). Springer. https://doi.org/10.1007/978-3-319-65368-6_6

Tanggaard, L. (2014). A situated model of creative learning. *European Educational Research Journal, 13*(1), 107–116. https://doi.org/10.2304/eerj.2014.13.1.107

Tanil, C. T., & Yong, M. H. (2020). Mobile phones: The effect of its presence on learning and memory. *Plos One, 15*(8), Article e0219233. https://doi.org/10.1371/journal.pone.0219233

Taylor, C. L. (2017). Creativity and mood disorder: A systematic review and meta-analysis. *Perspectives on Psychological Science, 12*(6), 1040–1076. https://doi.org/10.1177/1745691617699653

Taylor, I. A. (1975). An emerging view of creative actions. In I. A. Taylor & J. W. Getzels (Eds.), *Perspectives in creativity* (pp. 297–325). Aldine.

Taylor, S. I., & Rogers, C. S. (2001). The relationship between playfulness and creativity of Japanese preschool children. *International Journal of Early Childhood, 33*, 43–49. https://doi.org/10.1007/BF03174447

Taylor, V. F. (2018). Afraid of the deep: Reflections and analysis of a role-play exercise gone wrong. *Journal of Management Education, 42*(6), 772–782. https://doi.org/10.1177/1052562918802875

Thompson, D., & Meer, N. (2021). Blurring the boundaries of formative and summative assessment for impact on learning. *Practitioner Research in Higher Education, 14*(1), 28–40.

Thurm, D., & Barzel, B. (2020). Effects of a professional development program for teaching mathematics with technology on teachers' beliefs, self-efficacy and practices. *ZDM Mathematics Education, 52*, 1411–1422. https://doi.org/10.1007/s11858-020-01158-6

Tobia, V., Sacchi, S., Cerina, V., Manca, S., & Fornara, F. (2020). The influence of classroom seating arrangement on children's cognitive processes in primary school: the role of individual variables. *Current Psychology, 41*(9), 6522–6533. https://doi.org/10.1007/s12144-020-01154-9

Todd, E. M., Higgs, C. A., & Mumford, M. D. (2022). Effective strategies for creative idea evaluation and feedback: The customer's always right. *Creativity Research Journal*. https://doi.org/10.1080/10400419.2022.2025677

Toivainen, T., Madrid-Valero, J. J., Chapman, R., McMillan, A., Oliver, B. R., & Kovas, Y. (2021). Creative expressiveness in childhood writing predicts educational achievement beyond motivation and intelligence: A longitudinal, genetically informed study. *British Journal of Educational Psychology, 91*(4), 1395–1413. https://doi.org/10.1111/bjep.12423

Tor, N., & Gordon, G. (2020). Digital interactive quantitative curiosity assessment tool: Questions worlds. *International Journal of Information and Education Technology, 10*(8), 614–621. https://doi.org/10.18178/ijiet.2020.10.8.1433

Toraman, S., & Altun, S. (2013). Application of the six thinking hats and SCAMPER techniques on the 7th grade course unit 'Human and environment': An exemplary case study. *Mevlana International Journal of Education, 3*(4), 166–185. http://dx.doi.org/10.13054/mije.13.62.3.4

Torrance, E. P. (1965). *Rewarding creative behavior: Experiments in classroom creativity*. Prentice-Hall Inc

Treptow, J. M. (2020). *Sketchnoting as a reading strategy: Effects on motivation, self-efficacy, and comprehension in a high school English class* [Doctoral dissertation, Arizona State University]. ASU Library KEEP. https://keep.lib.asu.edu/items/158271

Tromp, C. (2022). Integrated constraints in creativity: Foundations for a unifying model. *Review of General Psychology, 0*(0). https://doi.org/10.1177/10892680211060027

Tseng, S.-C., & Tsai, C.-C. (2007). On-line peer assessment and the role of the peer feedback: A study of high school computer course. *Computers & Education, 49*(4), 1161–1174. https://doi.org/10.1016/j.compedu.2006.01.007

Tseng, S.-S. (2020). Using concept mapping activities to enhance students' critical thinking skills at a high school in Taiwan. *The Asia-Pacific Education Researcher, 29*, 249–256. https://doi.org/10.1007/s40299-019-00474-0

Tyagi, V., Hanoch, Y., Hall, S. D., Runco, M., & Denham, S. L. (2017). The risky side of creativity: Domain specific risk taking in creative individuals. *Frontiers in Psychology, 8*, Article 145. https://doi.org/10.3389/fpsyg.2017.00145

UNESCO International Bureau of Education. (2013). *Glossary of curriculum terminology*. http://www.ibe.unesco.org/fileadmin/user_upload/Publications/IBE_GlossaryCurriculumTerminology2013_eng.pdf

UNICE. (2000). *Stimulating creativity and innovation in Europe: The UNICE benchmarking report 2000*. https://www.businesseurope.eu/sites/buseur/files/media/imported/2002-03509-E.pdf

Van de Oudeweetering, K., & Voogt, J. (2018). Teachers' conceptualization and enactment of twenty-first century competences: Exploring dimensions for new curricula. *The Curriculum Journal, 29*(1), 116–133. https://doi.org/10.1080/09585176.2017.1369136

van der Lugt, R. (2003) Reconsidering the divergent thinking guidelines for design idea generation activity. In U. Lindemann (Ed.), *Human behaviour in design* (pp. 272–282). Springer. https://doi.org/10.1007/978-3-662-07811-2_27

van der Zanden, P. J. A. C., Meijer, P. C., & Beghetto, R. A. (2020). A review study about creativity in adolescence: Where is the social context? *Thinking Skills and Creativity, 38*, Article 100702. https://doi.org/10.1016/j.tsc.2020.100702

van Knippenberg, D., & Hirst, G. (2020). A motivational lens model of person × situation interactions in employee creativity. *Journal of Applied Psychology, 105*(10), 1129–1144. https://doi.org/10.1037/apl0000486

van Peppen, L. M., Verkoeijen, P. P. J. L., Heijltjes, A. E. G., Janssen, E. M., & van Gog, T. (2021). Enhancing students' critical thinking skills: Is comparing correct and erroneous examples beneficial? *Instructional Science, 49*, 747–777. https://doi.org/10.1007/s11251-021-09559-0

Vandercammen, L., Hofmans, J., & Theuns, P. (2014). The mediating role of affect in the relationship between need satisfaction and autonomous motivation. *Journal of Occupational and Organizational Psychology, 87*(1), 62–79. https://doi.org/10.1111/joop.12032

Vansteenkiste, M., Niemiec, C. P., & Soenens, B. (2010). The development of the five mini-theories of self-determination theory: An historical overview, emerging trends, and future directions. In T. C. Urdan & S. A. Karabenick (Eds.), *The decade ahead: Theoretical perspectives on motivation and achievement* (Advances in Motivation and Achievement, Vol. 16 Part A; pp. 105–165). Emerald Group Publishing. https://doi.org/10.1108/S0749-7423(2010)000016A007

Vernon, D., & Hocking, I. (2014). Thinking hats and good men: Structured techniques in a problem construction task. *Thinking Skills and Creativity, 14*, 41–46. https://doi.org/10.1016/j.tsc.2014.07.001

Vero, E., & Puka, E. (2017). The importance of motivation in an educational environment. *Formazione & insegnamento XV, 15*(1), 57–66. https://doi.org/10107346/-fei-XV-01-17_05

Victorian Curriculum and Assessment Authority. (n.d.). *Critical and creative thinking*. https://www.vcaa.vic.edu.au/assessment/f-10assessment/formative-assessment/formative-assessment-rubric-samples/Pages/CriticalandCreativeThinkingSamples.aspx

Vidergor, H. E., & Ben-Amram, P. (2020). Khan academy effectiveness: The case of math secondary students' perceptions. *Computers & Education, 157*, Article 103985. https://doi.org/10.1016/j.compedu.2020.103985

Visone, J. D. (2018). The development of problem-solving skills for aspiring educational leaders. *The Journal of Leadership Education, 17*, 35–53. https://doi.org/10.12806/V17/I4/R3

von Stumm, S., & Hell, B., & Chamorro-Premuzic, T. (2011). The hungry mind: Intellectual curiosity is the third pillar of academic performance. *Perspectives on Psychological Science, 6*(6), 574–588. https://doi.org/10.1177/1745691611421204

Vygotsky, L. S. (1980). *Mind in society: The development of higher psychological processes*. Harvard University Press.

Wallas, G. (1926). *The art of thought*. Jonathan Cape.

Wang, J., Wang, L., Liu, R.-D., & Dong, H.-Z. (2017). How expected evaluation influences creativity: Regulatory focus as moderator. *Motivation and Emotion, 41*(2), 147–157. https://doi.org/10.1007/s11031-016-9598-y

Ward, T. B., Patterson, M. J., & Sifonis, C. M. (2004). The Role of Specificity and Abstraction in Creative Idea Generation. *Creativity Research Journal, 16*(1), 1–9. https://doi.org/10.1207/s15326934crj1601_1

Waring, S. M., & Robinson, K. S. (2010). Developing critical and historical thinking skills in middle grades social studies. *Middle School Journal, 42*(1), 22–28. https://doi.org/10.1080/00940771.2010.11461747

Weiserg R. W. (2020). *Rethinking creativity: Inside-the-box thinking as the basis for innovation*. Cambridge University Press. https://doi.org/10.1017/9781108785259

Westby, E. L., & Dawson, V. L. (1995). Creativity: Asset or burden in the classroom? *Creativity Research Journal, 8*(1), 1–10. https://doi.org/10.1207/s15326934crj0801_1

Wheatley, K. F. (2002). Teacher persistence: A crucial disposition, with implications for teacher education. *Essays in Education, 3*, Article 1. https://openriver.winona.edu/eie/vol3/iss1/1

White, J. (2017). *The effects of guided and traditional note taking on student achievement in an eighth grade social studies class* [Unpublished Doctoral Dissertation]. Milligan College, Elizabethton, Tennessee USA.

Wiggins, G. A., & Sanjekdar, A. (2019). Learning and consolidation as re-representation: Revising the meaning of memory. *Frontiers in Psychology, 10*, Article 802. https://doi.org/10.3389/fpsyg.2019.00802

Wiliam, D. (2012). Feedback: Part of a system. *Educational Leadership, 70*(1), 30–34.

Willingham, D. T. (2019). *How to teach critical thinking* (Occasional Paper Series). NSW Department of Education. https://apo.org.au/sites/default/files/resource-files/2019-06/apo-nid244676.pdf

Witherby, A. E., & Tauber, S. K. (2019). The current status of students' note-taking: Why and how do students take notes? *Journal of Applied Research in Memory and Cognition, 8*(2), 139–153. https://doi.org/10.1016/j.jarmac.2019.04.002

World Economic Forum. (2020). *The future of jobs report 2020*. https://www3.weforum.org/docs/WEF_Future_of_Jobs_2020.pdf

Wu, Y., & Schunn, C. D. (2020). The effects of providing and receiving peer feedback on writing performance and learning of secondary school students. *American Educational Research Journal, 58*(3), 492–526. https://doi.org/10.3102/0002831220945266

Xue, Y., Gu, C., Wu, J., Dai, D. Y., Mu, X., & Zhou, Z. (2020). The effects of extrinsic motivation on scientific and artistic creativity among middle school students. *Journal of Creative Behavior, 54*(1), 37–50. https://doi.org/10.1002/jocb.239

Yap, C.-M., Chai, K.-H., & Lemaire, P. (2005). An Empirical Study on Functional Diversity and Innovation in SMEs. *Creativity and Innovation Management, 14*(2), 176–190. https://doi.org/10.1111/j.1476-8691.2005.00338.x

Yim, S., Wang, D., Olson, J. S., Vu, V., & Warschauer, M. (2017). Synchronous writing in the classroom: Undergraduates' collaborative practices and their impact on text quality, quantity, and style. In *Proceedings of the Conference on Computer Supported Cooperative Work* (pp. 468–479). Association for Computing Machinery. https://doi.org/10.1145/2998181.2998356

Yin, Y., Han, J., Huang, S., Zuo, H., & Childs, P. (2021, August 16–20). A study on student: Assessing four creativity assessment methods in product design. In *Proceedings of the International Conference on Engineering Design (ICED21)*, Gothenburg, Sweden (pp. 263–272). Cambridge University Press. https://doi.org/10.1017/pds.2021.27

Yuan, Y., Humphrey, S. E., & van Knippenberg, D. (2022). From individual creativity to team creativity: A meta-analytic test of task moderators. *Journal of Occupational and Organizational Psychology, 95*(2), 358–404. https://doi.org/10.1111/joop.12380

Zampetakis, L. A., Bouranta, N., & Moustakis, V. S. (2010). On the relationship between individual creativity and time management. *Thinking Skills and Creativity, 5*(1), 23–32. https://doi.org/10.1016/j.tsc.2009.12.001

Zenasni, F., Besançon, M., & Lubart, T. (2008). Creativity and tolerance of ambiguity: An empirical study. *Journal of Creative Behavior, 42*(1), 61–73. https://doi.org/10.1002/j.2162-6057.2008.tb01080.x

Zhang D., Zhou Z., Gu C., Lei Y., & Fan C. (2018). Family socio-economic status and parent-child relationships are associated with the social creativity of elementary school children: the mediating role of personality traits. *Journal of Child and Family Studies, 27*, 2999–3007. https://doi.org/10.1007/s10826-018-1130-4

Zhao, Y. (2020). Two decades of havoc: A synthesis of criticism against PISA. *Journal of Educational Change, 21*, 245–266. https://doi.org/10.1007/s10833-019-09367-x

Zielińska, A. (2020). Mapping adolescents' everyday creativity. *Creativity. Theories – Research – Applications, 7*(1), 208–229. https://doi.org/10.2478/ctra-2020-0012

INDEX

#
4Ps, the 55–81
6-3-5 method, the 111–12

A
ABC technique, the 127–8
academic testing 8
active cognitive strategies 203
active listening 37
activities 216–18
adaptive teaching 61–2
advertising 82
aesthetic creativity 4
affordances 31–4, 40
algorithmic thinking 88–9
ambiguity, tolerance for 81–4, 220
American musical theatre 85
analogous thinking 114–16
analytic rubrics 145–7
ancient civilisations 4
anonymity 98
argument mapping 104–5, 120
artificial intelligence (AI), 8–9, 226, 227, 230
arts, the 16–17, 216–17
assessment 22–3, 67, 113, 136, 206, 228
assessment tools 229–30
asset-based teaching and learning 178
assumptions 219
attitudes of a creative school 175
attitudes of creativity
    creative self-beliefs 55–9
    enthusiasm 67–8
    evaluation of 149
    intellectual curiosity 62–4
    intellectual risk-taking 65–7
    motivation 73–5
    openness 60–2
    parenting and 216
    persistence 76–7
    playfulness 68–72
    resilience 76–7
attributes of a creative school 175
attributes of creativity 149, 216
authoritarian parenting 216
automation 220, 227
autonomy 73, 78, 192, 216, 217

B
barriers to teaching creativity 18–23
behaviour, 'creative' 15–16
behavioural roles 45
Big-C creativity 14–15
big five personality traits model, the 60–2
blended learning 78–80, 179, 192
brains of creative people 15–16
brainstorming 109–14

C
The Catcher in the Rye 102
categorising 108
cause-and-effect diagrams 106–7
child autonomy 216
classrooms
    physical context of 30–31
    physical environment of 28–34
    social environment of 34–50
clusters (of desks) 30
cognitive capacity 95
cognitive flexibility 62
collaboration 41–42, 46–47, 163–167
collaboration competency 45–6
collaborative creativity, 41–50
collaborative note-taking 202
colour-coding 204, 205
combinatorial strategies (of recording) 100–7
communication 226
competencies 8, 9, 226, 228–9
competitiveness 5, 6–7
concept mapping 102–3, 120, 196–7, 205
conceptual understanding 192
concrete visualisation 99
conditional language 73
confidence 65, 216
consensual assessment technique (160–1
consolidation of knowledge 203–6
constructive feedback 37–8
constraints 31–3, 37–40
context of creativity 4
controlling feedback 37
convergent thinking 95, 120, 127–8
cooperation 42
cooperative revision 202

coordination 42
Cornell note-taking method, the 194–5, 205
COVID-19 pandemic 62, 215, 225, 230
creative capacity 206, 218–1
creative collaboration 41–50
creative competencies 8–9
creative consolidation 203–6
creative identity 56–9, 218
creative learning environments 172–4
creative metacognition 55
creative note-taking 200
creative pedagogies 225
creative problem-solving 226–7
creative process, the 95–132
    develop the final solution 128–30
    evaluation of 149–59
    four-stage model of 5
    generate ideas 97–119
    understand the problem 96–7
    validate the final solution 130–1
creative retrieval 206–9
creative self-beliefs 55–9
creative self-concept 55
creative self-efficacy 21–2, 55, 57–9, 216, 218, 220
creative solution diagnosis scale (CSDS), the 162
creative transfer 191–202
creativity
    applied science of 5
    as a competency 226
    assessment of 18, 19, 22–3
    attitudes of 55–80

    attributes of 81–9
    autonomy and 78
    brains of creative people 15–16
    as a competency 8
    context of 4
    definition of 3, 19–20
    development of 90–91
    evaluation of 135–68
    the future of in education 229–31
    holistic understanding of 6
    as a human quality 226
    influence of school management on 171–2
    myths about 14–18
    practical implementation of 22–3
    products of 159–62
    as a science 5–6, 229
creativity theory 229
criteria-based rubrics 161–2
critical feedback 77
critical thinking 7, 82, 122–6, 152–8, 191
croque method, the 209
cross-functional competencies 229
cue cards 205, 207
curiosity 62–4
curriculum 8–9, 19, 28

D

de Bono, Edward 109, 116
decision matrixes 120–121
decision trees 120
decision-making 122, 226
deductive reasoning 220
delayed gratification 221

demonstration 129
departments 180
developing the final solution 128–30, 158
developmental trajectory 182
diagrams 196, 205
digital brainstorming 110
digital competency 40
digital concept mapping 196
digital creativity 215
digital devices 7, 199, 215–16
digital literacy 228
digital home environment, the 215–16
digital mind mapping 198
digital note-taking 192–8, 199
digital play 71–2
digital summaries 205
digital technologies 40, 227, 230
digital transformation 229–30
directed brainstorming 113
discernment 122
distillation 112–113
divergent thinking 95, 97, 109, 230
diversity 41
divide and conquer method, the 202
dot points 196
drafting 158
drama 216

E

education
    competition in 8
    the future of 227–9
    the future of creativity in 229–30
    history of creativity in 6–9
    standardisation 8

INDEX

educational screen time 215
effectiveness 46–7, 130, 161–2
elaboration 203
elegance 161–2
empathy 42, 226
engagement 216–18
Enlightenment, the 4
enthusiasm 67–8
environment, the 6
evaluation (trialling) 128
evaluation of creativity 136, 144–9, 152–8
experimentation 68, 69, 214
exploration 214
exit slips 137
extrinsic motivation 73, 74, 217

F

Facebook 179–80
facilitation 96
fact-finding 95–6
fake news 122
fantasy 218
fear of failure 37, 38
feedback
    asking students for 61
    for collaboration 165
    formative feedback 137
    in a creative social environment 37–8
    intrinsic motivation and 217
    language for 42, 140
    peer-to-peer feedback and evaluation 139–42
    resilience and 77
finding the questions 96
fishbone diagrams 106
First Nations cultures 87

flexibility 95, 191
flexible learning spaces 29–30
flexible thinking 76–7
flipped learning 79–80
fluency 95
formative assessment 136, 230
formative feedback 137
four Ps, the 6
friendship 46
functional creativity 4
functional fixedness 219
future of education the 227–9
future of work, the 8–9, 225–7

G

games 48–50, 71–2
game-based learning 215
generating ideas 97–119, 150–1
generation (creative consolidation) 203
generative learning 190
generative notes 199
generative study 207
global economy 226
globalisation 85
graphic organisers 100–7
group brainstorming 111–14
group creativity 41 *see also* collaborative creativity
group passing brainstorming 113
guided brainstorming 113
guided note-taking 201
group size 45
Guilford, J P 5–6, 95, 96, 109

H

handwritten notes 192
hard skills 229
higher-order thinking skills 40

highlighting 203
hobbies 216–17
holistic rubrics 145
home environment, the 213–21
homework 215

I

idea evaluation tools 120–8
idea-finding 96
idea generation 76, 95, 97–119, 150–1, 219
idea generation tools 108–119
idea selection 76, 152–8
ideas recession 227
identifying problems in creative schools 176
individual brainstorming 110–11
imagination 214
implementation 22–3
improvisation 68
independence 77–80
independent learning 23, 189–209
indoor learning spaces 172–4
Industrial Revolution, the 5
Innovation Phase Assessment Instrument, the 176–7
inquiry 228
intellectual risk-taking 217
intelligence and creativity 6, 17–18
intellectual curiosity 62–4
intellectual risk-taking 65–7
interactive screen time 215
intercultural experience 85–9
interleaving 203, 204
international league tables 228
internet, the 7

263

interpersonal competencies 46
interpersonal skills 40
intrinsic motivation 73, 74, 217
Ishikawa diagrams 106–7
iteration 37–8

J

jigsaw technique, the 202
justification 219
justification of ideas 142

K

Kahoot! 71–72
keywords 196
knowledge 81, 219

L

language
    in advertising 82
    conditional language 73
    for discussing creativity 56
    for feedback 42, 140
    of pedagogy 218
    for peer evaluations 165
    for self-evaluations 165
    for teaching about creativity 182
laptops 192
league tables 8, 228
learning analytics 229–230
learning styles 203
lecture-style lessons 194, 199
left brain 16
lessons, context of, 30–1
lifelong learning 78
linear note-taking 194
lockdowns 62, 215

M

mastery 217
material affordances 31–4
mental illness and creativity 15
metacognition 41
metaphorical thinking 114–16
mind mapping 100–2, 198, 205
Minecraft 49–50, 205
mnemonics 207–209
modelling 129
mood (of classrooms) 34–5
motivation 73–5, 216–18
multicultural experience, *see* intercultural experience
music (as an intercultural experience) 85–6
musical instruments 217
musical theatre 85

N

negative feedback 37
negotiation 226
nominal group brainstorming 112–13
non-conformity of behaviour 15–16
non-lecture format lessons 199
non-linear methods of note-taking 196–8
non-linear pedagogy 62
note-taking 191–202
note-taking strategies 189
novelty 161–2, 218, 230

O

obstacles 46–7, 219
online instruction 192
open brainstorming 111
open inquiry model, the 228
open-ended questions 216
openness 60–2, 191, 214, 230
originality 95
Osborn, Alex 95–6, 109
outdoor learning spaces 172–4
overcoming obstacles 219

P

pandemic, the (COVID-19) 62, 215, 225, 230
parent–teacher interviews 213, 215
parenting 213–21
passive screen time 215
pedagogic approaches 23
peer-to-peer feedback and evaluation 37, 57, 128, 139–42, 164–5
peer-to-peer teaching 137–9
perseverance 218
persistence 76–7, 217
personal affordances 40
personal creativity 214
personality traits 60
photos (of notes) 206
physical classroom environment 28–34
physical education 68
pictorial strategies for recording ideas 99–107
PISA
    collaborative problem-solving framework 164
    tests 8
planning of collaborative activities 47–50
play 214
playfulness 68–72
Plowden Report, the 7
policy 19–20
posters 205

INDEX

PowerPoint 194, 205
Powtoon 205
pre-existing knowledge and skills 81, 219
Prezi 205
primary schools, critical thinking in 123–5
problem-posing 204
problem-solving
    cognitive model of 5
    creative problem-solving 226–7
    history of 4
    as a human quality 226
    intercultural perspectives on 85, 87
    and play 68, 69
problem-solving processes, 95–132
procedural roles 45
processes of creativity 95–132, 149–59, 176
products of creativity 6, 159–162
professional competencies 9
professional learning 13, 20–21, 177–85, 228
professional networks 179
Programme for International Student Assessment (PISA)
    collaborative problem-solving framework 164
    tests 8
prototyping 128, 158
psychological safety 35–6, 61, 65, 98–9, 118, 179, 214, 231
psychology 5

Q

questions (understanding the problem) 97

R

rapid prototyping 128
reading to children 216
real-world learning 228
reciprocal tutoring 137–9
recording ideas and information 98–112, 152, 191–202
recreation 216–18
reflection 132, 142–3, 203
reflective practice 137, 168
release of responsibility 200
relevance 161–2
remote learning 215, 225
Renaissance, the 4
rephrasing (of notes) 205
re-reading 203, 207
re-representation 203
research-based inquiry 228
research skills 40
resilience 76–7, 221
resources 31–4
retrieval practice 204
retrieval strategies 206–9
reviewing 203
right brain 16
risk-taking 35, 61, 65–7, 220, 230
role-play 69–70, 216
Romanticism 4
rubrics 140, 144–9, 161–2, 163–7

S

scaffolded inquiry model, the 228
scaffolding 78
SCAMPER 109, 116–19
scribes 99, 111
school climate 20
school culture 172–4
school leaders 176
school management 171–2
school-embedded professional learning 178
screen time 215–16, *see* also digital devices
seating arrangements 29, 30, 31, 34
secondary schools, critical thinking in 125–6
self-awareness 41
self-determined motivation 73
self-evaluation 142–3, 164–5
self-testing 204
silent brainstorming 111–12
single-point rubrics 148–9, 165–7
six thinking hats 109, 116
skeleton notes 201
sketch notes 199, 205
skills, pre-existing 81
social environment, 34–50
social loafing 113
social media 122, 215
social screen time 215
solving problems in creative schools 176
soft skills 228
Soviet Union, the 5, 6
space, organisation of 29–30, 31, 34
spoken strategies for recording ideas 99
sports 216–17
Sputnik I 6
standardisation of education 8
standardised tests 17, 228
STEM 47–50, 88, 227

student-centred learning 27, *see also* flexible learning spaces
students
- autonomy of 78
- creative identity in 56–9
- enthusiasm in 68
- evaluation by 137–42
- involvement of in the design of creative school environments 172–4
- motivation in 73–5
- openness in 60

study videos 205
summarising 108, 152, 205
summative assessments 136
synectics 114–16

T

T method of note-taking, the 196, 205
tablets 215
teacher-constructed social environments 34–50
teachers, *see also* professional learning
- adaptive teaching 61–2
- attitudes to gaming among 71
- creative competencies of 228, 230
- creative identity in 56
- creative self-efficacy of 21–2
- enthusiasm in 67–8
- evaluation by 136–7
- in flipped learning 80
- future role of 230–1
- motivation in 73
- openness in 60–1
- persistence and resilience in 77
- professional learning of 13
- release of responsibility by 200

teaching about creativity 182
teaching for creativity 183–5
teaching with creativity 179–81
teaching creativity 18–23
teamwork 165–7
technological change 226
television 215
testing 128
tickets 137
time 38–9
time pressure 221
tolerance for ambiguity 81–4, 220
tools for assessing creativity 229
transcribing 99
transferring information 191–202
trialling 128
trust 35
typed notes 192, 199

U

uncertainty 62
understanding the problem 96–7, 149
unfair marking 113
United Kingdom, the 7
United States, the 5, 6–7

V

vaccines 225
validation 129, 130–1, 159
van Gogh, Vincent 15
verbal ideas 99
verbatim notes 192, 206
video games 48–50, 71–2, 215
videos 199, 205
visual mnemonics 209
visual teaching tools 194

W

Wallas, Graham, 5
wellbeing 217
work, future of 225–7
working from home 225
written strategies for recording ideas 98–99, *see also* combinatorial strategies for recording ideas

Y

YouTube 215

Z

zoned classrooms 30

www.ingramcontent.com/pod-product-compliance
Lightning Source LLC
Chambersburg PA
CBHW051402070526
44584CB00023B/3253